Free
Labor
in an
Unfree
World

Free Labor in an Unfree World

White Artisans in Slaveholding Georgia, 1789–1860

MICHELE GILLESPIE

The University of Georgia Press *Athens and London*

Paperback edition, 2004

© 2000 by the University of Georgia Press

Athens, Georgia 30602

Designed by Kathi Dailey Morgan

Set in 10 on 14 Berthold Baskerville by G&S Typesetters

Printed digitally in the United States of America

The Library of Congress has cataloged the
hardcover edition of this book as follows:

Library of Congress Cataloging-in-Publication Data
Gillespie, Michele.
Free labor in an unfree world : white artisans in
slaveholding Georgia, 1789–1860 / Michele Gillespie.
xxii, 236 p. ; 24 cm.
Includes bibliographical references (p. [209]–229)
and index.
ISBN 0-8203-1968-6 (alk. paper)
1. Artisans — Georgia — History. 2. Slavery — Georgia —
History. 3. Working class — Georgia — History.
4. Georgia — Social conditions. I. Title.
HD2346.U52 G44 2000
331.7'94'0975809034 — dc21   99–28866

Paperback ISBN-13: 978-0-8203-2670-2
Paperback ISBN-10: 0-8203-2670-4

British Library Cataloging-in-Publication Data available

To my parents

Arlene Mary Gillespie and William Glenn Gillespie

with love

Contents

Tables

Acknowledgments

This book has been a long time in the making. In the process I have acquired my own family, the finest of friends, and innumerable debts.

Little did I know during my first weeks as an undergraduate at Rice University that taking on a work-study job at *The Journal of Southern History* would so profoundly shape my personal and professional life for the next two decades. It was here under the careful tutelage of Evelyn Thomas Nolen, Sanford W. Higginbotham, and John B. Boles that I developed a deep and abiding love for southern history and a respect for the profession. The wonderful courses I took with John B. Boles, along with the friendship, support, and mentoring I received and continue to receive from John have been mainstays in my intellectual and personal life. Evelyn Nolen, whose wit and wisdom continue to both delight and teach me, has been my other special source of such mainstays. I am also grateful to Allan Matusow, Richard Smith, and Patricia Seed for enriching and broadening my perspective on history in many important ways.

Princeton University offered me an incomparable graduate education with an incomparable community of scholars. Coursework, constructive criticism, and conversations with James Oakes, John Murrin, James McPherson, Sean Wilentz, and Christine Stansell have strongly influenced this project. It is to Allan Kulikoff, however, that I extend my deepest gratitude. His knowledge of southern history and southern sources, his commitment to this subject and its value, and his unswerving belief in me have shepherded this book from its inception to its completion.

Archivists throughout the South have been generous with their time and assistance. I would particularly like to thank the staff at the Southern Historical Collection at University of North Carolina, Chapel Hill, the staff at the Hargrett Library, University of Georgia, especially Linda Aaron and Larry Gulley (now deceased), the staff at the Georgia Historical Society, the staff at the Georgia Department of Archives and History, especially Dale Couch and Sue Watts, and the staff at the Museum of Southern Decorative Arts in Winston-Salem, North Carolina. Thanks also to Randy Reid, who generously shared his research on Howell Cobb with me, Marguerite Hodgson, who plied me with tall glasses of iced tea in her lovely home while I pored over her family papers, and Robert S. Davis for his advice and assistance.

At Agnes Scott College I have received critical support from a number of quarters. Elizabeth Mulherrin has handled all my interlibrary loan requests with gracious efficiency and exceedingly good humor. Sarah R. Blanshei, former dean of the College, and the Professional Development Committee generously awarded me three summer research grants and a semester's leave to keep this project on track. The staff in Information Technology Services, particularly Neta Counts, has saved me from more near disasters than I care to admit. My terrific colleagues in the history department, Kathy Kennedy, Violet Johnson, Mike Brown, and Penny Campbell, consistently championed my scholarship. And my students have been invaluable audiences and fine critics in their own right.

I have presented portions of this book as papers at a number of conferences and received especially helpful comments from Peter Coclanis, Christine Daniels, Sylvia Frey, Paul Gilje, J. William Harris, Stephanie McCurry, Howard Rock, Richard Stott, Harry Watson, and Betty Wood. I also received great comments from faculty and graduate student participants in the Beer Barrel Seminar at Rice University at an early stage in this project.

Portions of chapter 1 originally appeared as "Planters in the Making: Artisanal Opportunity in Georgia, 1790–1830" in *American Artisans: Crafting Social Identity, 1750–1850,* ed. Howard B. Rock, Paul A. Gilje, and Robert Asher, pp. 33–47, ©1995 Johns Hopkins University Press. A portion of chapter 4 originally appeared in *GHQ* 81 (summer 1997).

John B. Boles, Kent Leslie, Betty Wood, and Catherine Clinton have all taken time from their own work to read this manuscript in its entirety. Their invaluable insights have strengthened this book immeasurably.

My editor, Malcolm Call, has been the most consummate of gentlemen, not only appreciating the value of this book and its approach, but patiently cultivating its completion, for which I am most grateful. I am very thankful to Gillian Hillis and Jennifer Comeau, who together skillfully shepherded this book through the editing and production process.

I have appreciated the advice and friendship of many people over the long haul. To this end, I am especially grateful to Barbara Blatchley, Fitz Brundage, Christine Cozzens, Glenn Eskew, Randy Sparks, and Peggy Thompson. Last but not least, I owe a special thank you to Catherine Clinton, for her thoughtfulness, wisdom, and never-ending ability to make me laugh.

And finally, thank you to my terrific family: my parents, Mike and Arlene Gillespie, to whom this book is dedicated; my sisters, Heather Gaertner and Colleen Gillespie, whose collective irreverence knows no bounds; my sons, Michael Thomas and Matthew Colin, who never cease to amaze me; and my husband, Kevin Pittard, who sustains me.

Introduction

Even at the close of the twentieth century, the popular my-
thology surrounding the Old South remains a familiar mainstay
in American culture. This imaginary place harbored cavalier
gentlemen and languishing belles attended by devoted servants of African descent in white-columned mansions flanked
by sprawling live oaks. Beyond this world of honor and chiv-
alry lived the unfortunate poor whites, perpetually trapped in
squalor by their own ignorance. Since its publication as a book
and subsequent release as a film during the Great Depression,
Margaret Mitchell's *Gone with the Wind* has helped perhaps in
more ways than any other fictional account to burn this apoc-
ryphal image of antebellum southern society into the public
mind. In fact innumerable writers, historians, and critics have
spent entire careers tearing down Tara's false facade piece by
piece since *Gone with the Wind*'s debut.

Yet Margaret Mitchell and her devotees did manage to capture one aspect of the Old South that rings entirely true. Scar-
lett's father, Gerald O'Hara, like so many antebellum southern-

ers, was first and foremost a self-made man. This bull-headed Irishman, however stereotypically portrayed in the book and film, fled his homeland as a young man to make his way to Savannah. As a store clerk with a good eye for numbers, bargains, and cards, he soon secured his first slave and eventually a rather modest upcountry "plantation" in Clayton County.

From the most humble of origins, Gerald O'Hara would fashion himself into a planter of sorts over the course of his lifetime. He was not the genteel planter *cum* politician so enshrined in more embellished images of the glorious southern past, however, but the gritty, hard-scrabble migrant made good who more truly represents the antebellum southern experience of most white men.

While the legendary Old South may still appeal to the most romantic at heart, the stories of the Gerald O'Haras who populated this region reveal a profoundly different world—a far more interesting, dynamic, and complex one—than the static world ascribed to prewar Tara. To get at this new world and the reality of self-made men, this book highlights the experiences of one social group in particular: white artisans in a slaveholding society.[1]

Artisans have been essential actors in every aspect of early American history. Since the inception of the American colonies, artisans helped ensure the self-sufficiency of the villages and small towns that came to dot the Atlantic coast. Traditional craftsmen and craftswomen worked as smiths, bakers, coopers, sawyers, carpenters, furnituremakers, iron founders, shoemakers, hatmakers, spinners, saddlers, printers, jewelers, and even apothecaries, to name only the most obvious of artisan occupations.

Traditionally, young men, who have included the likes of Benjamin Franklin, Thomas Paine, and Paul Revere, signed on as apprentices with master craftsmen to learn the mysteries of a trade, receiving room and board for their services. Upon completion of their three- to seven-year indenture, apprentices were handed the tools of their trade by their masters, marking their transition to journeymen, and departed their masters' workshops in search of wage-earning work. Journeymen viewed this new stage of their working lives as temporary, for they hoped to save enough wages to secure master craftsman status and support a shop of their own. Thus, artisans in America who made the transition to independent master craftsmen have long embodied the self-made man.

With the advent of new technologies by the late eighteenth and early nineteenth centuries, and during a burgeoning commercial revolution, many artisans in the largest towns and cities of the New Republic found themselves—sometimes willingly and sometimes unwillingly—exchanging their traditional hand tools for machinery. This transition marked the earliest beginnings of industrialization in America and was accompanied by the breakdown of the traditional craft system that had been so indispensable in the establishment of the American colonies.

Artisans between the seventeenth and nineteenth centuries not only contributed to a successful domestic economy but were also among the most vocal and organized of political constituencies. For this reason their actions, which were integral to the patriots' victory in the American Revolution, the establishment of the earliest trade unions, and the shaping of Jacksonian democracy, have long been chronicled by historians.

This book presses in a different direction, however, from these earlier studies, by literally moving south. Through an examination of the distinctive nature of artisanal identity, status, opportunity, and politics between 1789 and 1860 in the maturing slave economy of one Deep South state, it seeks to show how white male artisans, in all their variety, responded to and acted upon the social realities of class and race.

White mechanics throughout the South occupied an ambiguous place in the antebellum social order. Unlike northern artisans, they earned limited respect for their labor in a slaveholding culture that often viewed work as menial, degrading, and the province of slaves. In general, skilled work performed by black artisans, slave and free, undercut the economic opportunities as well as the social status of free white artisans in the South. Hence the social system of slavery served as a perpetual reminder of white craftsmen's uncertain place in this unique region. The degree to which fellow whites encouraged competition between black and white artisans, through the training, purchase, and hire of slave artisans and through the hire of free black artisans at wages below those of whites, affected the kinds of choices white craftsmen in this region made about their livelihoods.

Given these troubling circumstances, white artisans at different points in their working lives and at different times and places in the southern economy had just cause to be critical of the slave system. White politicians were alert to artisans' disgruntlement for they knew that white artisans' protest against black competition could tip the delicately balanced apple cart that made up the white social order. At the same time, however, they recognized that white artisans, especially slaveholding white artisans, could benefit from the slave system like all other slaveholders. These complex truths forced white southerners to tread carefully around the issue of white artisans' status throughout the antebellum era.

Daniel Hundley, a native Alabamian, clearly understood the danger of denigrating white southern artisans on the eve of the Civil War. In his polemical defense of southern life, published in 1857 in the midst of the mounting sectional crisis, he assured his readers that artisans comprised an important sector of "the Southern middle classes." Southerners, he protested a bit too vociferously, did not equate white mechanic labor with black slave labor. In fact, he assured his readers, southerners had only the greatest respect for the artisan class. Unlike the "dull, restless" artisans in the North, who endured unemployment, poverty, and social ostracism, white artisans in the South, protected by the slave labor system from the hardships of a free labor economy, evinced a "smiling, rollicking spirit" indicative of their social position. Because Hundley and many other southerners recognized the danger that unsmiling white mechanics posed to the white social system, they sought to assure them of their inclusion in it.[2]

Hundley's pronouncements are important not only because they point to the interesting position that white artisans occupied in antebellum southern society. His writings also convey critical distinctions between northern and southern artisans. White craftsmen in the slave South did not evolve into a distinct proletariat by the time of the Civil War. The series of class struggles that brought rapid urbanization and industrialization first to England and then to the northern states, and that transformed artisans into workers, did not occur in the staple-producing, slave-labor region of the United States before 1860. Thus the artisan experience was fundamentally different in the South.

This distinction was not lost upon white southerners like Hundley who, in an effort to build a strong proslavery defense, convinced themselves that the slave system bestowed on all white men, including mechanics, a measure of economic opportunity and political equality unavailable to wage-earning white men in the North. Reliance on black slave labor, they argued, had produced a largely egalitarian society of independent white men—a *herrenvolk* society, as George Frederickson has argued. According to the logic of the political elite in the antebellum South, white mechanics had no need to protest the inequities they experienced as white men in a slave-labor system because there were none.

And there is some truth to this rationalization. Certainly many white artisans in Georgia did experience some measure of upward mobility and social respect during their lifetimes, especially in the earlier years of the cotton kingdom. By the late antebellum era, however, many did not, especially in the oldest cities in the state. As these craftsmen discovered, a white society dependent on slave labor did not always enhance *all* white men's economic opportunities, nor did it always ensure equal participation by *all* white men in the political process. Still, many mechanics found that their skills in time enabled them to become self-made men who differed in significant ways from their northern brethren in that they owned land and slaves in addition to and sometimes in lieu of workshops.

While historians have long acknowledged that class relations within antebellum white society were not harmonious, their tendency to limit descriptions of the social structure of the South to three static social classes—planters, yeomen, and slaves—has discouraged more careful analysis of class differences framed by racial realities over time. This examination of white artisans in Georgia from the end of the eighteenth century to the Civil War explores both the dynamic opportunities for upward mobility and the dynamic tensions between classes by demonstrating the many ways one social group defined itself in relation to changing structural realities and prevailing ideologies in the slave South.

That limited attention has been paid to white artisans as a social class in the South stems from several related but faulty conjectures. Since the publication of Carl Bridenbaugh's influential *Colonial Craftsmen,* some historians have argued that the slave labor system and the rise of the plantation economy discouraged the development of a significant population of skilled white craftsmen.[3] According to this school of thought, the desire to achieve self-sufficient plantations, where slave artisans performed all specialized tasks, precluded planter demand for skilled whites. Based on such limited opportunities to ply a trade, native-born young men must have steered clear of apprenticeships, while migrant artisans from the Northeast and Europe were loath to venture to any but the largest southern cities such as Baltimore or Charleston in search of work.[4] Given such circumstances, these historians surmised, skilled white mechanics must have been anomalies in a rural world of planters, yeoman farmers, and slaves.

Because they viewed white mechanics as anomalies, these scholars found little justification for examining their lives. Their alleged small numbers, near silence, and virtual invisibility in the historical record led schol-

ars to conclude that these men were marginal participants in the shaping
and perpetuation of the slave-based culture of the Old South. Yet as more
recent generations of historians have come to recognize, scrutinizing those
people at the so-called edges of social communities can often lead to new
ways of understanding the larger society they reside in.

Recently a handful of scholars have discovered that white mechanics
fully participated in this slaveholding agrarian society, at least in the upper
South. Their research indicates that white artisans played a significant role
in shaping the economic and political life of the eighteenth-century Chesapeake. These findings are important not only because they challenge earlier notions about the dearth of white artisans in the South, but because
they explore how white artisanal behavior was shaped by life in a slave
society. Taken together, Charles Steffan's and Tina Sheller's work, for example, provides a rich picture of Baltimore artisans' involvement in local
politics and party formation from the American Revolution through the
early Republic.[5] Detailed county studies by Jean Russo and Christine Daniels document the extensive participation of white artisans in the market
economy of the Chesapeake throughout the colonial period.[6]

Despite the importance of this work, and the lively debate it has
launched, it describes a single relatively unique region of the South. Only
two books extensively examine artisan experience outside the Chesapeake: Richard Walsh's older but still useful analysis of political organization among Charleston artisans during the American Revolution and
Johanna Miller Lewis's recent fine study of artisan economic activity and
market development in the North Carolina backcountry between 1750
and 1775.[7] These studies tell us about the political activities of artisans in
one urban center and the economic lives of artisans in one rural county
during the second half of the eighteenth century. But what were artisans
doing elsewhere in the lower South? How did white artisanal opportunities
change as the new cotton economy of the early nineteenth century began
to transform the region?

Unfortunately, answers to these questions have been hard to come by.
Virtually no work examines white southern artisans from the end of the
American revolution through the antebellum era, with the exception of
Ulrich B. Phillips's 1910 collection of primary sources on southern indus-
trial life, which documents the existence of a number of antebellum me-
chanics' societies and mechanic concerns, and Catherine Bishir's recent

work on the building trade in antebellum North Carolina, which adds significantly to our understanding of how economic developments, technological change, and the availability of labor shaped white carpenters' opportunities in a single state.[8] A few studies have focused on unskilled white workers in the late antebellum period. Roger W. Shugg, Richard Morris, and Herbert Aptheker recorded sporadic labor protests by white workers in the 1840s and 1850s in various parts of the South.[9] More recently, Fred Siegel, Ira Berlin and Herbert Gutman, Michael Johnson and James Roark, and other scholars have examined white workingmen's organized protests against competition from black workingmen in several southern urban centers during the turbulent 1850s.[10]

Together this body of work highlights the web of class and racial tensions that unsettled southern society on the eve of the Civil War. It is valuable because it recognizes the inherent challenge that white workingmen posed to the slave-labor system. The narrow time frame of these studies, however, along with their almost exclusive emphasis on major urban centers, especially Atlantic seaboard cities, limits the kinds of conclusions that can be drawn about white working-class identity and protest throughout the region and across the antebellum period. Yet the evolution – or de-evolution – of white male artisan status has important implications for understanding free labor in southern history.

What kinds of roles did white male artisans play in antebellum politics? How much autonomy to shape and define their own lives did these men experience as skilled free laborers in a maturing slave labor society? Though these white male artisans shared the double privilege accorded them by virtue of their white race and male status, what variations and differences distinguished them from other white men and from each other? And in what ways did slavery fundamentally define the kinds of lives these men could lead? Historians are agreed that the social system of slavery prevented the emergence of a white working class before the Civil War. But precisely how was this outcome effected? And in what ways did white artisans participate in it?

This study seeks to answer these questions by examining the experiences of white craftsmen in the towns and countryside of antebellum Georgia in light of the changing nature of artisanal opportunity in a cotton economy. It describes how artisans came to fit into the social and political order of slaveholding Georgia, and on whose terms. To this end, this study documents the relationship between white craftsmen and the economic and social conditions that simultaneously precipitated the entrenchment of black slavery and prevented the making of a white working class in Georgia in the decades before the Civil War and black freedom.

Perhaps even more important, this book reminds us that self-made men were not brash anomalies but part and parcel of the southern social landscape. As free laborers in an unfree world, their work, their goals, and their ideals ultimately contributed in profoundly important ways to the making of the Old South.

Free
Labor
in an
Unfree
World

1

Planters in the Making

Young Reuben King, a tanner by trade, arrived in Darien, Georgia on March 28, 1801, intent upon making this small, remote coastal community his new home. A year earlier, he had departed Sharon, Connecticut, at the conclusion of his apprenticeship and headed west to Pittsburgh by ship, stage, and foot. Discouraged by the low wages and competition he encountered there, he walked to Baltimore, earning enough wages along the way to buy his passage south. Although King scrambled to make a living as a tanner during his first five years in Darien, he eventually became a successful planter, with real and personal estates valued at more than $40,000 by the late antebellum era.[1]

Reuben King was one of many artisans from the northern United States and Europe who migrated to Georgia during the early republic. Drawn by the twin promises of new markets and widening opportunities, white artisans of all types, including masters and journeymen, the highly skilled and the virtually unskilled, found work and established shops in the port town

Savannah, the market-town Augusta, and the burgeoning Georgia countryside. Despite numerous hardships, including disease, debt, and competition with other artisans, slave and free, some of them accrued capital,
land, and slaves. The most successful of these white craftsmen, like Reuben
King, even became planters.

Although historians have argued that planters' growing dependence on
slave craftsmen over the course of the eighteenth century increasingly denied white artisans viable livelihoods in the Chesapeake, this was not the
case in Georgia. Limited white settlement, ample land, and rich rewards
from staple crop production attracted wave after wave of migrants to this
Deep South state—slaveholders and nonslaveholders alike. As established
urban centers expanded and new towns and villages arose to meet the
needs of the growing hinterland, Georgia in many respects came to resemble the bustling frontier west of the Appalachian mountains more than
the ordered slaveocracy of the Chesapeake by the close of the eighteenth
century.[2] Although a young white man's search for fortune would become
inextricably bound to westward travel in popular literature over the course
of the nineteenth century, venturing to the lower South in search of new
opportunities held plenty of promise on the eve of the cotton revolution,
as Reuben King soon discovered.

Georgia artisans, especially those seeking work in the emerging cotton
economy, experienced a set of circumstances quite distinct from those of
their northern counterparts. Although the lower South felt the impact of
the commercial revolution, and to a lesser extent the transportation revolution, the industrial revolution made limited headway in the region before 1860. While the transformation of master craftsmen into planters in
Georgia during the early republic mirrored the transformation of master
craftsmen into entrepreneurial employers in the North, the resemblance
ends there.

The marginal place of free labor in this slaveholding world discouraged
sustained class consciousness and class formation. Unlike the fledgling
middle class in the urban Northeast, which fostered the creation of a working class, the planter class in the South found little reason to press for the
establishment of more wage labor in a slave-labor economy. Moreover,
those master craftsmen who had become planters, as well as master craftsmen who hoped to become planters, conceived of themselves as members
of the "ruling race." They participated fully in the slave economy, relying

upon slave labor as much as free labor in their shops and using slave labor in their homes and fields whenever their financial resources allowed. In addition, even as opportunities for upward mobility for artisans dwindled after 1830, masters and journeymen in many trades did not experience the blanket devaluation of their skills that transformed northern artisans into wageworkers. The growth of the traditional staple-crop economy and the slave labor system in the South created unique opportunities for skilled, free white men to accumulate capital, land, and slaves. These sets of realities not only prevented the formation of a working class and fostered the transformation of artisans into planters in Georgia; they encouraged skilled white men to believe, at least through the first half of the nineteenth century, that they too could share in the rewards of the slave economy.

In many respects Georgia provided a unique environment for these migrant men. Made a colony by royal charter in 1732, Georgia quickly became a haven for deerskin traders bartering with Creeks, Choctaws, Chickasaws, and Cherokees and for planters securing title to fertile land along the coast. Although James Oglethorpe and his fellow Georgia trustees outlawed slavery and rum in the colony at its outset in the hope of building a self-sufficient, even prosperous, settlement of industrious farmers and tradesmen, the wealth to be made from rice plantations, where slaves labored, and from trade with Native Americans, mitigated against strict obedience to colonial law. Georgia's "Malcontents," those colonists who refused to respect the trustees' sanctions, helped make the youngest British colony in North America yet another jewel in the empire's mercantile crown by midcentury when the disappointed trusteeship surrendered its charter to the King.[3]

The colony grew rapidly over the next quarter century, as did the institution of slavery. Georgia's population exploded almost fourteenfold over this period, from only 3,500 white and black inhabitants in 1753 to 48,000 in 1773, nearly a third of whom were slaves.[4] Although the American Revolution thrust Georgia into a state of chaos, and temporarily discouraged settlement, migration to the new state increased even more dramatically at its conclusion.

Georgia colonists had been reluctant at first to respond openly to the abuses of the British Government that were rousing American colonists elsewhere into protest. The colony's tiny white population, meager financial resources, and vulnerability to attack by France and Spain as well as by Native Americans discouraged breaking ties with England too hastily. Georgians joined the independence movement at the last minute, nonetheless, sending three delegates to the Second Continental Congress in time to sign the Declaration of Independence. Despite the colony's strong personal and economic connections to England, the newly organized patriot leadership gathered a substantial share of popular support, especially in the upcountry surrounding Augusta.[5]

The revolutionary war shaped Georgia's future in several significant ways. British occupation and reoccupation of Savannah made the lowcountry a dangerous locale for patriots, which necessitated the removal of the Whig government to the upcountry. This change garnered new political importance for the upland region by war's end. Meanwhile, the bulk of the slave population in Georgia had been confined to the lowcountry along the Atlantic coast where war had been waged most fiercely. Thousands of slaves secured their freedom when planters fled their estates, leaving their slaves to fend for themselves. In what was a costly mass exodus for Georgia planters, at least 15,000 black Georgians escaped slavery by traveling south to east Florida or west to Indian country. Hundreds more slaves ran away to the British Army, which offered them their liberty in exchange for military service. The economic loss to whites and the social confusion that ensued would shape legal and cultural developments in the new state throughout the early republic.[6]

White male artisans fared well enough in Georgia during the colonial and revolutionary periods. They had been present in the colony from its inception as both indentured servants and independent craftsmen. Their limited numbers put them in constant demand. Despite their scarcity, white artisans, along with skilled slave artisans hired from South Carolina planters, moved the colony toward increasing self-sufficiency; they built homes, shops, wharves, boats, and warehouses and produced such essentials as shoes, cloth, nails, tools, candles, and barrels.[7] By mid–eighteenth century, white artisans were living and working in the Salzberg Lutheran settlement of Ebenezer, the Scotch-Highland settlement of Darien, the small port town of Sunbury, the bustling entrepôt of Augusta, and the seaport of Savannah. But after 1750, as the colony began to take new shape as a slaveholding society these men soon found themselves, as Betty Wood has argued, holding a mixed bag of opportunities.[8]

Growing reliance on black slave labor on coastal rice plantations had produced a number of skilled slave artisans in lowcountry Georgia, a circumstance that bore immediate consequences for white craftsmen by the late colonial era. In Savannah, the largest and most important urban center by far in Georgia, white artisans worked alongside slave artisans in a number of trades. Apparently upset more by the reduction in wages they suffered as a result of the increased labor supply than the social indignity of toiling with blacks, white mechanics vigorously protested the use of skilled and semiskilled slaves in Savannah before the colonial assembly. Their livelihoods, they argued, were being ruined by this unwanted competition. The Georgia Assembly responded to these protests in 1758 by passing an act that not only discouraged the employment of skilled slaves in Savannah, with the exception of slave shipwrights, caulkers, sawyers, and coopers, but pointedly invited white artisans to settle in Georgia towns. These same legislators feared, nonetheless, that white artisans could take advantage of this situation by raising their rates, so they appointed commissioners imbued with the authority to set wages. This legislation proved a minor victory at best for white artisans. Their wages were restricted, fellow townspeople generally ignored the act, and the practice of hiring out skilled slave artisans remained unaffected.[9]

Yet white artisans, like other new migrants, benefited greatly from the relative openness of Georgia society in the late colonial era, despite the difficulties created by competition with black artisans. Ambitious mechanics could take advantage of the abundant land and new markets in Georgia, unlike their artisan-brethren in the Chesapeake, who found themselves increasingly closed out of a society dominated by an established Tidewater elite. Moreover, master craftsmen in Georgia, if they desired, could take advantage of the slave economy by buying and hiring skilled slave artisans themselves, and in doing so, force the white journeymen they hired to accept reduced rates.

Thus, white artisans did not offer a sustained challenge to the emerging white social order or the new institution of black slavery in colonial Georgia despite the grievances they occasionally voiced. Although some white mechanics resented the competition they encountered with slave artisans, these same men also anticipated the day when they would be slaveholders, and perhaps even landholding planters themselves, and would want to use their black laborers as they saw fit. Competition with black artisans, under these circumstances, was an unfortunate hardship that propertyless white craftsmen endured on their climb up the social ladder. Fortunately for them, the American colonists' defeat of the British widened this ladder, permitting even greater numbers of white men, including artisans, to experience upward mobility in Georgia during the early republic.

By the late eighteenth century, geographic, demographic, and economic shifts already in progress in Georgia assisted many more adventurous artisans. Although lowcountry economic patterns had remained virtually the same since the colonial era, because seacoast planters continued to rely on extensive slave labor to cultivate staple crops of rice, indigo, and sea island cotton, great change was underway in the upcountry, where the forest was beginning to give way to the farmer's plow. By 1790, over half of the white population of Georgia, and slightly less than a third of the state's slaves, resided in the three newest and northern-most counties of the state, which were peopled by middling planters and hardscrabble Scotch-Irish farmers from Virginia and the Carolinas. Many of these settlers also spilled into middle Georgia, the lower half of the upcountry, inhabited by a third of the state's white population and a quarter of its slaves. In what marked an important departure from prerevolutionary demographic patterns, the expanding upcountry had become home to nine of every ten whites in Georgia, and just over five of every ten blacks.[10]

A series of treaties nefariously secured with Native Americans, principally the Creeks, had opened up greater and greater expanses of the Georgia piedmont to white settlement. The headright system of land distribution, which entitled the head of a family to two hundred acres for himself and fifty acres for each additional family member, bounty grants for soldiers who served in the Revolutionary War, and soon even a land lottery made cheap, fertile land available to eager pioneers. While some of these white migrants contented themselves with subsistence farming, others harvested cash crops. Tobacco prevailed during the late eighteenth century, but the fall in its market price, the invention of the cotton gin, and the rise of cotton prices ignited widespread interest in short-staple cotton during the first decades of the nineteenth century.[11]

The transition to a cotton economy, and the availability of land, increased the rate of settlement in the hinterland, nearly quadrupling the state's white population between 1790 and 1820.[12] Unlike lowcountry planters, whose enormous profits in rice, indigo, and sea island cotton mandated extensive investments in capital, land, and slaves to make money, upcountry farmers collected small-scale but respectable returns from tobacco and green-seed cotton, despite limited capital investment and limited labor. Farmers quickly realized, however, that the introduction of slave labor to their homesteads brought them even greater gains.[13]

By 1820, four out of five Georgia slaves toiled in the upcountry, a remarkable transformation from 1790.[14] While the lowcountry remained predominantly black, eight upcountry counties also claimed black majorities by this time. The dual enticements of land and cotton, key ingredients in the flourishing upcountry slave economy, had altered the state's racial balance from slightly more than one-third black in 1790 to slightly more than two-fifths black in 1820.[15]

These structural changes provided artisans and other migrants with opportunities unavailable to them in the older cities and towns along the Atlantic seaboard and in Europe. Disheartened by the existence of established proprietorships and manufactories in these places and frustrated by job competition, hundreds of men from Europe, New England, the mid-Atlantic, the upper South, and even nearby Charleston made their way to Georgia during the early republic. The nativities of these migrant artisans were as diverse as the trades they practiced, as evidenced in the many advertisements they placed in local newspapers. In Augusta, the painter William Anson announced his arrival from London, the blacksmith F. R. Gaddy told prospective clients about his Richmond experience, the jeweler Jeremiah Andrews described his Philadelphia training, the needleworker Miss Goddfrey related her familiarity with New York and London, the gardener John Barberon emphasized his experience in the West Indies and France, and the tailor Joseph Sudor respectfully informed the public of his recent arrival from Charleston. In Savannah, the watchmaker Thomas Lee claimed a Liverpool background, the baker Francis Herbert Berry his experience in a Charleston shop, and the hairdresser Lewis Cuigno his training in Bordeaux.[16]

As these advertisements suggest, most white artisans in Georgia probably were not natives of the new state. Many of them, like Reuben King, the Connecticut-born tanner who had settled in Darien, had traveled through a number of places before settling in Georgia. The tailor Benjamin Mullin had practiced his craft in New York, Baltimore, and Norfolk before opening his Augusta shop in 1799.[17] The silversmith John Ogier worked in New York City in 1791, Baltimore in 1796, Norfolk in 1803, and then moved to Charleston, before settling in Savannah where he died in 1814.[18] Will M. Theus's research indicates that all eighteen Savannah furniture-makers in the early republic whose nativities he could identify were non-Georgians; eight of the eighteen were born in Europe.[19] Similarly, George Barton Cutten identified 46 silversmiths in Georgia during this same period; eighteen came from Europe, eleven from New England, eight from the mid-Atlantic states, and six from Maryland, Virginia, and the Carolinas. Only three were native Georgians.[20]

White artisans practicing commonplace trades such as blacksmithing and baking were nearly as likely to be non-Georgians as white artisans engaged in elite crafts like furnituremaking and silversmithing. Although artisans in nonelite trades often lacked the resources, family connections, and training characteristic of luxury craftsmen, they too chose to make their way to Georgia. A master tailor, for example, advertised the excellent journeymen he had hired from cities stretching up and down the Atlantic coast.[21] Three carpenters from Connecticut settled in Darien in 1802 at the request of town fathers eager to see their community grow.[22] The vernacular architecture of Savannah, which included New York-style stoops and dormer windows, Rhode Island gambrel roofs, and New England porticoes built in the immediate wake of the Savannah fire of 1796, attests to the presence of newly arrived northern-born and northern-trained carpenters from a variety of locales eager to take advantage of the city's misfortune.[23]

It is important to point out that for craftsmen in elite and nonelite trades alike, relocation to Georgia could be a risky endeavor and in some cases a last resort, as Reuben King's early experience in Darien suggests. Upon the completion of his apprenticeship in Connecticut, King had settled his local debts and "against the advice of my best friends . . . although I was steadfast in my opportune undertaking" departed for Pittsburgh in the spring of 1800. Arriving with thirty cents in his pocket and a trunk full of tools, leather, and partially made shoes, he hoped to earn enough wages as a journeyman to establish a partnership in a tanning business with his best friend. But wages proved much lower than he had anticipated and competition for jobs much stiffer. After three months, he decided to strike out on foot for Baltimore, selling shoes along the way to pay for his meal and board, and on occasion fleeing highway robbers. On reaching Baltimore, he worked long enough to purchase the cost of his ship passage to Georgia.

His first five years in Darien were rocky ones, despite his belief in the growing opportunities available to him, for Darien was a small port town that served coastal planters south of Brunswick. At times aided by an older brother, Roswell King, who lived nearby, Reuben King spent two years building a tanyard only to lose part of it in a sheriff's sale to pay off his debts and part of it to the ravages of a hurricane. Yet King remained undaunted for the most part, supporting himself both in the tradition of a tanner by peeling bark, sinking vats, curing hides, and making shoes, and in the tradition of a farmer by cultivating corn and watermelons, picking berries, grazing cattle, and netting fish. An ambitious and energetic man, he also took on such odd jobs as piloting boats, cutting timber, and measuring lumber for his neighbors. When his financial resources sank especially low, he bound himself out for a year to a local merchant, and having learned something of the business, later opened a store of his own, one that sold supplies, groceries, and liquor as well as shoes and leather, although this effort soon failed as well. Eventually, of course, more propitious circumstances transformed him into a planter, but his first years in Georgia were undeniably difficult ones.[24]

Like King, artisans who arrived in Georgia during the early republic had to assess and then adapt themselves and their skills to the needs of the local economy—needs that were fundamentally different, in most cases, from the needs of the far more commercially and culturally sophisticated towns and cities they had departed. They also had to be prepared to weather rough times. But patience under these circumstances generally paid off. The growing size and wealth of the state's white population generated new demand for a variety of artisanal skills. This demand took a number of forms.

Increasing emphasis on the production of staple crops encouraged the expansion of marketing and transport facilities in the two largest urban centers in the state, Savannah and Augusta, and to a lesser extent in smaller towns like Darien. This expansion increased the demand for artisanal work in all its variety. As more staples were brought to market, more wharves, warehouses, public buildings, and other public works were erected by artisans skilled in the building trades. In 1798, for example, the Augusta City

Council offered "ready money" to carpenters willing to build a city well.[25] The rise in urban construction, in turn, generated demand for such necessities as tools, nails, bricks, and lumber, which were supplied by local artisans engaged in such trades as blacksmithing, brickmaking, and sawyering. At the same time, as trade expanded, more artisans were needed to build and repair the boats, wagons, and other vehicles that transported these goods, generating new demand for shipcaulkers, shipwrights, blacksmiths, and wagonmakers. As the staple economy matured, artisans with some mechanical proficiency were needed to produce tools, equipment, and machinery for agricultural households, plantations, sawmills, and gins. The invention of the cotton gin alone created new demand for machinists able to repair and replace worn parts, but artisans also built and repaired saw mills and flour mills throughout this period.[26]

Trade expansion affected demand for artisanal skills in other ways as well. Growing numbers of urban inhabitants sought provisions from bakers and butchers as well as attire provided by tailors, seamstresses, and shoemakers. New wealth among a growing urban class of planters and merchants eager to acquire the accoutrements appropriate to their elevated social status—whether in the form of silver, jewelry, portraits, furniture, pianos, carriages, or ostentatious urban homes—generated demand for a whole host of luxury craftsmen. Thus, urban artisans in a variety of trades both benefited from and participated in this expanding market economy.

Most migrant mechanics, not surprisingly, first sought work in Savannah or Augusta, where the rippling effect of this expansion quickly reached the greatest number of people. Although distinctly different places in many respects, both towns shared one central function—the marketing of the staple crops cultivated in their regional economies.[27] Savannah was the largest export center south of Charleston and the tenth largest city in the country in 1800.[28] Visitors to the lovely city, including George Washington, marveled at its fine harbor, with its impressive number of square-rigged vessels at anchor and its extensive command of the outlying countryside. Travelers and inhabitants alike were certain that the city's future was a bright one given its superior resources and excellent location.[29] Eighteen miles above the mouth of a powerful river whose headwaters lay 125 miles northwest, Savannah offered safe harbor to ocean-going vessels as well as access to the Georgia and South Carolina upcountry.

At the end of the eighteenth century, Savannah performed all the traditional functions of a port city. It exchanged, collected, stored, and distributed the state's commodities: rice, indigo, sea island cotton, and lumber from the lowcountry, as well as tobacco, upland cotton, grains, deerskins, and other pelts from the upcountry. These commodities were sent up the coast or across the Atlantic on the approximately four hundred ocean-going ships that passed through the harbor each year. Since the port's primary purpose was the distribution of commodities intended for distant markets, the town's mercantile, transport, and warehousing facilities were well developed. In contrast, especially when compared to cities like New York, Philadelphia, Baltimore, and Boston, its manufacturing capacities were virtually nonexistent.[30]

As a result, artisanal production in Savannah was tied to the needs of this particular distribution system and to the consumption patterns of the planters and merchants who resided there. Artisans in the construction and service crafts maintained and expanded the physical infrastructure that made this trade possible. Artisans who produced consumer goods and luxury items served the coastal planters who marketed their crops in Savannah, the merchants who arranged the sale and shipment of these crops, and the other urban dwellers who supported this trade. While many of these wares were imported from the North, the West Indies, Europe, and Africa, others were too costly or too fragile to import. During the early republic, many of these goods, such as clothing, furniture, silver, and carriages, were made locally by artisans, though almost always copied from European styles. Artisans also provided this planter and merchant elite with such luxury services as house building, wallpaper hanging, and watch repairs.[31]

To a much lesser extent, Savannah artisans in nonluxury trades counted on the patronage of a group of citizens at the other end of the social scale. Poor nonslaveholding "crackers," who had pushed their two-wheeled carts loaded with eggs, chickens, hides, fruit, and tallow for as many as ten days through the piney woods to the coast, sold their goods in the town market several times a year. In many instances, these poor whites found themselves competing with slave families who sold similar items from wheelbarrows and wagons on the outskirts of town. Once the poor whites had managed to sell their produce, despite this competition, they used the proceeds to fill their carts with a minimal amount of storegoods, including basic necessities made by local artisans that they could not fashion for themselves, to take back to their distant homes.[32]

Despite growing demand for artisanal goods from across the social spectrum, white artisans in many trades in Savannah constantly confronted competition posed by the institution of slavery, which in some cases fundamentally affected how and even whether some white male artisans could make a living. Not only did slavery sustain the regional economy; it also shaped all aspects of urban daily life. White artisans who lived and worked in the city year round felt slavery's sting in a number of significant ways. Savannah residents had relied on skilled and unskilled urban slave labor in their public and private lives throughout the last half of the eighteenth century. By 1800, 2,367 slaves, almost half the city's population, lived and worked in the busy town.[33] Slave men performed a variety of urban jobs, including skilled work, like boat-building, brickmaking, butchering, and blacksmithing, as well as unskilled work like loading ships, carrying cargo to warehouses, digging ditches, and running errands. The preponderance of wealthy planters and merchants in Savannah meant that many slaves, male and female, also worked as house servants assigned to gender-specific tasks. Slave men served as valets, carriage-drivers, hostlers, and gardeners. Slave women worked chiefly as domestics, and sometimes at artisanal tasks, such as sewing and hatmaking, which were performed in private homes for private consumption. Whether slave work was public or private, however, all evidence indicates that the institution of slavery was deeply embedded in the social and economic relations of the city by the end of the century. Thus, the presence of urban slavery fundamentally affected the kinds of work white artisans performed in Savannah, as well as white artisanal attitudes toward slaves and slavery.[34]

Slavery's centrality to Savannah's economy was evident in another critical form as well. The city operated as the nexus for all slave trade in Georgia. Planters in the lowcountry, who had relied on field hands to perform arduous physical labor in the rice and indigo fields since the mid–eighteenth century, continually sought new slaves to add to their growing plantations. In addition, after the American Revolution, the settlement of the upcountry, along with the introduction of staple production in this region, brought increased demand for slaves. Trade in African slaves, and later American-born slaves, was yet another important commodity in the commercial exchange of Savannah, one that affected white male artisans in contradictory ways.[35] On one hand, the rising trade in slaves meant that an increasing number of specialized slave artisans could be sent to the city to hire out their time during the off-season, creating more competition for artisanal jobs. On the other hand, the constant trade in black slaves reminded white artisans that they too shared in the privileges accorded the white race—the right to own slaves and the right to the wealth that could be accrued from their labor.

Although a busy export center that relied on skilled and unskilled labor, black and white, as well as slave and free, at the turn of the century, Savannah's engagement with the trans-Atlantic world hindered urban growth in those areas unrelated to the market exchange of commodities. This reality had important implications for white artisans. While the dynamism and diversity of many urban economies were at least partially encouraged by the investments of local merchants, this was not the case in Savannah.[36] Most of the so-called merchants of the town were in fact agents for commission houses in Charleston, Liverpool, and Glasgow. Profits secured from the sale of Georgia's commodities, therefore, were usually destined for distant coffers, and not for reinvestment in the local economy. However charming visitors found Savannah's symmetrical streets and squares lined with exotic chinaberry trees, and however promising the fine harbor and new wharves and warehouses, the dirty, cumbersome roads of shifting sand and the town buildings not nearly "so elegant as those of Charleston" served as physical reminders to visitors and inhabitants alike that Savannah had yet to achieve the importance of the leading port cities of America and Europe.[37] While Savannah's size and function provided the greatest number of artisans, white and black, slave and free, with the greatest number and variety of work opportunities in Georgia, the city's economy and population grew relatively slowly after 1800, necessitating fewer workshops and manufactories than in comparable cities elsewhere. Many white artisans, daunted by the city's second-class status, competition with black artisans and the other hardships they encountered there, ventured to the upcountry market-town of Augusta in search of work.

Located at the fall-line of the Savannah River, Augusta had been a convergence point for trails leading north and west to Creek, Choctaw, and Chickasaw lands. Under James Oglethorpe's orders, soldiers had erected a fort on this site in 1736 to protect trade with the Indians.[38] By the mid-eighteenth century the little village that had grown up alongside this fort, labeled by traders and merchants as "the key to the Indian country," not only catered to the bartering business but linked a growing population of upcountry farmers in Georgia and South Carolina to the port cities of Charleston and Savannah.[39] The end of the revolution brought a steady rush of tens of thousands of these settlers to the surrounding upcountry, often with slaves in tow, drawn by the Georgia headright system, by bounty claims awarded to war veterans (although these claims were often purchased from veterans by speculators), and eventually by a land lottery system, which awarded virtually free plots of land, secured through treaties with Native Americans, to household heads.[40] By 1790, more Georgians lived in this region than in the older lowcountry settlements along the Atlantic.[41]

Indeed, Augusta briefly challenged Savannah for the position of preeminent Georgia town following the removal of the capital from Savannah to Augusta in 1786.[42] By 1800, nearly one hundred stores and workshops lined the main thoroughfare. At the end of every harvest season, scores of upcountry farmers led oxen harnessed to rolling barrels of tobacco down Broad Street to one of the three warehouses along the river where, following its inspection and sale, the crop awaited shipment downstream by flatboat.[43] Farmers used their tobacco profits to buy goods and supplies from the town's shopkeepers and artisans. The cultivation of green-seed cotton, which began to dot the rolling hills of the upcountry soon after the invention of the cotton gin, brought a new set of farmers and buyers to the river port, doubling the town's population from an estimated 1,100 residents in 1790 to 2,270 in 1800, just over half of whom were white.[44] By 1810, Augusta's role as cotton exchange was so assured that little boys could climb aboard wagons bearing cotton and "run a mile down Broad Street . . . without ever getting down off the cotton bags."[45] Augusta, in less than a century's time, had become a thriving entrepôt and even an upcountry cultural mecca of sorts, one that included several churches, two newspapers, an academy, and a theater.[46]

White artisans venturing to Augusta at this time were fortunate. The youthful town lacked the workshops, manufactories, and warehouses of older urban centers that had begun to trap artisans elsewhere into perpetual journeyman status.[47] Many Augusta artisans engaged in commonplace crafts found that their clients included the town's population as well as farm families from the countryside. Artisans engaged in luxury trades relied upon a small but wealthy clientele of planters and merchants for work. As with Savannah, a dearth of sources prevents precise tabulation of the artisan population and its occupational distribution. Although newspaper advertisements reveal much about master craftsmen in luxury trades, they fail to identify masters in more commonplace ones who relied on handbills or word of mouth to secure work. Moreover, the advertisements fail to identify journeymen in general. Available sources do suggest, however, that Augusta artisans, like their Savannah counterparts, employed their skills in a wide array of trades: construction, clothing, leather, food, shipbuilding, forging, furnituremaking, printing, and clock and jewelry crafts.[48]

The unique nature of Augusta's local economy mitigated against too many artisans practicing highly specialized crafts. Unlike Charleston or Savannah, Augusta did not boast a population of fabulously wealthy rice planters. Nor did it cater to the needs of businessmen sent to American port cities from the merchant houses and banking establishments of Glasgow and London. Augusta remained an entrepôt, albeit a thriving one, that served an upcountry of largely self-sufficient farmers. Demand for artisanal goods and services came largely from these men, and to a lesser extent, from townspeople, planters, and merchants.[49] Although the successful cultivation of tobacco and cotton created a modest but growing planter class increasingly able to afford their goods and services, most artisans, regardless of craft or status, adapted and expanded their skills or developed new ones in a community where specialization could prove a drawback. In this regard, perhaps no Augusta artisan was quite as versatile as Mathias Beaver, who advertised his services as a shipwright and boat builder as well as a clock- and watchmaker in 1813.[50] Still, most artisans could anticipate stretching their skills to fit the changing and occasionally limited needs of this local economy.

By the late eighteenth century slavery, though not as deeply embedded in the social and economic life of Augusta as in Savannah, was rapidly becoming so. Unlike lowcountry Georgia, slavery was a relative newcomer to the upcountry. Area farmers, mostly newcomers themselves, had acquired slaves slowly. Unlike the lowcountry, where wealthy planters invested in labor forces of anywhere from several dozen to several hundred slaves to cultivate large labor-intensive crops, upcountry planters relied on an average of a half-dozen slaves to cultivate smaller, less labor-intensive crops of tobacco, grains, and upland cotton.[51] By 1800, slavery in Augusta was not as established as slavery in Savannah. Although the proportion of urban slaves in Augusta was comparable to the proportion in Savannah, totaling nearly half of the town's population, this was a brand-new development.[52]

Augusta's increasing importance as a commercial center, which was reflected in its many stores and shops, its warehouses and wharves, and its growing white and black population, did not result in the town's severance of all its ties with its frontier past. Newspaper accounts relate that men still attended church with their dogs, although this was frowned upon, one or two men were rumored to have traded their wives for slaves, and brawlers continued to gouge eyes and bite off ears. The humorist, minister, educator, and lawyer, A. B. Longstreet, who grew up in Augusta during this period, described the upcountry town at this time as a bawdy place where the lower sort feverishly bet on mounted contestants engaged in yanking the greased heads off strung-up geese. As Longstreet's story suggests, the town had yet to shake off its frontier roots at the end of the eighteenth century.[53]

Many migrant white artisans made this upcountry town their new home, despite its relative coarseness, in their quest for new opportunities. Other artisans believed that the older and more sophisticated city of Savannah held the most promise. Still others, like Reuben King, headed to the small towns and villages of the Georgia coast and countryside instead. Regardless of where they chose to settle in Georgia, however, white male artisans learned that finding new opportunities in this expanding slaveholding economy often depended less on character, ambition, and industry than on timing and circumstance. While the growth of staple-crop economies in Georgia meant new demand for a wide variety of artisanal skills and services, not all white artisans benefited from this development, despite their hopes to the contrary. And even those artisans who managed to take advantage of these structural realities and transform themselves into planters experienced some setbacks. Certainly, they did not experience the loss of status characteristic of independent craftsmen in the urban Northeast where the rise in new technologies and manufactories made some artisanal skills, such as shoemaking, increasingly obsolete after 1820. They did, however, experience a complicated set of pressures that discouraged many of them from pursuing their artisanal occupations.

Artisanal opportunity was inextricably tied to planter wealth. The rise and fall of staple-crop prices on the world market, as well as the political decisions that affected access to this world market, had a fundamental impact upon the planter class and the state of the local slave economy. Since white artisans in Georgia, especially urban artisans, participated in this market economy by often accepting payment in cash for services rendered, their fortunes rose and fell with the fortunes of the planter class. Artisanal opportunity was also tied to changes in style and taste, the number of imported and manufactured goods sold by local merchants, and competition from fellow artisans, black and white, slave and free. These factors affected individual white artisans in different ways depending upon time period, skill, status, and location.

That most of these artisans suffered personal and economic setbacks at various points in their careers, whether in Savannah, Augusta, or the countryside, is clear from the sources. Poor health, uncertain income, and mounting debt struck most Georgia mechanics, rich or poor, at some time during their careers. Illness was ubiquitous in Savannah's mechanic community. The rice swamps and open ditches that surrounded three sides of the city made it a treacherous place to live, one where "none will venture," according to a traveler's account, during the disease-plagued months of summer and early autumn. As late as 1820, after city officials had launched one of the most ambitious disease prevention programs in the South, six hundred residents died in a five-month period during a yellow fever epidemic. Journeymen were especially vulnerable to disease, and not simply because they lived year-round in the city. Although authorities removed all standing water and garbage from much of Savannah, they neglected to perform these preventive measures in the poorer wards where many wage-earning mechanics lived.[54] But journeymen elsewhere in Georgia were no less immune to local fevers and agues. Reuben King, who frequently fell ill and sometimes lay bedridden for a month at a time, worriedly recorded in his journal that in 1803 six local white craftsmen, all once strong and vigorous, had died in a single nine-month period.[55]

At times money woes proved as incapacitating as sickness. Georgia artisans were subject to a series of economic changes outside their control. Factors beyond the regional economy, like a drop in European prices for staples, an increase in the availability of northern manufactured goods, and the national depression in the wake of the War of 1812, affected the consumption patterns of artisans' customers. Local circumstances, such as a flood or a drought, affected artisan livelihoods as well. But perhaps the most profound changes imposed on artisans resulted from the decisions the planter class made about spending its wealth—decisions which often put white craftsmen at their mercy.

Artisans certainly recognized their dependence on the planter class. As a "Mechanic" claimed in a letter to the editor of the *Columbian Museum and Savannah Advertiser*, "The planter takes his money, buys more negroes, goes on a frolic to the northward," but when the carpenter he hired requests his wages for work performed, the planter puts him off. When the carpenter seeks legal redress, he discovers that "the courts are tedious and will tire the carpenter out before the planter."[56] Reuben King observed that it was difficult to distinguish gentlemen who honored their debts versus those who absconded without making payments owed:

> I have resolved to trust no person this year on Book Account and not to tan on Shares In my Opinion it is an imprudent thing for Merchants or mechanics to give Credit in this Country Thare is a number of Sole vagabonds that git thare living by Swindling or rather by runing in debt without any intention to pay &c—This Country differs from many others The inhabitants are generally liberal and a Man well dressed passes for a gentleman with out further acquaintance—[57]

Even bona fide gentlemen planters of longstanding acquaintance were often late with their payments. Fairly typical was the experience of a Savannah cabinetmaker owed more than $250 for work completed in 1802 and 1803; he received his due only upon the settlement of his patron's estate in 1805.[58] While such payment practices did not undermine the businesses of successful master craftsmen, they proved especially disheartening to struggling craftsmen like King.

Mechanics coped with these payment problems in a variety of ways. An Augusta tailor informed the public that "he intends working for the future at the most reduced prices for prompt pay."[59] The Savannah trunkmaker Willard Sears offered a 25 percent discount to those customers who paid quickly.[60] When income was slow in arriving, mechanics often moved their shops. The Savannah watchmaker Edward Griffith believed that his new address, "nearer to the Merchants and Planters Coffee-House," would bring better clientele to his store.[61] Other mechanics unable or unwilling to relocate chose to expand their skills. Francis Girondon of Savannah offered his services to the public as "an armorer, founder, and mechanist [who] repairs umbrellas in the neatest way."[62]

Sometimes, mechanics' efforts to adapt themselves to the vagaries of their local economy proved futile. John Richards, an Augusta gunsmith forced to divide his last twelve hundred dollars among his creditors, poured out his financial woes in an unusual newspaper announcement attesting to his sterling character. "Assiduity has been my study, and fidelity my prop. Fortune's frowns are daily crowding in upon me. . . . I hope my creditors will take one serious moment to deliberate upon my indigent circumstances at present, and be so amicable as to withdraw their suits against me."[63] He then recommended that young artisans who hoped to avoid his misfortune invent a cotton machine "that shall work without the impelling power of water, fire, beasts, or humans."[64] Richards clearly recognized that an artisan's success was linked to his ability to meet the new demands of this cotton economy. Reuben King found himself in similarly desperate straits when, after working industriously for several years at his Darien tanyard, he was unable to collect monies owed him. "I am now all Most discouraged," he recorded in his journal. "I am without Money without Credit and Nothing to Sell."[65]

Unlike Richards and King, some artisans experiencing financial woes did not choose to deal with their creditors so honestly. When Augusta watchmaker Charles de la Place's debts proved insurmountable, he left town for parts unknown, taking with him watches entrusted to him for repairs.[66] Sudden departure, with or without stolen merchandise, proved the only choice for many mechanics confronting hard times. Their names and addresses appeared once, sometimes twice, in Savannah and Augusta newspaper advertisements and local records before disappearing, like the men themselves, without a trace.[67]

As Richards, King, and other white artisans in Georgia came to recognize, their fortunes were tightly bound to local circumstances like weather and disease, the production of staple crops, the ups and downs of the world market, and more often than not, the spending power, consumer habits, and payment practices of wealthy whites, especially planters. While the 1790s were flush years for the regional economy, the embargo and the War of 1812 played havoc with crop prices over the next two decades. Upland cotton, at 30 cents a pound in 1800, fell to 16 cents in 1810, slipping to a frightening 12 cents in 1813, before bouncing back to 29 cents in 1816.[68] Many farmers, small planters, and artisans struggled to pay their debts under these circumstances; only some of whom were rescued by the state legislature's Debtors' Relief Law of 1809.[69]

This series of local, national, and international economic realities affected white artisans in different ways depending upon the trades they practiced. Unlike the North, manufacturing in Georgia was in its nascence during the early republic, despite some political pressure to develop this sector of the economy. As Georgia, along with the rest of the nation, found itself forced into some measure of self-reliance after 1808, state leaders began to promote a more diversified economy. In his 1809 message to the state, Governor Jared Irwin urged Georgia's citizens to "cherish every institution for the promotion of agriculture and domestic manufactures."[70] Despite this pronouncement and others like it, however, manufacturing establishments were virtually absent in Georgia at this time. In 1810, the U.S. Census Bureau, in its *Statement of the Arts and Manufactures,* reported that one cotton establishment, one forge, one nailery, one bloomery, one soap and candle-making establishment, one brewery, one sawmill, two gun powder establishments, 31 tanneries, and 126 distilleries comprised the sum of Georgia's manufactories. Although these figures are misleading in that every indication suggests, for example, that more than one sawmill operated in Georgia in 1810, the census-takers were basically correct in concluding that workshop and home production, not manufacturing, accounted for the vast majority of nonagricultural goods produced in Georgia.[71] Local demand, particularly in the upcountry, simply could not sustain all the ironworks, sawmills, and brickeries launched by eager investors. Newspapers throughout this period contain at least one or two advertisements in every issue offering these establishments for sale at public auction. The repercussions for rural white artisans in traditional crafts are obvious. Numerous millers, sawyers, and brickmakers found themselves without jobs.[72] Yet it would be inaccurate to state that all artisans suffered equally during this era. Technological developments and international politics, for example, actually created work for mechanics, stonecutters, and coopers during the first decades of the nineteenth century. Although a relatively simple device, the cotton gin, a machine purchased by farmers and planters across the piedmont, necessitated some measure of mechanic know-how to erect and repair. The brand-new grist-mill industry that emerged during the War of 1812, when Georgians were forced to grind their own grains, also created work for skilled men.[73]

As these white artisans discovered, the changing demands of the staple-crop economy, along with developments in the world market and national politics, profoundly affected the nature of rural artisanal opportunity. Meanwhile, Georgia artisans producing luxury crafts also discovered that changes in production, particularly in the free-labor economy of the northern United States, affected artisanal opportunity as well. After 1800, growing numbers of master craftsmen in Savannah and Augusta began to import manufactured goods from northern cities and abroad. Savannah silversmiths, for example, received silver articles from New York to resell under their own manufacturer's mark.[74] In 1799, Savannah silversmith Frederick Marquand entered into a partnership with Connecticut-born Josiah Penfield. Together they gradually replaced their own original silver with articles imported from a New York company owned by Marquand's relatives.[75] Likewise, Savannah furnituremakers also began to import furniture from New York by ship at this time.[76] Benjamin Ansley, a respected Savannah artisan, formed an agreement with John Hewitt to ship him ready-made furniture.[77] In addition, the designation "Northern-made" began to appear on advertisements for carriages and riding-chairs.[78] Manufactured imports were not always limited to expensive luxury items. Shortly before 1800, several shoemakers in both Savannah and Augusta offered for sale huge numbers of ready-made shoes from Philadelphia and Boston intended both for Georgia slaves and "ladies and gentlemen."[79] The effect of these importations was twofold. On one hand, an elite group of master craftsmen with connections and credit transformed themselves into artisan-merchants. On the other, urban journeymen-shoemakers subsequently suffered from a dearth of wage-earning positions.

Georgia artisans during the early republic confronted a complicated set of circumstances that brought some men great distress. Yet many white artisans in a wide array of trades prospered over the course of the era. Newspaper advertisements provide a rough guide to the population figures for master craftsmen residing in both Savannah and Augusta; these figures increased dramatically between the 1790s and the 1810s despite so many economic uncertainties. The number of Savannah master craftsmen in the construction and forging trades who placed newspaper advertisements increased 7 percent between one decade and the next; the number of cabinetmakers, chairmakers, and upholstery-makers who placed advertisements increased 40 percent; and the numbers of silversmiths and watchmakers 54 percent.[80] A similar shift occurred in Augusta, though the upcountry town lacked Savannah's ties to the great planter wealth of the lowcountry. For example, the number of master craftsmen advertising furniture and carriages increased 63 percent from the 1790s to the 1800s, a change that suggests where the new wealth of upcountry planters was being spent.[81]

The Chatham County Tax Digests for 1798 and 1799, the only ones extant during the early republic that include occupations as well as taxpayers' names, indicate that the wealth of urban white artisans as well as their numbers were on the rise. Out of 1,301 returns in 1799 representing those residents of Savannah and surrounding Chatham County prosperous enough to own taxable property (houses, lots, stock in trade, carriages, slaves, etc.), mechanics' returns comprised a respectable 16 percent. By contrast, planters' returns comprised 13 percent; merchants' returns, 14 percent; and shopkeepers' and professionals' returns the bulk of the remainder.[82] The tax digests also demonstrate rapid growth in the number of taxpaying artisans in luxury and nonluxury trades over a single year's time. The number of taxpaying tailors and butchers, for example, more than doubled between 1798 and 1799; the number of taxpaying luxury tradesmen also grew substantially. Overall, the number of taxpaying artisans increased 29 percent from 1798 to 1799.[83]

Savannah master craftsmen in a variety of trades, as this evidence suggests, did make money, as did Georgia artisans elsewhere. How these artisans organized their households, along with how they used their new wealth, reveals much about the ways in which these migrants adapted themselves as well as their skills to their slaveholding world. These men quickly came to recognize that their status as white men was inextricably tied to the structure of the household in which they lived, and in particular, to their position within that household. It was here in the household, the nexus of all social relations in the South, that men, women, and children learned and acted out the hierarchical set of roles assigned them by virtue of their race, class, and gender.

The social system of slavery, then, revolved around the relations of production and reproduction that took place within the household, generally headed by a white property-owning male whose individual rights and authority over his dependents received special sanction from the state. This system nurtured a paternalistic ideology that legitimated and indeed created social expectations of white male dominance over the household, and by extension, southern society. This ideology, in turn, helped perpetuate the notion of egalitarian relations among free white men.[84]

Southern white male artisans eagerly established households of their own to serve as vehicles for increasing their productive capacities and for cementing their status as independent white men. Like artisans in free labor economies, these southern artisans used newly earned capital to build substantial households of varied composition—households that could include wives, children, journeymen, apprentices, free blacks, and slaves.

Many white male artisans in a number of trades in both Savannah and Augusta began fashioning their households by first securing apprentices shortly after their arrival in Georgia. The inclusion of an apprentice in a new craftsman's shop provided him with relatively inexpensive help, broadcast his confidence in his ability to support an added household member, and gave him legitimacy as a master craftsman competent enough to train a young man in "the mysteries of the trade."[85]

Likewise, the hiring of journeymen also signaled a master craftsman's confidence in his skills as well as the future success of his shop. Shortly after his arrival in Georgia in 1797, Edward Griffith advertised for "one or two journeymen silversmiths" to whom he would pay twenty dollars per month plus board and lodging. A boot- and shoemaker with a small workshop in Savannah sought two or three journeymen and two or three apprentices in 1797.[86] The Savannah artisan John Gardiner sought "3 or 4 journeymen who are good workmen." The Augusta mechanic William Savel announced the success of his new business while also notifying the public that he had acquired "a number of workmen."[87]

Throughout the early republic, master craftsmen sought help from white apprentices and journeymen in many trades ranging from printing, tailoring, and tin-plating to coach-trimming, bricklaying, and plastering.[88] Artisans who took on apprentices and hired journeymen in Georgia demonstrated their status as masters in a craft tradition that stretched back to medieval Europe. At the same time, they demonstrated their status as masters in the slaveholding tradition of the South. Though not all artisans owned slaves, they could share in the status of "master" by virtue of their household dependents—including journeymen and apprentices.[89]

Whereas master craftsmen's reliance on apprentices and journeymen was an important stage in establishing themselves as bona fide artisans and masters in their new locales, artisans' growing reliance on slave labor marks an even more important development in their adoption of southern mores. The use of slave labor by white artisans, while not unheard-of in northern cities during the late eighteenth century, was becoming increasingly atypical during the course of the early nineteenth century. The staple-crop economy in the slaveholding lower South, in contrast, encouraged urban townspeople as well as planters to hire and buy skilled and unskilled slaves (and to a lesser extent, to hire free blacks). Prospering white artisans, like most other men with capital in this staple-crop region, chose to participate in the slave economy. It is difficult to determine precisely how many white artisans owned or hired slaves (and what kinds of slaves they owned or hired) during this period, but the available evidence suggests that an individual artisan's ownership of slaves provided a strong indication of his rising economic and social status, whether or not he purchased skilled slaves, who were more costly. Male field hands sold for approximately $450 in 1800—as much as a modest town house and lot—and slave artisans and trained domestic slaves generally proved even more expensive.[90]

Most migrant artisans needed some time to accrue enough capital to afford an unskilled bondsperson. The purchase of a skilled slave artisan or domestic servant, however, required even greater investment. Thus, although silversmith Devine Lambertoz arrived in Savannah in 1795 and immediately signed on a white apprentice, a full eight years elapsed before he acquired his first slave, a domestic.[91] Likewise, the silversmith Joseph Rice, who appeared in Savannah in 1787, quickly obtained apprentices, then "excellent workmen," but some years passed before he acquired "a valuable young Negro man," presumably a skilled slave.[92] While taking on apprentices and journeymen may have increased an artisan's productivity and indicated that artisans shared in white southern men's "master" status, the purchase of black slaves helped further define white master craftsmen as legitimate members of a social order that increasingly viewed artisanal work with some ambivalence.

While slave ownership promoted white artisan status and increased artisanal production, it also engendered a whole series of tensions within the artisan class. Although a significant social distance separated master craftsmen such as the silversmiths Lambertoz and Rice from their skilled slaves, this was not always the case for white journeymen in nonelite trades who lacked the capital to establish their own shops and buy slaves. Thus, skilled white and black laborers often worked alongside each other in a variety of situations. The brickmaker George Miller employed ten white men and six of his own slaves at his Savannah brick factory. The Chatham Steam Saw Mill operated with the assistance of three white sawyers and eight slave sawyers, as well as two slave women and four slave children. Four white men, two slave men, and two "boys," the race of the latter unclear, ran a Chatham County iron foundry. The L. Baldwin Company's candle- and soap-making establishment employed three white men and one slave.[93]

While these sources demonstrate that whites and blacks, as free and unfree skilled laborers, worked together in early-nineteenth-century Georgia shops, it is not clear whether workers shared the same tasks and skills or were assigned them according to a racial hierarchy. Nonetheless, white men working in these situations must have been aware of the lack of boundaries separating them from the slaves with whom they worked. In a society that degraded the kinds of labor that slaves performed, it must have been important to these white journeymen to distinguish themselves from skilled slaves based on a conception of racial difference. Such work experiences must have compelled white journeymen to hire or even to buy slaves of their own if the opportunity ever presented itself.

Newspaper advertisements seeking the return of skilled runaway slaves, along with occupational information from registries of free blacks, also make it clear that master craftsmen consistently relied on skilled black labor that they either owned or hired. In runaway advertisements in Savannah newspapers, lowcountry planters frequently reported that their skilled slave artisans had fled to Savannah and sought urban work while pretending to be free.[94] Many of these runaway slave artisans were well known in the city, much to their masters' chagrin, and knew how to find work and hide themselves from their masters in the relative anonymity of an urban milieu.[95] Of course, not all slave artisans who worked in the city were runaways. Many slave artisans had leave to find work in Savannah during dull periods on the plantation. Other slave artisans belonged to local residents, including merchants, shopkeepers, and artisans. On the whole, nevertheless, male slave artisans appear to have represented a relatively small proportion of the city's slave population and tended to be clustered in labor-intensive and low-status trades such as brickmaking and construction during the early republic.[96]

Augusta's population of slave artisans seems to have been smaller than Savannah's. Though Augusta whites hired groups of slaves for heavy, monotonous work such as felling timber and attending cotton gins, little evidence exists to suggest widespread reliance on the work of slave artisans at this time. An examination of advertisements for runaway slaves placed in Augusta newspapers reveals that few runaway slave artisans attempted to pass themselves off as free blacks or as slaves permitted to hire out their own time in Augusta, though this was a commonplace practice in Savannah.[97] In fact, most runaways from the Augusta countryside bypassed the upcountry town to head directly to Savannah or Charleston, where larger black communities, more job opportunities, and more anonymity awaited them.[98] Or they headed west toward Indian country.[99] Furthermore, slave artisans were simply rarer in the upcountry, and therefore were less likely to be hired out in Augusta during the off-season; their talents often proved too specialized for the small-scale upcountry plantations and farms that prevailed there.[100] Upcountry plantation development also discouraged the establishment of a significant skilled free black population in Augusta.[101] Between 1800 and 1840, the free black population never exceeded 6 percent of the total population of Augusta; Savannah's free black population exceeded that figure only once, in 1810, when it rose to 10 percent of the city's inhabitants.

The existence of a Register of Free Persons of Color for Chatham County (Savannah) in 1817 permits some speculation about the degree of competition between white journeymen and free black artisans in this port city during the latter days of the early republic. Artisanal occupations were listed for 21 percent (44) of the adult free black men on the register. The nine occupations that these forty-four men claimed can be collectively characterized as commonplace trades. Half of the men worked as either tailors or carpenters. Likewise, the 1819 Register of Free Persons of Color for Richmond County (Augusta) listed twenty-one artisans, all of whom worked in nonluxury trades, half as carpenters. While Savannah free blacks worked in artisanal occupations generally considered distasteful, dirty, servile, or simply less prestigious (i.e., butchering, bricklaying, and shoemaking), it is important to note that several Augusta free blacks worked in relatively elite trades such as harnessmaking and saddlery. This

Table 1. Population in Savannah and Augusta, 1800–1810

	1800	Percentage	1810	Percentage
Total Population				
Savannah	5,146		5,215	
Augusta	2,215		2,476	
White Population				
Savannah	2,598	(50.5)	2,490	(47.7)
Augusta	1,159	(52.3)	1,109	(44.8)
Slave Population				
Savannah	2,367	(46.0)	2,195	(42.1)
Augusta	1,017	(45.9)	1,321	(53.3)
Free Black Population				
Savannah	181	(3.5)	530	(10.2)
Augusta	39	(1.8)	46	(1.9)

Sources: Second Census of the U.S., 2N, 4N; Aggregate Amount of Persons Within the United States in the Year 1810, 80.

suggests that the predominance of trained white journeymen in Savannah may have discouraged white masters in elite trades that required specialized skills from hiring free black artisans, while the lack of skilled men of either race in the smaller town of Augusta allowed free black artisans entry into more select trades.[102]

While white journeymen in elite trades may have suffered little or no competition from free black artisans, these registries point out that some competition must have existed between white journeymen and free black artisans in nonelite trades, especially in Savannah. Such competition must have proved especially frustrating to white journeymen who assumed that their whiteness would secure them work. Instead, they discovered a society in which a small population of free black artisans not only found artisanal work but could accrue wealth and status. The Savannah free black resident Louis Mirault, for example, owned a small but flourishing tailor's business in 1806. Twenty-two years later, his estate included property valued at $1,000, six slaves, and over $200 due him by some forty customers. Free black artisans like Mirault must have represented a disproportionate share of the wealthiest of Savannah's free blacks since most professional and business careers were generally closed to them. Rivaling the combined wealth of much larger free black communities in Richmond and Petersburg, twenty-two Savannah free blacks owned sixty-four homes and lots between them, and from one to fifteen slaves each (many of whom were probably family members purchased from white slaveholders) by the 1820s.[103]

Despite their wealth, this small group of free black men and women occupied an ambiguous place in Savannah. On one hand, their social activities, according to local reports, resembled those of whites and in at least some cases even received white sanction. Free black men in Savannah reportedly "duelled like white gentlemen." The wealthiest of free black families held parties, filled with "dancing and making merry," attended by whites and blacks alike. On the other hand, the local government passed numerous restrictions based on free blacks' racial identity rather than their status as free people in an attempt to limit their physical mobility and economic opportunities.

Some of these laws, like annual registration, curfews, and limitations on the size of black gatherings, were attempts to guard against insurrection, particularly in the wake of the slave revolt in St. Domingue in 1794 and Gabriel's attempted revolt in Virginia in 1800. Other laws took advantage of free blacks' marginal status. For example, free blacks were forced to work with slaves on the city's fortifications during the War of 1812.[104] They also had to endure marked attempts to curb their economic freedoms, which suggests that white craftsmen resented the competition created by black craftsmen who performed artisan work without the supervision of a white employer. In 1809, slaves were prohibited by city ordinance "from carrying on any mechanick or handicraft trade of themselves." Eight years later, the city council expanded this law to include all free blacks. These laws, however, were rarely enforced, an indication of one way that the white elite played white and black labor against each other for its own political and economic gain.[105]

Although at least one historian has suggested that skilled job competition between blacks and whites was not a problem in Savannah—because whites had access to widening professional and commercial opportunities—these ordinances suggest a more complex picture.[106] At least some white mechanics resented black mechanic competition enough to convince their city councilmen, several of whom had been master mechanics themselves, to act on their behalf.[107] The 1809 and 1817 city ordinances against independent slave and free black mechanics indicate that Savan-

nah city councilmen attempted – at least in theory – to promote white mechanics' economic interests over the economic interests of black mechanics. In Augusta, no such ordinances existed. Competition from slave and
free black artisans, their numbers much smaller, apparently posed less of
a threat to white mechanics.

Another factor that complicates any reading of white mechanic response
to skilled slave and free black competition is slave ownership among white
craftsmen. Extant records certainly indicate that master craftsmen in a
number of trades owned slaves. White journeymen seeking employment
from such masters, and hoping to become masters themselves, could not
afford to voice their antagonism to competition from skilled blacks too
loudly if they hoped to secure work as wage-earners themselves. White
journeymen carpenters, for example, were forced to compete for work
with slave carpenters because many master carpenters owned or hired
skilled slaves. The Augusta carpenter James Harrison owned – in addition
to two town lots and many upcountry acres – 11 slaves, at least some of
whom must have helped him at his trade.[108] The Savannah carpenter Asa
Hoxey owned 10 slaves in 1820.[109] Although the Augusta carpenter William Dearmond was not a wealthy man at his death, his estate included
"negroes" as well as "horses, hogs, household and kitchen furniture, carpenter's tools, etc."[110] An inventory of his estate indicates he owned a number of duplicate carpentry tools – including 22 chisels, 6 handsaws, 4 axes,
4 augurs and 4 adzes. This inventory suggests he must have handed his
tools out to slave carpenters he hired rather than white journeymen carpenters who would have been expected to carry their own set of tools from
job to job.[111]

While the hard labor and seasonality of the carpentry trade made the
use of slave labor an obvious choice for masters, many artisans in other
trades were equally dependent upon slave help. The Augusta baker J. B.
Larey owned 3 slaves, the Augusta shoemaker Reed Collins owned 12
slaves, the Savannah shoemaker John Miller owned 6 slaves, and the Augusta blacksmith Lud Harris owned 3 slaves.[112] The Augusta cabinetmaker
John Harwood owned five slaves in 1809, and a Savannah cabinetmaker
owned 14 slaves in 1812, according to his estate records.[113] While the task
assignations of these slaves cannot be determined, it seems fair to assume
that at least several of these slaves were expected to perform errands if not
specific skills in the workshop. Such evidence suggests that white journey-

men seeking positions were forced to accept the fact that master craftsmen relied on the labor of skilled slaves as well as skilled free laborers. Accordingly, wage-earning artisans sought to transcend their dependent status at all costs, directing their energies toward becoming master craftsmen, with property and dependents of their own. Creative uses of available labor, in all its variety, helped some men make this transition, as was the case of Reuben King.

As a journeyman tanner new to Georgia, King quickly learned that his own labor, even when applied six days a week, was not adequate to the task at hand—establishing his own successful tannery. Impecunious upon his arrival to Darien, he could not afford to hire or purchase virtually any kind of laborer, slave or free, black or white. He could rely on, however, a series of relationships and exchanges to secure the assistance he so desperately needed. During his first few months in Darien, he frequently worked for his brother at such tasks as planting mulberries, erecting a cowpen, and making brick, after the two agreed they would form a tanning business in which Reuben was the junior partner. King also helped out his neighbors by hoeing their corn, catching their runaway cows, and cutting timber.[114] His efforts were repaid when his brother and several neighbors began to frame his tanning house.[115]

After nine months in Darien, King not only continued to assist his neighbors and kin, who assisted him in return, but he began to employ laborers as well. Over the next four and a half years he hired 24 white journeymen and 2 free black men—most for several days, a handful for a month or more, and one white laborer for slightly over a year—to perform carpentry, tanning, and currying tasks for him, depending on their skills. He paid them mostly in cash, occasionally in goods such as lime, and in a few instances, in his own labor.[116] During this same period, he also hired six slaves from neighbors for several days at a time and trained three apprentices: a mulatto youth in the tanning trade, a slave boy with only one leg in the shoemaking trade, and a white boy in the tanning trade, the only one of the three for whom King signed a legal contract of indenture.[117]

King's financial resources and local circumstances shaped the kinds of choices he could make about securing laborers. But his relationships with his relatives and his neighbors may have played an even larger role in these choices. Reuben's brother Roswell, for example, relied on Reuben's labor in return for "the hides and bark that is now on hand and the use of the tan house and two lots for the term of three years."[118] This rather unequal copartnership, which rested on Reuben's skilled labor and Roswell's resources, gave Roswell the upper hand; he appears to have used this upper hand to force Reuben to take care of a reluctant apprentice, a young free black man who probably was Roswell's son.[119]

Stephen, the recalcitrant mulatto apprentice, stood at the center of what was a complicated situation, one bound as much by social relationships and expectations as by economic ones. To King, these relationships blurred the lines that traditionally distinguished sex, race, and class from each other in southern society. King's ability to make independent choices, then, including what kinds of laborers to engage and for how long, was somewhat constrained by the particular circumstances and relationships that characterized his life in Georgia. While not all migrant white artisans in Georgia were so dependent upon a relative, they undoubtedly found themselves, especially early in their careers, confronting such complicated social circumstances—circumstances over which they had quite limited control.

Despite his difficulties with Stephen and with his brother, King remained ambitious and industrious, intent upon achieving financial security by the age of thirty-one. "I con[si]der the first part of my life from the age of 21 years untill 31 being ten years which I think will be the Most Laborious part of my Life With a flattering Idea at the end of this term I shall be so independent as to labour only when it is agreeable," he wrote on his 26th birthday in 1805.[120] To achieve this end, he engaged apprentices and journeymen of both races whenever his finances allowed. But he also believed that his future success rested upon the acquisition of a wife as helpmeet. He observed in his journal:

> I am this day 26 years of age 5 years I have been out of my Aprinticeship I have not accumilated much property for that length of time It may be justly observed that a Single man Seldom obtains property so fast as one married allowing them to be equally Industrus[121]

King illustrates another aspect of building a productive artisan household—the important interrelationship between marriage and work characteristic of all preindustrial households, including those of white artisan men in the South. Marriage, in light of the many limitations that migrant white mechanics encountered in Georgia, promised these men an added measure of financial security. It not only increased the economic security of a household by, at the very least, doubling its productive capacity, but earned the household head a modicum of social respect in a world that aligned political and social privilege with independence and property. After all, a wife, who was socially and legally defined as a dependent, constituted an abstracted kind of property in the southern mind-set. Moreover, marriage could also produce children, whose labor could prove useful and whose presence symbolized a white man's status as provider for a growing brood of dependents.[122]

Despite his failure to achieve economic independence during his first five years in Georgia, Reuben King eventually married, had children, bought slaves, and became a wealthy planter. His experience as a household head with impermanent dependents, in the form of apprentices, white wage-earners, free black wage-earners, and hired slaves, helped him make the economic and social transformation from virtually propertyless journeyman to propertied planter. Many other artisans managed this transformation during the early republic as well. It is easiest to chart this transformation in terms of the acquisition of land and slaves, as in the case of Holland McTyre, who first advertised his carriage-making shop in Augusta in 1795. Two years later he owned three slaves, but no other taxable property. By 1809, he was married and had acquired approximately four hundred acres in Richmond County, some four hundred upcountry acres elsewhere, and eleven slaves. McTyre continued to add slaves to his holdings, owning twenty-three by 1818.[123] Nicholas Long's career resembled McTyre's. The Augusta coachmaker owned no real estate in the mid-1790s but possessed three slaves. By 1808, he held close to four hundred upcountry acres and eleven slaves. Twelve years later, he possessed more than eight hundred acres in three upcountry counties, twenty-three slaves, and a carriage.[124]

Other artisans in luxury trades patronized by rich planters and merchants worked to achieve the accoutrements of planter status, though their gains were more modest than those of McTyre and Long. The riding chairmaker Joshua Pharoah, after twelve years of residence in Augusta, owned 100 Richmond County acres, a house, two thousand dollars in inventory, two unimproved lots in nearby Harrisburg, a carriage, and one slave. The cabinetmaker William Barnes owned approximately 150 upcountry acres, eight slaves, and a carriage by 1812, while the Savannah chairmaker

Henry Densler owned more than 100 upcountry acres, along with five slaves.[125] H. Bunce, a clock- and watchmaker, owned four slaves and over 200 acres in Richmond County within eight years of his arrival in Augusta.[126] William Allen, a cabinetmaker and upholsterer, acquired more than 900 acres in Burke County between 1789 and 1795. At his death in 1801, he bequeathed to his brother three slaves, 300 acres on Butler's Creek, and "his horses, cattle, hogs, plantation tools, and household furniture." [127] As these examples suggest, during the early republic, master craftsmen in luxury trades could accumulate land and slaves and thus establish their own plantations, however modest.

Yet artisans in trades that did not cater exclusively to the planter elite and that did not produce high-priced goods could also hope to acquire land and slaves as well. The potter and tile-maker Nathaniel Durkee owned virtually nothing in 1800.[128] By 1818, he claimed four hundred acres in Wilkinson County, four slaves, six hundred dollars' worth of town lots, and one hundred dollars' worth of inventory.[129] Jacob Dill, a blacksmith, came to Augusta in 1807 and bought a house within two years of his arrival. By 1816, he owned nearly two hundred upcountry acres, twelve hundred dollars in inventory, six slaves, and a carriage, as well as his home. By 1830, Dill's property included seven more slaves.[130] The stonecutter Garret Laurence, who arrived in Augusta in 1811, owned six slaves, one hundred acres in Richmond County, and more than two thousand acres in Wilkinson County by 1818. Within twelve years, he had acquired three more slaves.[131] Even women artisans occasionally appear in the records as planters in the making. Mrs. Jones, an Augusta mantua-maker, owned a female slave in 1820.[132] Jane Whiteford, a Savannah milliner, acquired four hundred upcountry acres in Washington County in 1788.[133]

White male artisans in elite and nonelite trades worked to become planters. They generally followed a prescribed set of patterns to achieve this status. Upon arrival in Augusta or Savannah, they hired apprentices and journeymen as soon as they could afford them. As they accrued capital, they hired and bought slaves, working to increase their slaveholdings over time. They married and had children. They also invested in town lots and upcountry land—real estate usually destined for residence but sometimes purchased for speculation.

It would be misleading to suggest that all artisans made the financial and social headway indicated by the evidence here. Nevertheless, it is clear that many artisans in a wide range of trades hoped to become independent planters. Although in 1820 not one of a group of Augusta and Savannah artisans (a bricklayer, a stonecutter, an artist, a potter, a bookbinder, a herald painter, and two watchmakers) owned a single slave, each possessed between fifty and three hundred upcountry acres.[134]

Still, some journeymen experienced few gains after years of toil. The clock- and watchmaker John Cortelyou arrived in Augusta in 1803. Six years later he owned no property and managed to pay only his poll tax. The Augusta bookbinder Peter Browne, the cabinetmaker James Alexander, and the blacksmith Gideon Sealy also proved unable to accumulate capital over a similar time span, although Browne eventually acquired one hundred upcountry acres in Franklin County.[135] These men had to hope that the future would bring them better fortune.

Competition from free black and slave artisans must have lessened the opportunities for upward mobility for some white journeymen in nonelite trades such as tailoring and carpentry. By the 1820s and 1830s, the growing availability of ready-made clothing from New York City, ready-made boots and shoes from New England, and ready-made cabinets and furniture from the North would also serve to discourage artisans in luxury and nonluxury trades alike. The end of the land lottery system in 1832 added yet another roadblock to artisans' hopes for prosperity.

Yet the economic opportunities that many white artisans discovered during the early republic, including slaveholding, landholding, and eventually entry into the planter class, began to wane only with the maturation of the cotton economy, the extensive settlement of the upcountry, and the flood of low-priced, northern-made, manufactured goods into Georgia. By 1820, many white mechanics had secured a place for themselves in Georgia's slaveholding economy. They had used their artisanal skills to build productive households that enabled them to accumulate capital; many had exchanged this capital for land and slaves. By shrewdly taking advantage of widening economic opportunities, some artisans had adapted themselves to the peculiarities of this slave economy by transforming themselves into planters. These same men proved equally adept at taking advantage of widening political opportunities.

It is clear that artisans in a number of trades found themselves at the whim of forces beyond their control. Planter spending habits, competition from other artisans in the same trade, the presence of skilled black labor, changes in production, and the vagaries of the world market could all play havoc with a southern artisan's prospects. Yet it is also clear that artisans in Georgia in the early republic used their skills to create new opportunities for themselves that stretched well beyond their workshops. Hiring and owning slaves as well as buying town lots and upcountry acres at this critical juncture in Georgia's history helped many of these men transform themselves into planters in the making.

2 *Artisanal Politics*

By the last quarter of the eighteenth century, the political reins of the lower South were held by powerful planters and merchants. In a society where political deference was the rule, planters often managed to secure local office election year after election year; they frequently faced no challengers. The arrival of new numbers of migrant mechanics to Augusta and Savannah in the late eighteenth and early nineteenth centuries began to reshape the power of this political elite. Artisans who were planters in the making with political ambitions of their own soon recognized that organization of the local artisan community could lead to an important block of votes. Although artisan political leaders ultimately sought the respect and opportunities available to the planter elite, for brief periods of time they assiduously courted the artisan vote and cultivated a distinct strand of artisanal politics.

Throughout the early republic, white male artisan leaders in Augusta and Savannah not only demonstrated their familiarity with the principles of artisanal republicanism espoused in the

more established cities of the Northeast and Europe. In what was a significant development, they used these principles to create a place for themselves within their slaveholding world.[1]

This transition occurred at a unique juncture in time and place. The
political, economic, and social changes that characterized life in Georgia
on the eve of the cotton revolution proved a powerful antidote to a sustained artisanal class consciousness. Class-based identity was discouraged
in a society where politics was characterized by an emerging Democratic-
Republican Party consensus at the national level, where opportunities for
upward mobility were abundant for white men, and where the enslave-
ment of black men and women shaped all social relations. Under these
circumstances, white artisans over the long run came to conceive of themselves not as laboring men bent upon advancing their own interests and
ideology but as new members of the white social order. In the end they
willingly exchanged their skills, their pursuits, and even their ideas about
the nature of acquisitiveness to gain entrance into the planters' world.

Historians traditionally have assumed that the slave labor system and
the rise of the plantation economy prevented the emergence of an artisanal political community in the South.[2] But the evidence suggests a more
complicated scenario. Artisan leaders in Georgia carefully constructed a
political community for themselves, however short-lived. They then used
that community, along with widening economic opportunities, to establish
themselves as bona fide members of this slaveholding society.

The structure of the economy of upcountry Georgia during the 1790s
had provided white artisans with an unprecedented number of opportunities. Demand for their abilities and limited competition enabled many artisans to make the most of their skills. Accordingly, the desire for a political
community and upward mobility, not the deep-rooted economic woes that
shaped artisanal politics in seaboard cities to the North, proved the primary motivation for artisans' organization of the Mechanics' Society of
Augusta (MSA) and the Savannah Mechanics' Association (SMA) in the
last decade of the eighteenth century.

Unlike master craftsmen in the urban Northeast, whose economic options and political power were increasingly circumscribed by market
changes, artisans in Augusta and Savannah, and especially the leaders of
the mechanics' societies in each of these places, established shops, accrued
capital, land, and slaves, and transformed themselves into substantial mid-

dling men with, in some cases, real political power. As a result, these men in time came to cast aside their artisanal beliefs and traditional modes of craft production to embrace a more conservative brand of republicanism and planter ambitions.

Historians of the early republic have located the origins of a national postrevolutionary artisanal class consciousness in the political responses of urban artisans to changes in production. Yet this illuminating body of work has been limited to urban artisanal experience in such places as Lynn, New York, Newark, Philadelphia, Baltimore, and Cincinnati.[3] The political beliefs and actions of white artisans in less urban settings, particularly those situated in slave economies in the Deep South, where changes in production were negligible, remain unexplored.[4] The mechanics of Augusta and Savannah, despite the relative smallness of their urban locales, their diverse origins, their craft practices and their limited numbers, built self-conscious communities based on the principles of artisanal republicanism. Why did these artisan newcomers embrace artisanal republicanism so readily and how did they manage to build their mechanics' societies and artisan communities so quickly?

Certainly, the artisanal republicanism of their brethren to the North offered these men a framework that gave political and social meaning to their labor.[5] Like most citizens in the wake of the revolution, American artisans believed that republican thought, which would become the basis for the Democratic-Republican Party at the national level, rested on a set of political conceptions considered vital for the maintenance of their new republic. Citizens must participate in politics, work to preserve the commonwealth, subordinate private ends on behalf of the public good, and establish their independence from the political desires of others.[6] But artisans pushed these republican beliefs further to create their own version of republicanism. In New York, Philadelphia, and Baltimore, they reshaped this prevailing political discourse into an ideology of their own.

By the late eighteenth century, urban artisans in the North not only sought to protect the moral health of the government (like all good republicans), but criticized increasingly inegalitarian social relations brought on by the early inroads of the market revolution. Asserting that good republicans must respect the right to *equal* representation for all citizens and honor the dignity of labor, this artisanal republicanism of the late eighteenth century incorporated Jeffersonian ideas about small producer independence alongside Paineite arguments for *equality of opportunity.*[7]

An artisanal republicanism particular to the realities of urban Georgia during the early republic took shape in both Augusta and Savannah. Dating the precise beginning point of this ideology in each city is difficult to do. Yet circumstantial evidence surrounding a special election in Augusta indicates artisans may have begun to conceive of themselves as a unique political community in this market town as early as 1790.

On February 8 of that year a group of citizens waited for news of the day's special election outside the markethouse in Augusta. Upon learning the returns, the men hurried to the home of the town's newest alderman, Josiah Shoemaker, a tailor and habit-maker by trade. There they strapped Shoemaker into a chair set atop two poles and carried him in his makeshift throne through the streets, stopping to deliver loud jeers at each of the incumbent aldermen's homes. After a final victory shout at the mayor's door, the jubilant men returned to Shoemaker's to toast their good fortune.[8]

This event appears to mark the beginning of an organized artisanal community in Augusta. Although the historical record is silent on the occupations of the participants in this celebration, it seems highly likely that most of these men were white mechanics. An artisan had been elected to local office, an important achievement in a political community traditionally ruled by planters and merchants.[9] A year later, Augusta artisans would establish their own mechanics' society. Throughout the 1790s, the artisans who led this society used their institution to build an artisan community that embraced the principles of artisanal republicanism; they then used it to launch themselves into local office. Eventually, however, these same men deserted their community. After 1800, Augusta artisans increasingly exchanged their carefully crafted artisanal identity for a new role rooted in the independence of white property-holding men in a slaveholding society.[10] Indeed, by 1804, the Mechanics' Society of Augusta (MSA), once the heart of the artisan community, was defunct.[11]

Thus it took a corrupt local election proceeding and the apparent complicity of the state government before Augusta artisans began to embrace these artisanal republican principles and to recognize their shared interests as a class. The impetus for these developments, the special election of Edward Shoemaker, originated in an act of the Georgia legislature, passed on December 23, 1789, which incorporated Savannah as a city and Augusta as a town.[12] At first intended only for Savannah, Augusta's inclusion was secured due to last-minute lobbying efforts by the town's British merchants. The act called for an immediate election of city council members in each place. On the day of this hastily called election, held only eleven days after the bill's passage, Augusta merchants won all seven of the newly created aldermen's seats.[13]

Within twenty-four hours a petition signed by "Fifty-Five Respected Property Owners" was submitted to Governor Edward Telfair in protest. This remonstrance demanded inquiry into the validity of the poll proceedings and the eligibility of two aldermen thought to be British citizens.[14] These petitioners represented a broad social spectrum. While property-holding, in the form of lots, land, slaves, and stock-in-trade, distinguished these men as economically privileged, not all were planters or merchants. At least nine artisans signed the remonstrance, six of whom would help organize a mechanics' society a year later.[15]

Not surprisingly, Governor Telfair failed to take the petitioners' grievances seriously. Georgia citizens generally expressed limited interest in state and local politics during the 1780s, though this situation would change dramatically over the next decade. After the American Revolution, local government had been minimal and elections too few to arouse much excitement, especially when the same members of the local elite ran for office year in and year out. Moreover, high property-holding qualifications had prevented common men from declaring their candidacy. This system cemented the political power of the local elite so that deferential politics, despite the ideals of the American Revolution, remained the rule in Georgia.[16]

Although Governor Telfair had agreed to an investigation, he ruled in favor of the merchant aldermen at the close of the three-day hearing, despite his solicitor-general's recommendations to the contrary. The governor dismissed the petitioners' charge of poll fraud on the ground that the votes challenged by the petitioners were too few in number to alter the results. He dismissed the question of eligibility when one alderman thought to be British produced proof of admission to a Charleston club that prohibited foreign members. The other alderman in question resigned of his own accord, a tacit admission of his British status.[17] Telfair made public his approval of the election results in an address to the citizens of Augusta published in the local paper on January 16.[18]

Many Augusta citizens were incensed by the governor's ruling. Given such a blatant exhibition of cronyism between the state and the local merchants, these townspeople were quite willing to challenge the old rules of deference. The mechanics, shopkeepers, and planters of the town interpreted the governor's decision as a betrayal of the public's welfare and a tacit admission of patronage. "The privileges of a free people have been violated, arrogance encountenanced, and the public good sacrificed for private interest," proclaimed an editorialist in *The Augusta Chronicle and Gazette of the State*.[19] Under the pseudonym "Cleon"—presumably borrowed from the name of the spokesman for the shopkeepers and artisans of Athens during the Peloponnesian War—another critic penned a scathing verse about the incident:

Sometime ago, no matter where—
(About the place we little care)
The supreme power met to debate
Reform, and rule, and judge the state;
And made such laws, as to them should
Seem most to injure the public good.[20]

To these children of the War for Independence, Governor Telfair's promotion of monied interests, especially *British* monied interests, smacked of the most vile corruption. "Ill-fated Americans! Are these the effects of your memorable struggle to liberty?," demanded "An Examiner." "To what purpose is it that your exertions, added to the will of Providence, have left you in a state of freedom and independence, if you are still to be controlled by the adherents of that government which exerted its utmost strength to bind you and your children in lasting slavery?"[21] Obviously, this reference to slavery was not made lightly. A white southerner's greatest fear, given his intimacy with the peculiar institution, was to be denied freedom in any form.

Georgia politics at the conclusion of the revolution not only was shaped by local factions but also was beginning to reflect political developments on the national front. Factions in Augusta in the 1790s revolved around what one historian has described as a conflict between "the old Whig stock" and "the new Tories."[22] The pro-Federalist British merchants, or "new Tories," earned the enmity of those Augusta citizens who identified themselves with a rising planter elite that scorned the Washington administration and anyone with British connections. While these fledgling Jeffersonians had approved the ratification of the U.S. Constitution in 1788, in the belief that a strong federal government would protect them from threats along their state's borders, the administration's handling of Indian concerns and land issues soon convinced them to cut their Federalist ties. Washington's involvement in shaping the terms of the New York Treaty in 1790, which handed pieces of Georgia back to the Creeks and laid the claim for the federal government's sovereignty over lands lying west and south of the treaty boundaries, further alienated land-hungry upcountrymen. By the winter of 1789–90, the Whig faction in Augusta, many of whose members were speculators and planters, was openly hostile to the Federalist party and its local faction, which was comprised mostly of merchants.[23] Augusta artisans, far more dependent upon the Whig faction for patronage than upon the merchants, and familiar with the republican principles the Whig leaders espoused, joined the Whig side.

These Whigs, armed with their classic republican arguments and frustrated by the governor's willingness to side with the merchants, hoped their strong rhetoric would force the governor to renege on his decision. The mechanics of the town, eager to diminish the authority of a class of townspeople not only associated with the Federalist administration but whose means of livelihood, the import and sale of British goods, often threatened their own, chose a more direct route.

On February 8, the date of the special election to fill the solitary seat vacated by the admitted British alderman, mechanics secured their own political representation by electing tailor Edward Shoemaker to the position. While the Whig faction had joined forces against the merchants, the mechanics who gave three victory shouts at each of the presiding aldermen's doors clearly interpreted this victory as their own. So great was the effect of their protest that Shoemaker went on to serve the town without incident to the end of his term in 1792 and was hailed at his death two years later as "the late worthy alderman." In contrast, the six contested merchants-turned-councilmen bowed to public demand by resigning as a body six months after their election.[24] Although opposition to the merchants had come from all quarters, it was Augusta's artisans who had translated republican protest into action. Shoemaker's election scored a significant moral victory for the Whigs of Augusta, encouraged the demise of the British merchant oligarchy, and spawned an artisan consciousness as well.

While it would seem that the role of the mechanics in the destruction of the merchants' hold on Augusta politics should have led to a local political scene characterized by a homogenous Whig faction of artisans, shopkeepers, and planters, this did not prove to be the case. Instead, the mechanics of Augusta chose to view themselves as a self-conscious community with their own leadership and following in the wake of this incident. This community took formal shape a little over a year later when fifteen artisans, including six signers of the "55 Propertyholders' Petition," organized the Mechanics' Society of Augusta.[25] For the next thirteen years, most of these men (with the addition of one more), served as the elected leadership of the MSA, which held quarterly meetings, elected officers annually, hosted dinners, marched in public festivities, and routinely celebrated their society's anniversary, St. Tammany's Anniversary, and the Fourth of July. By 1800, they had even erected their own Mechanic Hall.[26]

The existence of a mechanic organization does not in and of itself constitute conclusive proof of an artisanal community. The extant records of this organization, however, indicate that these men viewed themselves as ardent artisan-republicans. Alfred Young has defined artisanal republicanism as a set of four "consciousnesses" unique to the artisanal world. While the relatively small numbers of artisans in any given trade in Augusta prevented the emergence of a visible "craft consciousness" in the form of trade union organization—the first of Young's useful criteria—artisans in the MSA did embrace what Young has described as a mechanic's interest consciousness, a producer's consciousness, and a citizenship consciousness.[27]

These mechanics promoted the dignity of their efforts in a society that viewed laboring with one's hands as a servile enterprise to be reserved largely for slave labor. According to the MSA charter, these artisan leaders erected their organization with the intention of "plac[ing] their craft on a more respectable and social footing than heretofore," which implicitly suggested that they sought to distinguish their labor from that of the black residents in Augusta.[28] Their choice of the singular in the word "craft" served as a deliberate reminder to the townspeople and to each other that no matter what their individual skills, no matter how much (or how little) income their work generated, all Augusta mechanics shared in the artisan order, thus giving evidence of a producer's consciousness.

These same members drank celebratory toasts at called meetings in honor of "the [mechanic] arts" and "mechanism and the sciences."[29] Such proclamations, evidence of a mechanic's interest consciousness, served to underline their independence. Although not all mechanics owned land, slaves, capital, or stock-in-trade, all owned their tools and their skills, forms of property which in republican tradition entitled all mechanics—including white journeymen who labored alongside slaves—to citizenship and respectability.[30] In contrast, slave artisans held no property, not even the tools with which they labored, an important distinction in a society where white journeymen might find themselves laboring alongside skilled slaves.

In addition, the MSA leaders hoped to build a supportive community for each other. Accordingly, their charter established "through their united exertions and contributions a lasting fund for the relief and support of their unfortunate brethren, or their families, who may become objects of charity."[31] These artisans acknowledged that they were at the mercy of the clients who patronized them unless they worked together to help each other out.

While white artisans in Augusta recognized their shared interests as a class by establishing a mechanic society that upheld the dignity of their labor, implicitly distinguished their labor from that of blacks, and supported each other in times of need, their commitment to their brand of artisanal republicanism was also evident in their verbal demonstrations of "citizenship consciousness." Referring to themselves as "the Sons of Liberty" and "the Sons of America," these artisans claimed their right to participate in the political sphere as independent, virtuous men. Moreover, they pledged to support struggles for political equality and to challenge local and state political actions they deemed corrupt (although with the exception of Shoemaker's election, there is no evidence to indicate that they ever actually acted upon these pledges).[32]

At every MSA meeting, members honored the president of the United States, Congress, the governor, and Georgia. They honored the men who fought and fell "in defense of American freedom" during the American Revolution. As war veterans and as militiamen themselves, the mechanics sought to actively preserve the independence and liberty they willingly defended on the battlefield and the muster ground.[33] Moreover, like the members of the Democratic-Republican Societies which proliferated from 1793 to 1800 (who were also principally artisans who considered themselves heirs of the Sons of Liberty), the members of the MSA hoped to protect citizens' liberties from unjust and corrupt leaders. "May the genuine principles of rectitude and philanthropy in future govern all legislative, judicial, and executive bodies," they toasted at their meetings.[34] One of the central concerns of the MSA, as expressed in the convivial pledges these artisans made to each other at their gatherings, was to preserve a moral ethos: "May merit always prevail in every public or private dispute. . . . May the *honest* hearts never want. . . . Disappointment to those who would exchange the cause of their country for selfishness and sordid gain."[35]

The members of the MSA were also champions of political equality. Their society embraced the French Revolution for its commitment to liberty and equality. Initially adopting a moderate stance, toasting both the king and the National Assembly in 1791, the artisans moved to a more radical position by 1793, proclaiming, "May the hard fate of Louis the XVI be a lesson to kings, monarchs, and emperors." The MSA urged the American government to take no action that would undermine "that spirit which has excited France" and wished "perdition and a total loss of property" for Americans who sought normal trade relations with Great Britain during its war with France.[36] This insistence on political equality characterized society meetings throughout the 1790s. As late as 1804, the organization remained a strong supporter of Thomas Paine and his ideas although most Americans had long since rejected them.[37] As these examples suggest, Augusta mechanics were not excluded from the wide-ranging social and political debates of the decade. Their political positions closely resembled those of the emerging Jeffersonian Republicans.

On occasion, the tenets of artisanal republicanism shaped moral and political debate in Augusta during the 1790s at the insistence of Augustans who were not artisans, which suggests the degree to which the townspeople recognized them as a distinct community. When George Washington, borne across the state in his immaculate white coach-and-four, visited Augusta in the spring of 1791, state politicians concluded the president's three-day tour with a subscription ball.[38] This gala affair was hosted by some of the wealthiest men in Georgia, who apparently expressly forbade mechanics from attending. The decision of the governor and the state's political elite, mostly staunch Federalists, to exclude Augusta mechanics, those "honest and industrious men" with "unspotted characters," according to one editorialist, was perceived to be a serious breach of public ethics, since the president, a promoter of mechanics, frequented their workshops and mills on all his tours through the country.[39] The mechanics themselves, however, were quiescent at least in print on the subject, presumably reluctant to associate themselves with the premier Federalist in the new nation.

Augusta artisans were also silent as local politicians, eager to influence their ballot choices, campaigned for their votes. During the course of the 1790s, campaigning for election to office in Georgia had been transformed from a refined gentleman's game to a rollicking free-for-all of name-calling, barbecues, and stump speeches. Ambitious candidates, eager to court the votes of relatively large groups like the mechanics of Augusta, played on artisanal notions of political virtue. An exchange of letters in the *Augusta Chronicle* indicates the intent of a pair of competing candidates to use principles they ascribed to artisans to secure their votes. R. Dickenson, the inferior court clerk for Richmond County, running for a state assembly seat in 1793, accused his opponent, Philip Clayton, "You are giving Barbecues in the country for electioneering purposes, feasting the *honest* mechanicks in town, . . . and holding forth every specious allurement for favour and popularity." To which Clayton replied, "The mechanicks of this town are not like *yourself;* they stand on too *respectable* a footing for any man to offer them a *bribe.*"[40]

MSA leader William Dearmond found himself relying on this respectability when called before a military tribunal in 1798. Accused of neglectful duty, contemptuous and willful disobedience, and even mutiny after failing to process his troops as ordered during a parade, the captain of the Richmond Light Horse was forced to explain his conduct to his superiors. The accusations against Dearmond seem ill founded based on the exchange of letters between military officers that followed this event.[41] Indeed, Lieutenant Colonel Commander Robert Watkins, an Augusta lawyer, state legislator, Federalist, and public enemy of Republican Party leader James Jackson, was responsible for bringing these charges against Dearmond, which suggests that party politics rather than military manners shaped the tribunal.[42] Apparently, Dearmond had not received the orders to move his troops forward. His explanation for his failure to act had been terse. His superior officer had been displeased by this attitude. To defend himself before these officers, Dearmond cited his exemplary service to the nation as patriot, soldier, and most importantly, an artisan:

> In closing my defense I can say that I feel neither hatred[,] malice [n]or revenge but at the same time I must say that my feelings had been much injured. These feelings you must yourselves possess and thus feeling you will receive me in a proper light Having served my country faithfully both as a Soldier and a Mechanick in the worst of times and for many years I did hope that my character as both was irreproachable, nor do I know to the contrary.[43]

Dearmond alluded to the partisan battles that seemed to be at the root of the tribunal by concluding, "These are not the times to erect fudes [feuds] among citizens but to cultivate harmony . . . which of these fall to my lot is for you to say."[44] Testimony from fellow mechanic, MSA leader, and Adjutant to the Richmond County Militia, Baxter Pool, later corroborated Dearmond's statement. "William Dearmond . . . conduct[ed] himself . . . to the best of my observation and opinion, as becomes the good Soldier and the worthy Officer."[45] Although the outcome of the tribunal has not been preserved, Dearmond certainly believed that his fine mechanic's character would see him through, a point he makes in his statements to these officers.[46]

While fellow Augustans recognized the existence of a distinct artisan community in their town and the principles that this artisan community subscribed to, the artisans themselves, with the exception of Shoemaker's election, did not appear to translate their ideological avowals of artisanal republicanism into programmatic action, unless one counts the transformation of MSA leaders into local politicians. In many respects, this transition marked a logical progression. The MSA gave its leaders experience, visibility, platforms, and followers in a society that traditionally reserved positions of public power for planters and merchants. The MSA served to politicize its members by encouraging them to recognize their shared interests as a class; this development, in turn, secured the MSA leaders new power for themselves.

Over half of the MSA leaders went on to hold some form of public office, in addition to MSA positions, between 1790 and 1810. Machinist and inventor William Longstreet was perhaps the most popular of these artisans turned politicians. Elected alderman in 1792, 1798, 1808, and 1809, state legislator in 1794, and appointed justice of the peace, Longstreet al-

lowed his home to be used as the polling location for the third ward and a
base of operations for the town tax collector.[47]

The silversmith John Catlett's rise to local power occurred later than
Longstreet's but was equally illustrious. Appointed justice of the peace in
1805 and chosen president of the Augusta Jockey Club in 1806 (a position
of great prestige), Catlett was elected alderman and appointed mayor in
1808.[48] The carpenter Robert Cresswell served on the city council in 1798
and 1806.[49] The shoemaker Francis Vallotton proved an able district poll
manager for many years.[50] All of these men were MSA officers. An MSA
charter member, Thomas Bray, was appointed clerk of the market.[51] The
carpenter William Dearmond, the carpenter Baxter Pool and the shoemaker Joseph Stiles, all MSA officers, were each elected militia captains, a
traditional route to political office.[52] Isaac Wingate and Thomas Bray, both
MSA charter members, sat on the board of the Richmond Academy.[53] Yet
in a sign of things to come none of the elected artisans ever initiated laws
that specifically reflected concern for their artisan constituency. In fact,
John Catlett passed an ordinance for a bread assize (a requirement that all
loaves of bread sold by local bakers conform to a uniform weight and size
to prevent cheating customers) when mayor in 1808, a decision that served
to alienate him from the local bakers.[54]

Meanwhile, an artisanal elite and a mechanics' society were also emerging in Savannah. Despite the obvious demographic and economic differences between the two urban centers, the strategies and ideologies of
these two groups of artisans largely mirrored each other, although the port
city was a physically larger place, contained more people, and was more
firmly embedded in the institution of slavery than Augusta. Moreover,
many more mechanics of diverse nativities, occupations, resources, and
incomes, as well as political attitudes, resided in Savannah, making efforts
to cultivate a cohesive political community of artisans more difficult but
not impossible.

White artisan organization, in fact, occurred in Savannah at an earlier
date than in Augusta. Savannah's white mechanics had protested the use
of skilled black artisans in the city as early as 1758. Almost thirty years
later, in 1786, sixty-six Savannah mechanics had joined together to protest
the state's paper money act. Frontier trouble with Indians and Spaniards
required money for troops that the state treasury could ill afford. Some
politicians had suggested that paper money be printed to solve the prob-

lem; this proposal, however, only served to divide Georgians geographically. While upcountry men heralded the plan—because they would benefit from increased military support—lowcountry men despised it. "The friends of paper money," argued a Savannah editorialist, "can be reduced to the following classes: 1st debtors 2nd Speculators, and 3rd brokers." He added, "Its enemies are, all *honest* lawyers, Doctors, Parsons, Mechanicks, and Farmers," indicating that as in Augusta, the merchants were in many respects a class unto themselves.[55]

A slight majority of upcountry votes allowed passage of the money act. But in short order, the "Sixty-Six Savannah Mechanics" invited Chatham County residents to a series of "Whig meetings" to protest the new money. Their sentiment struck a common chord, for within a few weeks even the Chatham County Grand Jury was voicing its opposition to paper emission.[56]

The mechanics' political success convinced local politicians, who were generally planters, merchants, and lawyers, to take mechanics' concerns more seriously. Tax-paying Savannah mechanics, representing about a quarter of the adult white male population in Savannah by 1798, comprised an important block of votes.[57] Accordingly, planters, shopkeepers, *and* mechanics were all "worthy of judgement as citizens," at least according to some residents.[58] Savannah mechanics, like Augusta mechanics, were often viewed as political peacemakers able to surmount individual differences in the interest of republicanism, as the words to this "Mechanics Song," published in Savannah's *Georgia Gazette* in 1789, suggest:

Ye merry mechanicks come join in my song;
And let the brisk chorus come bounding along;
Tho' some may be poor, and some rich there may be,
And yet all are contented, and happy and free . . .
Each tradesman turn out with his tool in his hand,
To cherish the arts
And keep peace through the lands.[59]

Individually affected by the political economy of slavery in different and even conflicting ways, white artisans in Savannah nonetheless were described by local politicians and civic leaders who were seeking their support as a single political force that sought freedom and peace and deserved full participation in the public sphere. A series of events with profound political repercussions during the 1790s persuaded some mechanics to put the politicians' lofty rhetoric to the test by running for office themselves. In the process, some of these Savannah artisans discovered that their new-found political strength could be used to augment their individual public influence and private wealth.

The Savannah Mechanics' Association was organized in 1793 in the wake of an infamous local event known as "The Nelson Incident." As in Augusta, Englishmen controlled many Savannah merchant-houses. And also as in Augusta, this reality did not endear the British to all Savannah residents. As late as 1793 some residents strongly supported France and continued to do so after the execution of Louis XVI. Two hundred Savannah citizens, with many mechanics among them, assembled at the court-house on January 31, 1793, to rejoice over the course of the French Revolution and "the late happy events in favor of the freedom of France." They marched to Christ Church accompanied by the firing of artillery.[60] Moreover, they sang "Ca Ira," the national song of France, a symbol of the French people's unity, because it had been sung by all classes in Paris on July 9, 1790, as they prepared the Champ de Mars for the first celebration of Federation.[61]

On July 20, 1793, six months after the two hundred Savannah citizens had commemorated their support of France, French privateers off the Georgian coast were captured and brought into the city by British supporters. Three of the captured men commissioned by the Republic of France were taken to jail. The fourth member of this party was released but delivered to a mob who tarred and feathered him and then paraded him through the streets. During their public ridicule of the unlucky privateer named Nelson, the pro-British mob sang a derisive version of "Ca Ira," another practice borrowed from France, a version that reflected French citizens' latest fears and disenchantment over the now dangerous course of their revolution.[62]

This display by British supporters disgusted many of the loyal French advocates in the city who believed the anonymous mob members were bankrupt merchants of British birth and British connection and their store-boys. Offended by this "stain on Georgians who purportedly value republicanism and honor," these French supporters accused the pro-British men of "mak[ing] a mockery of republicanism."[63] The entire Nelson affair, so dubbed for the name of the shamed privateer, became a watershed of sorts in Savannah politics.

The French supporters, avowed republicans and inheritors of Georgia's Whig legacy, contended that only a "depraved place" would abuse men representing a government that had so helped and inspired Americans. That British merchants could take the law into their own hands and receive no admonishment from local authorities, these republicans believed, signaled Savannah's rule by a "monocratic junto." Concluded one critic, "It is a melancholy reflection, to Georgians possessing the principles of republicanism, or the principles of honor, that such an outrageous violation of both, should be transported and applauded, in the only part of our State which our Northern brethren affect to think in any way civilized." [64] In November 1793, Nelson and the other privateers were acquitted and the incident eventually forgotten, but not before even some Augusta citizens had aired their opinions. As might be expected, they sided with the pro-French republicans of Savannah, dispensing much venom on Savannah's merchant class before the trial in the editorial pages of the local newspapers. [65]

The Nelson affair and the furor surrounding it created two political camps in Savannah—British merchants, speculators, and their sympathizers versus mechanics, professionals, and planters. Like the British merchant election in Augusta, the Nelson incident three years later had provided the grounds for republican opposition to Savannah merchants, speculators, and politicians suspected of placing their own interests ahead of those of the public. Their republican opposition labeled them "the Free and Easy Club" because they were "free and easy with the citizens [rights]." [66] The affair, with its five months of public debate, probably helped instigate the subsequent formation of the Savannah Mechanics' Association (SMA). Although no explicit evidence links the Nelson affair with the consequent incorporation of the SMA in December of 1793 (two years after the first meeting of the MSA), logic suggests the connection. At this latter time, thirty artisan-petitioners received official sanction from the state legislature. [67]

Except for the carpenter William Lewden, the first president of the SMA and a three-term city councilman, and the cabinetmaker Gabriel Leaver, who owned a large plantation, available evidence indicates that the other

SMA petitioners were unremarkable men of moderate wealth with little previous involvement in local politics at the time of their signing.[68] While Lewden's three-term election to City Council suggests that Savannah artisans had already formed a loose union at the polls, the creation of the Mechanics' Association signaled a more sophisticated politicization and socialization effort by a self-selected group of tradesmen. Within two years of the SMA's incorporation, an event larger and more profound than the Nelson affair pushed Savannah's artisans more firmly into the local political world. The event that instigated this change was the Yazoo crisis.

In 1789, three land companies supported by South Carolina, Virginia, and Tennessee politicians and speculators purchased 15.5 million acres from the Georgia legislature only to see the sale fall through. Five years later, four new land companies, after some successful bribing of state politicians, convinced the Georgia Assembly to pass a bill selling them 50 million acres of Georgia's western land claims for the sweet bargain of half a million dollars.

Once this law, which virtually gave away Georgia's "Yazoo" lands, became public knowledge, Georgia's citizens were outraged, especially when they learned that many of their legislators had received stock in the Yazoo companies in return for their votes. Eventually James Jackson resigned from his U.S. Senate seat to run for state legislature, which led to the repeal of the Yazoo Land Act in 1776.[69]

Although many other Georgians were enraged by state leaders' land abuses, Savannah citizens spearheaded the protest against Yazoo in the spring of 1795. They sent remonstrances to the Georgia legislature demanding that their "servants correct acts . . . designed to benefit private members . . . in a measure so momentous to the common rights and interests of the People."[70] SMA mechanics were among the leaders of this protest. Newly elected city councilman Balthasser Shaffer, a Savannah tailor and member of the SMA, authored a circular intended for "the honest and industrious Mechanics and Planters of Chatham County" that criticized "the Free and Easy Club's" role in Yazoo. After identifying a group of representatives and local politicians involved in the sale, Shaffer asked citizens to vote against them in the next election. He requested that voters support the popular democratic leader General James Jackson, U.S. Senator, for state legislator. Jackson promised to force the state to rescind the infamous Yazoo Act if elected to the new office.[71]

Whether penned by real mechanics or nonmechanics who shared mechanics' views, a series of letters to the editor reiterated Shaffer's points. "A Mechanic" warned citizens that "if the speculators succeed, we shall not much longer be freemen, for the legislature may as well sell us as sell our rights."[72] "A Real Mechanic" agreed. Yazoo speculators "would ruin the country, without regarding oaths or the principles of honor, to make their own fortunes." He added, "These are the kind of men that made paper money, by which the merchants and the hard working mechanics were paid off with one-fourth of what was justly due them, to the disgrace of the State."[73]

Savannah artisans did not simply argue their positions in circulars and editorials. They also organized among themselves. On November 5, 1795, a committee representing "a considerable portion of the citizens of Chatham County" requested General Jackson's resignation from the Senate to enable him to be elected to the state legislature so that he could rectify the Yazoo fiasco, "knowing his moral heart [is] in the right place." The committee was comprised of five men, four of them leaders of the SMA, and two of these four, Shaffer and Lewden, city councilmen. Jackson officially agreed to their request and was subsequently elected to the state legislature.[74] The following year, after the Yazoo Land Act was declared void and the papers burned, a relieved "Free Man" boasted, "each industrious man enjoys the fruits of his own labor, in security and peace."[75]

While the Yazoo crisis galvanized the artisan community, and subsequently helped it secure a new measure of political clout, the great Savannah fire of 1796 and the resolution of the problems it created also demonstrated Savannah artisans' growing influence, which was not always welcome in the larger political community. On November 26, 1796, a huge fire raged through the town, followed by a smaller one on December 6. In all, 229 homes were destroyed, and only 179 left standing.[76] People went homeless, business ground to a halt, and almost no one was spared from loss. Over the next few months, contributions from around the new nation poured into the city to help Savannah rebuild. The distribution of these funds turned into a hotly contested issue when the city council determined that these monies would be given to victims at the rate of 10 percent of their loss.

Poorer residents protested. Although "A Citizen of Savannah" was grateful for the contributions, he considered the distribution system farcical.

Was it fair, he queried, to give a family whose simple dwelling and furniture was valued honestly at $400 a measly $40 when a family owning several homes and stores, not all of which were burnt, whose loss was estimated at $4,000, received $400? Admonishing city council for its lack of judgment in setting policies that favored the rich over the poor, the editorialist reminded the aldermen of their ideological and moral responsibilities. "Let the remainder of the monies be divided among the lot holders who need assistance to rebuild on their lots," he advised. "But as to the affluent and independent man . . . I trust he will bear his loss, with that fortitude which becomes the dignity of his nature." [77]

Savannah's mechanics adhered to this view. Like most residents of moderate income, they had lost shops and residences. The distribution of fire funds seemed questionable to them as well. "A Mechanic" published an allegory comparing the fire to a drought. Who suffered more in this drought, he asked hypothetically. The fish in the sea, wealthy Savannahians, or the fish in the pond, poor Savannahians? [78] Artisans continued to criticize the distribution system and to demand retribution. Three years after the fire, chairmaker Simon O'Connor was among a number of workingmen who "would not relinquish their right to any further sums that they may be entitled to from the donations to the sufferers by the 26th November, 1796 [fire]." [79] That mechanics desired a system of retribution based on social justice marked an unusual turn, indeed a radical departure, from contemporary ideas about equality. By recognizing themselves as fish in the pond and planters and merchants as fish in the sea they hoped to illuminate the *inequality* that prevailed in their everyday world. This recognition suggests that these men were reshaping their political and social ideas in a society organized around hierarchical social relations. Theirs was not an easy task.

Beside the inequitable distribution of contributions, the Savannah fire also unearthed two other disturbing situations that shaped white artisan livelihoods. A grand jury presentment argued in October 1797 that the fire had so damaged certain parts of the city that election of aldermen by wards was no longer appropriate. Accordingly, they urged the institution of "at-large" positions. [80] Events suggest this was probably a pointed attack against the rising political power of the mechanics, for the 1798 tax list indicates that some wards were becoming increasingly populated with workingmen. News of the fire had brought carpenters and builders and other construction tradesmen from as far away as Boston in search of employment and high wages. Those who prolonged their stay created a new source of artisan votes, a situation that undoubtedly did not sit well with the merchant class.[81]

Fortunately for the artisans, the presentment was never passed. But in addition to this political challenge, artisans also suffered from a social one—xenophobia. Arising out of rumors that "foreigners" (those who were not southerners) had started the 1796 fire, some established Savannahians blamed any and all "Spaniards, Frenchmen, Dutchmen, Scotchmen, or New Englandmen, or any but Georgians." An editorial by "Satan" in 1798 mocked long-time Savannah residents who promised to "lynch" all "foreigners" responsible for the devastating fire.[82] Since so many of the arriviste tradesmen were indeed "foreign" by this definition, it would appear that these would-be lynchmen were reacting to perceived dislocations in their city—the rise of democratic rule in the wake of the Nelson Affair and the Yazoo Crisis, the physical and financial ruin caused by the fire, and the influx of common men, usually non-Georgian, nonslaveholding white mechanics.

National political events and their repercussions had thrown many citizens squarely into the Democratic-Republican Party. Savannahians, especially artisans, shopkeepers, and small merchants, were no exception. This Democratic-Republican tide, along with the desire to secure individual rights after a period in which local and state political elites threatened to usurp them, compelled the majority of Savannah citizens to vote for Jefferson and herald his presidency. Thus, by 1801 "A Friend to Equal Rights" could confidently announce the "triumph of republicanism over aristocracy" in Savannah.[83] "Federalist" was now a dirty word, and the first edition of the *Republican,* whose very existence and political bent acted as another sign of Democratic-Republicanism's triumph, contained a critique of these hated men. "It is laughable to the aristocrats how they labor to get the name republican," sneered the lead article.[84] The *Republican* also printed Thomas Paine's letters and writings, observing that some men "had reason to fear the return of *commonsense* to America at this *crisis,* conscious that all attempts against the *rights of man* will be exposed."[85] Even an English visitor to Savannah and the surrounding area was amazed at the universality of "Democratic opinion" and "notions of equality."[86]

Because Savannah's mechanics had been among the most vocal and organized of opposition throughout the 1790s, they were rewarded for their efforts with the responsibility of community leadership. For example, when news of Washington's death reached the city, a funeral procession was arranged, with judges, civic leaders, officers, lodge members, *and* the SMA leading the rest of the citizens through the streets in mourning, though it is important to note that the SMA was the *last* organization to precede the people. It is unclear whether this was a deliberate decision to show that the artisanry still lacked the status awarded those groups preceding it or whether the artisans themselves chose to hang back because of their ambivalence over Washington's federalist leanings.[87]

Meanwhile, in the intervening years since the SMA had been incorporated, the twenty-eight unremarkable charter members had begun to prosper politically and financially. Seven members secured city council seats over this period; almost no year between 1791 and 1820 passed without an artisan alderman in office. Moreover, artisans also served as election superintendents in many of the wards. Thus, in 1800 and 1801, William Eppinger, Balthasser Shaffer, William Lewden, and William Spencer, all SMA members, were selected to monitor Heathcote, Percival, Derby, and Warren wards respectively.[88]

After 1794, artisan leaders in both Savannah and Augusta found themselves, along with their Whig cohort, increasingly caught up in state and national issues that eventually drew them into the new Democratic-Republican Party. Their swing away from factional politics based on local leaders and issues and toward party politics with a national emphasis began with Georgians' growing distrust of the Washington administration. However, the Yazoo land sale of 1794–1795, orchestrated by state leaders (including the artisan leader from Augusta William Longstreet, who was one of the few politicians to emerge politically unscathed by the scandal), and the aggressive opposition to the sale led by Senator James Jackson in 1795–1796, brought most artisans into the national Democratic-Republican Party fold by the end of the eighteenth century.[89] Like Georgia's Democratic-Republican electors in general, these white male artisans came to hold opposition to large-scale land speculation and respect for the tenets of republicanism as their guiding political principles in the wake of the incident, eroding their separate identity as an artisanal community.

The new popularity of the Democratic-Republican Party, along with statewide interest in national issues, served to unify Georgians despite class and geographic differences from this point forward. Growing southern opposition to national policies viewed as pro-British during the Adams administration, particularly the Jay Treaty, which left out southern requests for British compensation for slaves stolen during the American Revolution, further served to bring Georgians together. As the political tensions between the Federalists and Democratic-Republicans escalated, and to some extent took on a regional nature, Georgians joined other southern Democratic-Republicans in voicing their opposition to the Alien and Sedition Acts. With the nation on the verge of a great crisis, southerners, desperate to preserve their liberty, helped assure the Democratic-Republican Party victory by voting overwhelmingly for Thomas Jefferson, a fellow southerner, in the election of 1800. Georgia, the fastest-growing slave economy in the region, contributed to this Jeffersonian triumph.[90]

The escalation of political opposition from abroad during Jefferson's and Madison's presidencies also brought together planters, merchants, and mechanics in support of national domestic and foreign policies pursued by a Democratic-Republican administration.[91] Savannah's and Augusta's artisan-politicians were drawn into this statewide movement. The growing influence of the Democratic-Republican Party throughout Georgia meant that local factions, whether based on class differences or personality conflicts, were increasingly inviable. Thus, these artisan-leaders, elite master craftsmen, appear to have used their status as artisan-republicans to gain access into a political world hitherto denied them. Ironically, upon gaining these positions, they came to identify themselves more with the newly established Democratic-Republican Party than with the mechanics who had voted them into office.

This phenomenon of artisan-leaders turned local politicians no longer interested in artisan concerns explains in part why the MSA and expressions of artisanal republicanism deteriorated after 1804. The unwillingness of the artisan leaders to sustain their community over time was not due to party politics alone, however. Indeed, this unwillingness stemmed from a series of interlaced developments that promoted a shared social identity for all white men at the expense of a separate artisanal community. White Georgians' opportunities for upward mobility, their fear of slaves and the white superiority this fear engendered, along with their political cohesiveness in the wake of the Yazoo scandal, seriously discouraged internal divisions along class lines. The effects of these developments on the artisans, when taken together, illustrate how the making of a social identity based on slave labor profoundly discouraged class consciousness.

Free labor's political identity was fundamentally challenged by artisanal opportunity for upward mobility. This challenge in turn was predicated upon an important set of economic transformations that made Georgia's social structure especially dynamic and fluid during the early republic. The existence of staple-crop economies, the availability of inexpensive land in the upcountry, and limited competition from urban artisans, white and black, slave and free, enabled these skilled migrants to acquire capital, land, and slaves between 1790 and 1810, and to become planters or at least planters in the making. For especially successful artisans clearly managed to put aside their leather aprons and tool boxes and enter the planter class.[92] It is important to note that the leaders of the MSA and the SMA were at the very forefront of this transition, showing not only how wealth and politics worked hand in hand in the construction of the Old South, but how aware artisans were of this reality.

Perhaps the most adventurous of these self-made planters was the afore-mentioned Augusta artisan, William Longstreet. Born in New Jersey in 1759, Longstreet moved to Georgia with his wife and infant son in 1785.[93] A leader of the MSA as well as a local politician, he made his living in Augusta as a machinist and inventor who built and sold cotton gins and engines. He also earned money from the operation of two cotton gins and a saw mill. Longstreet was an innovator. He was one of the first men to introduce steam engines to the upcountry. He built a steamboat patented by the Georgia Legislature that plied the Savannah River several years before Robert Fulton's invention. Although his efforts were routinely mocked by fellow Augustans, his stock-in-trade from these ventures was valued at a hefty $5,000 by 1809.[94]

Longstreet was also an ardent land speculator, not unlike many upcoun-trymen in this era. During his twenty-nine years in Georgia, he bought and sold at least 1,200 acres of upcountry land and town property.[95] According to a biographer of the Longstreet family, "[H]e was a business man of an almost shocking degree. . . . Always he was trading, giving people power of attorney, buying a residence and selling it soon to some advantage, re-moving to another only to repeat the process, his money eye always wide open."[96] Longstreet used his "money eye" to pursue planter ambitions in

1800 when he moved his family, along with ten slaves, to a South Carolina farm some fourteen miles from Augusta. This venture failed, however, so Longstreet returned his family to Augusta in 1805 where he resumed his speculative pursuits, thanks at least in part to his wife's willingness to run a private boarding house to maintain the household economy.[97]

Unlike Longstreet, who was ultimately a successful businessman if not the most successful of planters, silversmith John Catlett, another MSA leader and local politician, glided easily into the ranks of the planter class. The Virginia-born Catlett probably arrived in Augusta around 1786. Over the next two decades, he owned a "wet-goods" store, held a partnership in a tinsmithing shop, and like Longstreet engaged in a variety of real estate transactions, including appraisals, rentals, and sales.[98] In the early 1800s, he invested spare capital in the newly formed Planter's Bank, operated a plantation with the help of fifty-three slaves, and owned some five thousand acres in three upcountry counties that produced upwards of 150 bales of cotton by 1810.[99]

While few artisan leaders could match Longstreet's success as a speculator or Catlett's as a planter, other MSA officers also enjoyed prosperity.[100] Robert Cresswell, a carpenter by trade, owned five houses and lots as well as 1,750 acres in Washington County valued at $23,000 at his death in 1816.[101] In addition to their urban properties, which included at least one house and lot for all but one of the MSA leaders, twelve owned significant amounts of upcountry land. Silversmith Thomas Bray held nearly 1,000 acres, tailor John Cook 260 acres, carpenter William Dearmond 200 acres, carpenter Conrad Liverman over 2,000 acres, miller Hugh Magee nearly 3,000 acres, Angus Martin 600 acres, carpenter Baxter Pool 1,100 acres, Edward Primrose over 200 acres, and shoemaker Frances Vallotton 700 acres.[102]

SMA artisan-leaders also achieved considerable financial success. The wealthiest of members was probably William Spencer, who owned eleven slaves and whose estate was valued at just over $4,000 after his death.[103] Three members acquired taverns or grog shops during their careers.[104] John Miller, a shoemaker, had enough capital by 1800 to switch his business to the importation of ready-made shoes, which he sold to upcountry shopkeepers.[105] In fact, the majority of these men owned more taxable property in 1806 than in 1798.[106] At least nine men had acquired a few hundred acres of land. In short, while none of these men had joined the ranks of the wealthiest of Georgia planters and merchants, almost all had made great financial strides between 1793 and 1806.

Unlike artisans in the North who invested their profits in businesses and shops, these artisans chose to invest much of their wealth in land, which could be cultivated, rented, mortgaged, or sold at a later date when land values escalated, which they invariably did. Land ownership remained the key to prosperity and social status in the South. Artisans were quick to recognize this reality.

Slave ownership provided another important route to wealth and status. In many respects, slave ownership was the best kind of investment because slave property could be liquidated easily or hired out to raise cash. More-over, ownership of female slaves of childbearing age raised the possibility of owning additional slaves at very little cost. At least eleven of the sixteen MSA leaders owned slaves between 1790 and 1810. By comparison, just over half of the Augusta taxpayers owned an average of seven slaves apiece in 1800.[107]

Economic opportunity ate away at the very core of these artisan com-munities by transforming artisan leaders into entrepreneurs and planters; local political opportunity and national party developments had proved equally insidious. Given these realities, it is not surprising that an artisan community could not be sustained in Augusta by the early nineteenth cen-tury. Over time, the leaders of the artisan community, an elite group of financially comfortable men who participated in local politics, found that their loyalties had become more firmly tied to the planter society they had successfully entered than to the artisan interests they had once honored. They had gained political experience as local leaders and financial expe-rience as artisans, speculators, and planters. More important, they had acquired slaves and land, the two most important prerequisites for social prestige in the lower South.

The rise of an artisanal elite that assimilated itself into the dominant slaveholding class by the early nineteenth century occurred both in Savan-nah and Augusta. The departure of this artisanal elite from its class moor-ings weakened any semblance of class identity that remained among non-elite white artisans. This phenomenon was especially visible in Savannah in 1802 when a group of 42 white male carpenters, in an apparent effort to capture both a class *and* a trade identity, sought and secured the incorporation of their own Savannah House Carpenters' Association from the state legislature. This organization's primary goal was ostensibly a professional one—to establish social respect for its members—according to its charter, which duplicated the SMA charter, except for the exclusion of a relief fund. Undoubtedly, many of these petitioners had arrived after the 1796 fire, had little savings, had no connections to fall back on between jobs, and thus could ill afford dues for relief monies. Also, carpenters were the likeliest of all artisans and mechanics to suffer from black competition.[108] It should come as no surprise then that only a few of the petitioners were financially comfortable by SMA standards. According to the 1806 tax list, only four petitioning carpenters were assessed taxes over $10.[109]

The Carpenters' Association, like its petitioners, did not fare well. In fact, it disappeared from the records shortly after its incorporation. Four of its petitioners had also been SMA members, two of whom, Asa Hoxey and Francis Roma, were fairly prominent businessmen. The Carpenters' Association's quick demise suggests the difficulty encountered by white mechanics in a slave society trying to establish a class identity. Trade associations simply could not prosper in these circumstances. Mechanics' societies had a difficult enough time.

The demise of the Carpenters' Association and the MSA and the artisanal communities associated with them did not stem from economic and political developments alone. The implications of living in a society shaped by slavery also undermined the independence of the artisan world. Artisans were as inextricably tied to the social system of slavery as other white men in the South. They owned and hired slaves who worked in their homes, workshops, and fields. They ascribed to a planter worldview based upon the dominance of white men over black men. Every aspect of daily life was shaped by the realities of slavery, a crucial factor that served to bind mechanics to other white men despite their class differences.

To acquire their substantial holdings, most MSA leaders had depended on slave labor. To maintain and enlarge those holdings, they expected to rely on more slave labor. While they embraced notions of equality and independence in their avowals of artisanal republicanism in their mechanics' society meetings, these men did not believe such values applied to the slaves and free blacks who worked among them. For them there was no contradiction. They willingly accepted the racial order that separated black men from white. To do so, they had to assume a belief in white superiority. This decision was made easier by the fear that characterized white relations with blacks throughout the late eighteenth and early nineteenth centuries in the lower South.

While both the ownership of land and slaves signaled entry into the elite social order of the South, the proof of an individual's commitment to that order was best demonstrated through slave ownership. This must have been especially true for migrant artisans at a time and place when their commitment to slave labor may have been viewed with suspicion. Indeed, by the late 1790s, Virginia Federalists feared that Democratic-Republicans would abolish slavery altogether. Gabriel's conspiracy and his subsequent trial in Richmond indicated that slaves certainly believed that the egalitarian principles espoused by their fellow white workers justified bringing slavery to an end.[110] While no evidence indicates that white residents in Augusta feared the impact of white artisan avowals of republican ideals and political egalitarianism on their slaves, such pronouncements must have been ill suited to a climate where whites were increasingly worried about revolts. Ownership of slaves by MSA leaders must have convinced white Augustans not to doubt artisan commitment to a society ruled by the white race.

The impact of the American Revolution had set into place a series of social and economic changes that further entrenched the slave regime in Georgia, even as slaves acquired a new measure of assertiveness.[111] As slave numbers increased and staple prices rose at the end of the eighteenth century, Georgia slaves asserted their new autonomy through acts of resistance that ranged from illicit commercial exchanges to running away.[112] Such examples of autonomy, fed by growing concerns about slave rebelliousness, threatened white authority. These concerns were fueled by the memory of maroon societies in the marshes along the lower Savannah River. Runaways from coastal South Carolina and Georgia had sacked nearby plantations for provisions and new runaways in the wake of the war.

By 1786, local militia were intent upon securing the capture of one particularly bold group of "armed Banditti," who called themselves the "King's Englishmen." These men resisted capture until the spring of 1787, when Georgia troops imprisoned their leaders, "Captain Cudjoe" and "Captain Lewis," following bold attacks on nearby plantations by nearly one hundred armed runaways.[113] The fear excited by maroon societies, along with rumors of foiled slave insurrections, was compounded by events in the French West Indies, where slaves in Haiti, inspired by the French Revolution, had launched a spectacularly successful revolt of their own, forcing planters to abandon their stakes.[114] Lowcountry Georgia responded to these events with a series of prohibitions that included banning entry of ships bearing slaves from the West Indies, registering free blacks, and banning free blacks from entry into the state.[115] Intent upon maintaining authority over unfree black labor at all costs, even upcountry Georgians feared the implications of black revolt in Haiti.[116]

A rash of slave and free black trials, and in some instances executions, marked white efforts to contain black autonomy.[117] An Augusta free black man accused of horse-stealing was tried, convicted, and executed in the summer of 1793.[118] Several of Augusta's artisan leaders participated in these efforts to contain black rebelliousness. When a slave named George was brought to trial that same summer for "harboring and assisting a runaway" and opposing the runaway's capture by brandishing a gun, William Longstreet served as one of two justices of the peace at his trial, Isaac Wingate as Grand Jury member, and Conrad Liverman as witness. George was convicted and though not executed was sentenced to banishment from the United States after a public whipping at the markethouse and several street corners.[119]

These attempts to prevent black resistance served to cement social relations among whites and to reduce division. White communal fear of black freedom brought whites together as a race, ultimately generating a racist justification for the perpetuation of slavery that would shape proslavery ideology and southern nationalism throughout the antebellum and Confederate eras. Under these circumstances, white artisans had little room in which to nurture an artisanal class-consciousness.

White workingmen were a significant portion of the population in urban Georgia. They were powerful enough to organize their own communities and to embrace their own ideology. Indeed, for one brief decade, Augusta artisans sustained a political community of their own. Savannah's artisan community lasted slightly longer but was led by artisans-turned-entrepreneurs, who expressed virtually no interest in a distinct artisanal ideology by 1810. A complicated set of developments encouraged successful craftsmen to cast aside their artisanal identity in exchange for acceptance in the racially based white social order. The pull of a southern political consensus shaped around the ideals of the Democratic-Republican Party, opportunities for upward mobility, and the embeddedness of a social system based on slavery served to unify the interests of white men across class differences. It was this set of circumstances, and not planter self-sufficiency, that explains the failure of white artisans to sustain their political communities in Georgia on the eve of the cotton revolution.

In the end, these artisans willingly exchanged their artisanal ideology, their artisanal skills, and their artisanal identity for inclusion in the dominant social order of the South. Urban workingmen adhered to the principles of artisanal republicanism in cities throughout the early republic, but the circumstances in which artisanal republicanism triumphed in Georgia were the exception rather than the rule. In both Savannah and Augusta artisan-leaders used republican ideology to serve their particular needs—both to politicize the mechanic community and to earn political and social respect in their slaveholding world by carving out a critical niche for themselves among the planter class.

That these artisan-leaders chose to conceive of themselves as white men of the dominant social order rather than a distinct class of white artisans has important implications for understanding antebellum political culture in the South. Historians have pointed to the 1830s as an era in which a "democratic revolution" of sorts occurred in southern politics. Southern leaders, responding to growing northern sentiment for abolition, formulated a quasi-egalitarian ideology that united white men as members of the master race.[120] The actions of Georgia's artisans not only suggest that the foundation for this development was laid much earlier, but that these white artisans were not deceived into thinking of themselves as members of the white social order by a persuasive planter elite. Instead, they were active participants in ensuring their own inclusion in that order. Though the maturation of the cotton economy would bring economic change and a diminishment of opportunities to white artisans in Georgia, their belief that they had established a place for themselves within the social and political order of slavery would continue largely unabated through the antebellum era.

Like many arriviste men in the emerging South, Georgia artisans quickly learned how to advance themselves in their new culture. They recognized that the key to economic success and political power was tied to the ownership of land and slaves. While artisans were quite willing to ply their trade in this new slave economy as well as organize mechanics' societies and participate in local politics, the most ambitious and acquisitive among them used their trade and their mechanic identity as a bridge to the planter class. Thus free labor was not so much foiled by the pervasiveness of slave labor in the South during the early republic. Instead, free laborers recognized that in a slave labor economy their artisanal work and their identity was best used as a means to an end.

3 *The Spread of Production*

By the 1820s white master craftsmen had begun to carve out a significant place for themselves across Georgia. Many had secured some measure of political power for themselves and accumulated new wealth, even transforming themselves into planters in the process. The conditions that made these aspirations possible—planter consumption patterns, town growth, the new cotton economy, and the expanding upcountry— began to affect the different regions in different ways between 1820 and 1860. As a result, depending upon their trade and locale, not all white artisans experienced the degree of social and economic mobility in the antebellum era that had been available between 1789 and 1820.

In the decades that followed, artisans' economic opportunities would be profoundly influenced by the significant changes that characterized Georgia at this time. The spread of the cotton economy through middle Georgia and down to the southwest corner of the state had critical implications for artisanal demand and the spread of production in general. This chapter documents both how and why urban growth and manufacturing growth were circumscribed in antebellum Georgia as well as the repercussions of these limits in respect to artisanal work.

Between 1820 and 1860 white artisanal opportunity continued to be shaped in fundamental ways by the plantation economy. First and foremost, the failure of the plantation economy to encourage significant urban growth in the antebellum era marked one of the most significant factors shaping artisanal opportunity in this period. The fluctuating supply and demand of the world cotton market and the profitability of plantation slavery in Georgia, along with the circumstantial reality of cheap, new land suitable for cotton cultivation, formed a strong deterrent to the kind of urban growth common in the antebellum Northeast and the Midwest. Although the plantation system of the South was sustained by the world economy, described by one historian as "an enclave within the capitalist market," slavery prevented the South's complete immersion in the marketplace.[1] This reality meant that white artisanal opportunity was inextricably linked to the plantation and to slavery. In the North cities had come to dictate the economy of the surrounding countryside through developments in technology, the growth of manufacturing, and the availability of capital. This change had led to increasingly complex urban functions, involving the processing, producing, marketing, and distributing of goods and services, and in fact turned some artisans into entrepreneurs and manufacturers and others into members of the working class. In either case, in the northeastern United States artisan livelihoods became bound to urban development over the course of the late eighteenth and early nineteenth centuries.

This phenomenon simply did not develop in the deep South. Plantation slavery bred innumerable obstacles to the kinds of intense urban development that characterized early-nineteenth-century New England. One of the principal obstacles to southern urban growth was the lack of capital. In the early nineteenth century, southern cities had surrendered control over the sale of their local products, particularly cotton, to the monied agents of commission houses outside the South in places like New York, Liverpool, and elsewhere. As a consequence, merchants extended credit to southern retailers and wholesalers. These men in turn were forced to sell on credit to cotton growers until the harvest and sale of the annual crop. Profits that might have been invested in manufacturing in the urban

South were often retained to pay interest to outside creditors or to purchase stock.[2]

Historians have blamed more than the New York merchants' monopoly of the carrying trade for the slow rate of urban growth in the South. They also have fingered the self-sufficiency of nineteenth-century plantations where skilled black craftsmen proved able substitutes for small town services. They blame the numbers of slaves, poor whites, and subsistence farmers who lacked the cash to buy goods from the towns and the absorption of capital into slaves instead of manufacturing.[3] It is important to stress that these obstacles in and of themselves did not block the kind of urban growth that was occurring in the North. More accurately, they were symptomatic of the tremendous control that plantation slavery exerted on cities and towns, and hence on white artisans who sought to make their living in Georgia.

While aspects of the capitalist market came to be present in the antebellum South and in Georgia—in the form of commercial centers, financial institutions, canals, and railroads—they never presided over or came to characterize the productive relations in this economy before the Civil War.[4] Because cities and towns in Georgia promoted the trade of the planters in the countryside, their primary functions were as suppliers and distributors. The manufacturing that was fostered in these cities was shaped by these functions. The ties that bound these places to the national market were exceedingly weak.

These ties bore very little relationship to the ties that characterized market relations in the cities of the Northeast and growing urban centers of the Midwest. All were in the process of moving from commercial to industrial economies by the 1840s. Unlike cities in Georgia, they boasted surprisingly complex interdependencies with each other. Aided by middlemen and forwarding agents, these urban places experienced tremendous growth (as measured by population and the expansion and diversification of commerce and manufacturing) as a result of "the movement of [their] agricultural commodities, natural resources, and industrial goods" to broad markets beyond traditional hinterlands.[5]

Antebellum Georgia, including Savannah and Augusta, but also towns like Athens, Macon, and Columbus, did not participate in this evolving "city-system." Instead, these places acted as market centers for regions of staple-crop production, a relationship that was more typical of eighteenth-century urban development in the North.[6] Thus while northern communities began to witness the emergence of a working class of urban wage-earning men, southern communities did not.

The desire to produce short-staple cotton for the growing European market together with the knowledge that upcountry land yielded respectable cotton crops had worked to unify white Georgians' economic interests, including those of mechanics, during the last decade of the eighteenth century and through the first decades of the nineteenth century. With cotton as their common bond, white Georgians from a wide spectrum of social classes continued to march westward across the state in succeeding decades in search of more land for cultivation. Small farmers came first, followed by planters and their slaves, but merchants, shopkeepers, artisans, and mechanics, men whose livelihoods were sustained by this expanding agricultural world, quickly followed them.

While long-staple, sea island cotton had been cultivated on the coastal islands of Georgia and South Carolina since the 1780s, it did not prosper in the upland. Experimentation with short-staple, green seed cotton produced a variety that grew well in the upcountry but whose sticky green seed required too much labor to separate from the cotton strands to make it profitable. Then in 1793 Eli Whitney contrived a very simple piece of machinery that divided the seed from the cotton. This simple mechanical device produced a great revolution in the southern economy and the southern way of life, for the cultivation of green seed cotton was relatively easy, it could grow almost anywhere, and profits could be earned from even the smallest of cotton patches.

Georgia emerged as the world's largest cotton producer in the 1820s, and though new southwestern states soon eclipsed the state's cotton production, Georgia held her own. The state was second only to Alabama in cotton cultivation, producing half a million bales in 1850, and fourth to Alabama, Mississippi, and Louisiana, producing over 700,000 bales in 1860.[7]

The land that made this degree of productivity possible was exacted from Georgia Indians in the late eighteenth and early nineteenth centuries. Treaties reluctantly signed by the Creek Indians in 1802, 1804, and 1805 had extended Georgia's boundaries to the Ocmulgee River. The state had distributed these lands through a lottery system that allowed men of modest means to acquire land. Subsequent treaties and the use of federal force

soon guaranteed more Indian soil for greedy white Georgians and migrants alike, allowing the state to claim the Pine Barren and Wiregrass regions inhabited by the Creeks in 1814 and the mountainous North Georgia
lands of the Cherokees in 1817, 1818, and 1819 as its own.[8] White settlement in these sections, without the attraction of the rich loam of the piedmont, was sporadic until farmers realized that these lands could comfort-
ably sustain livestock and yield respectable grain crops. The growth of the
white population in North Georgia was also hastened by the discovery of
gold in the Cherokee hills in the late 1820s, which hastened the removal
of the Cherokees via the infamous Trail of Tears.[9]

Meanwhile, the cotton belt borders were stretched further west and
south after the state assumed title to Creek land between the Ocmulgee
and the Flint rivers in 1821 and the Flint and the Chattahoochee rivers in
1826 and 1827. Ideal for growing cotton and veined with several large
rivers suitable for water transport, the extensive new piedmont eventually
drew the bulk of the state's population to its fertile lands. By 1820 one-
fourth of the state's population already lived west of the Oconee River.[10]

Although the state had restricted the size of the original lottery grants in
an effort to discourage land speculation (in the wake of the Yazoo scandal)
and had thereby limited wealthier men's access to large properties, this
situation did not hamper planters for long. Greed became the name of the
game. The buying and selling of titles to land grants subsequently proved
commonplace. As a result, the most desirable pieces of land were rapidly
gobbled up by prominent white settlers, their black slaves, and cotton
seed. Even less desirable properties experienced this transformation almost as quickly.

Most new inhabitants of the widening upcountry came from the eastern
part of the state and the coastal lowcountry as well as from Virginia and
the Carolinas. But northerners and Europeans also migrated to the Georgia upcountry. Together, these immigrants constituted a mixed bag of social classes. Some were hardscrabble farmers seeking economic independence. Others were the unpropertied progeny of plantation families eager
to reproduce the lifestyles of their forebears. Regardless of their origins,
all, including white mechanics, sought to take advantage of the new opportunities available to them. As this hodgepodge began to shape an agricultural economy out of these formerly timbered Indian lands, they forged a
new Georgia society and reshaped politics as well.[11]

The settlement of these fresh lands necessitated town building. While Savannah and Augusta remained the largest and most important market centers in the state, the peopling of the upcountry encouraged towns to spring up.[12] This growth was stimulated by state conflict over political representation as upcountry politicians sought to keep pace with their powerful lowcountry counterparts and in general by state politicians' desire to establish law and order in favor of planters' interests in these new regions in the burgeoning cotton economy. Plantation counties, located primarily in the lowcountry before 1810, with their small white populations and large black populations, had received a disproportionate share of political power compared to the new settlers of the upcountry who initially owned far fewer slaves.[13]

The method of determining apportionment for state representatives, borrowed from the federal government's ratio for ascertaining population, favored planter counties with black majorities. The number elected from each county depended on the size of the white population and the size of the black population figured with the three-fifths federal rule.[14]

Since the revolution, Georgia citizens had maintained a political alliance between rich and poor that hinged on their shared conceptions of republican ideology. All white men, whether or not they were slaveholders, believed they all shared the right to political equality under this conception. Upcountry citizens, with their smaller slaveholdings, periodically challenged the unequal white representation implicit in this system. Their arguments were based on an underlying belief in white egalitarianism.[15]

State senate representation was determined more equitably. Beginning in 1798, every county, whether large or small, was allowed to elect one, and only one, state senator. By establishing relatively small counties—and therefore many counties—in the newly ceded lands, the number of upcountry senators was increased. In time, this strategy produced a majority of upcountry legislators in the state senate, counterbalancing the previous era's overrepresentation of lowcountry planter counties in the state assembly.[16]

The establishment of so many new counties was attributable to another factor as well. As the expanding edges of the upcountry were often virtual frontier zones where settlers skirmished with Indians (and sometimes with each other), the state hoped to instill law and order in these outlying borders. Legislators, who readily acknowledged that the organization of county seats hastened the settlement process, gave the location of the new county seats supreme consideration. They worried about the healthiness of a place before decreeing it the site of a future town and appointed town commissioners to preside over the sale of town lots to discourage speculation.

The legislators also put a great deal of thought into the physical layout of these towns, reserving specific acts for themselves, like determining the size of lots, the style and construction of the courthouse and jail, the location of public buildings, and the situation of streets, parks, and squares.[17] They recognized that the erection of courthouses permitted systematic and uniform practices for legalizing and recording land deeds, that the construction of jails meant criminals were speedily and publicly punished (a deterrent to other offenders), and that building schools and churches promoted community pride. In short, legislative town planning, they believed, hastened the process of settlement.[18]

Ostensibly the primary function of the courthouse town—often hardly more than a village—was to serve the surrounding county residents. Although these places generated some manufacturing and commerce, urban products and services were limited to the local economy, which had significant implications for mechanics. Indeed, the most important role of the county-seat town was to act as social, cultural, and political gathering point for the inhabitants of the countryside. Production was not a priority. Courthouse towns experienced boom periods that reflected upswings in settlement. But the inevitable maturation of plantation society ultimately restricted county-seat growth. With each succeeding land lottery, a portion of the populace chose to move on to the newest frontier. This westward migration eroded the county population. Declining numbers meant fewer clients to patronize the goods and services available in the courthouse town. These circumstances limited white mechanics' opportunities. They also circumscribed the number of master craftsmen in any given trade who could support themselves in this limited economy. Thus many mechanics, along with other less established urban residents, were compelled to move on as well.

This boom and bust cycle shaped local population and growth. The inevitable migration out of the courthouse towns, caused by the absence of cheap land in the countryside, along with the declining populations that accompanied these changes, became commonplace. For example, to demonstrate the scope of this movement, Sparta, the courthouse town of Hancock County, was inhabited by more than three hundred residents in 1810, only to lose 20 percent of its population in only a decade's time. The population of Waynesborough, the courthouse town for Burke County, declined 26 percent and Marion, the courthouse town for Twiggs County, declined 36 percent over this same period. Although Louisville, the former capital of the state and the courthouse town for Jefferson County, experienced a 17 percent rise in population between 1810 and 1820, those numbers dropped 10 percent by 1830.[19]

The maturation of a county's plantation economy, with its subsequent westward migration, triggered population declines in the populations of older courthouse towns throughout eastern and middle Georgia. With these changes the courthouse town economies began to slow as well.[20] Thus, while plantation agriculture supported much of the Georgia economy by the 1820s, the rural nature of this economy, along with the availability of new lands, played a hand in discouraging urban growth, as measured in population and commercial and manufacturing developments. While population growth occurred in new places to the west, it was not sustained in old ones. This pattern, which continued throughout urban Georgia during the antebellum period, meant that artisanal opportunities, while promising in the first years of a courthouse town's establishment, were bound to wane over time, forcing artisans to move elsewhere or change occupations.

Another series of towns, also state-planned, revolved around the needs of rural dwellers. Legislators, planters, and farmers alike encouraged the development of planned trade centers designed to serve the expanding cotton economy.[21] Moreover, unlike the stagnating county-seat towns, these trade centers were better situated, for in short order, the railroad proved to be the key to the growth of these new communities. At first, many artisans and merchants newly located to these trade centers were unhappy at the arrival of the train, which introduced competition with larger merchants in Savannah, Charleston, and even more distant places like New York. Over time, however, local merchants and artisans learned to accommodate their businesses and their local economy to the iron horse and reaped considerable profits from their efforts.[22] In fact, many master craftsmen transformed themselves into merchants who were able to sell manufactured goods newly available to them through railroad transport.

By 1860, the major antebellum cities and towns of Georgia included the planned trade centers of Savannah, Augusta, Macon, Columbus, and Atlanta, and to a lesser extent, the college town of Athens and the state capital of Milledgeville. Excluding the port city, Savannah, the capital, Milledgeville, and the latecomer, Atlanta, the remaining four of these seven leading antebellum towns originated as distribution points near the fall-lines of significant rivers.

Originally, location on these headwaters enabled towns to act as market centers for inland cotton, as well as for grains, lumber, hides, and supplies in the years before the railroad, because they could rely on water transport to move their products to market. These locations also encouraged the establishment of a limited number of manufacturing enterprises that relied on power generated by running water. Though relatively rudimentary urban functions when compared with the far more sophisticated urban economies of the Northeast, river transport and water power encouraged the growth of a handful of fledgling Georgia towns that eventually transformed themselves into significant urban locales by the 1840s and 1850s.[23]

Three towns, Augusta, Macon, and Columbus, were located in prime cotton-producing areas, and their initial development hinged on their ability to facilitate cotton's shipment to market. Augusta, a late-eighteenth-century tobacco center, was transformed into an early-nineteenth-century upland cotton center and finally—when the bulk of the state's cotton no longer passed through Augusta's markets—into a factory center by mid-century. Augusta's transformation was so successful that the city became known as "the Lowell of the South."[24]

Macon, established in 1823 on the banks of the Ocmulgee, constituted the buckle of Georgia's cotton-growing belt by the late antebellum years. Because this town was located near some of the largest cotton plantations in the state, Macon evolved into an important trade and transportation hub by the 1830s.[25] By the end of that decade, Macon cleared one-third of the state's cotton crop, over 100,000 bales, through its markets, floating most of it downriver by steamboat to the port of Darien.[26]

The advent of railroads capable of hauling cotton almost nonstop to the sea briefly threatened Macon commerce. "The Georgia Railroad has already injured the place some and when it is completed they must feel it more sensibly," wrote a visitor in his journal in 1842. "It will then be an easy matter for the large planter to ship his cotton to Savannah and attend to the sale of it himself . . . and while there they will supply themselves with goods as the assortment will always be much larger and prices as cheap."[27] As a result of the railroad's impact on commerce, city fathers encouraged the development of local industry. Manufacturing endeavors proved so successful that by the 1850s Macon had emerged as the heavy machine center of the deep South.[28]

Columbus was laid out in 1828 alongside the Chattahoochee, an impressive river that winds its way down from the north Georgia mountains into Appalachicola Bay to form a significant portion of the western border of the state. Like Augusta and Macon, Columbus was forced to convert itself into an extensive factory town. In fact, with the construction of dams to provide water power for industry, Columbus rapidly emerged as the second-largest textile producing city in the South.[29]

Throughout most of the antebellum period, Augusta, Macon, and Columbus all shared a similar history as distribution centers for the agricultural world that surrounded them. The functions and services of these places closely resembled the functions and services of late-eighteenth-century Augusta, with its tobacco and upland cotton hinterlands, and Savannah, with its rice, indigo, and sea island cotton-producing lowcountry.

In the early 1840s the after-effects of the 1837 national depression, including the subsequent drop in cotton prices, along with the perceived threat to commerce posed by the railroad, compelled town leaders to advocate the diversification of their traditional market center economies. Accordingly, they urged the establishment of manufactories. Only limited diversification took place, however. Manufacturing remained small-scale and closely tied to the staple-oriented economy. Urban manufactures either supplied plantations with tools and equipment or processed plantation products.

Milledgeville and Athens were secondary market centers in contrast to these fall-line towns. Both places depended more upon their respective functions as home to the state capital and the state university than upon their geographic locations and economic services. Though legislators had hoped that Milledgeville's placement near the Oconee River would encourage the exchange of cotton following the state's decision to move the capital here in 1807, it was the new capital's willingness to serve the needs of the state legislators that made its economy viable. These visitors to Milledgeville were prosperous men with time and money on their hands. As many a traveler noted, the streets were full of their vehicles and horses.

Legislators and men interested in politics "lounged about" on verandas of boarding houses and "on chairs in the open air." Thus, Milledgeville's economic functions were largely service-oriented and aimed at an unusual clientele.[30]

Athens also sat on the Oconee, though some sixty miles north of Milledgeville. Before 1800 state legislators had settled upon the future site of Athens as the location for a state university. Until the late 1820s, however, Athens was little more than a sleepy village until a few enterprising men came to recognize the potential of the Oconee River that bordered the town and decided to use the shoals to power mills. By 1837 five textile mills operated within twenty miles of the university. With the arrival of the railroad in 1840, Athens became an increasingly important center for transportation and industry.[31]

Milledgeville and Athens were shaped by the countryside surrounding them; Atlanta was not. Incorporated only in 1847, the former hamlet turned into a burgeoning town on the eve of the Civil War because it serviced the railroad industry at the crossroads of three separate lines. Atlanta was the exception to the rule for its local economy bore very little resemblance to the local economies of the more traditional market centers of Georgia.[32]

By 1840 federal census-takers included Macon and Columbus, along with Savannah and Augusta, on their list of Georgia cities. Milledgeville and Athens did not yet qualify as urban, and Atlanta did not as yet exist. The majority of the inhabitants of these four cities were white, but the older the city, the closer the percentage of whites and blacks and the higher the percentage of free blacks. While this same situation basically held true for urban Georgia in 1850, a number of developments in each of these cities altered the demography.

Atlanta, a brand new town in 1850, was nearly three-quarters white. Several reasons explain this high proportion. Not only was Atlanta in fairly close proximity to traditionally nonslaveholding north Georgia, but the nature of the Atlanta economy, with its emphasis on railroad industry, attracted a large number of white mechanics to the youthful town and few planters and slaves.[33] In Macon the proportion of whites to blacks did not change over the decade because demand for slave labor in the countryside outstripped urban demand following the recovery of cotton prices by the mid-1840s. In comparison, the proportion of whites in Columbus dropped by 4 percent as urban dwellers found an increasing number of ways to use black labor. Meanwhile, the older urban locales of Savannah, Augusta, and Milledgeville remained white majorities by a slight percentage. Again the proportion of free blacks in the urban population was likely to be higher in older cities.

By 1860 the proportion of blacks in urban Georgia had dropped significantly, a phenomenon that was occurring in other cities across the South. This did not mean that slave labor was incompatible with urban Georgia. Instead, rising cotton prices had increased demand for slave labor in the countryside during the 1850s. This external agricultural demand depleted the urban slave populations, but this demand was reinforced by internal shifts in the urban world. Rising slave prices and hiring rates, along with greater rural demand for slaves, juxtaposed against increasing availability of urban migrants and declining wage rates for whites, created high urban elasticities. Unlike the countryside, where there were few substitutes for slave labor, cities could substitute any number of newly arrived migrants and foreign workers for slaves.[34]

Meanwhile the proportion of free blacks in these major towns and cities was on the decline. The proportion of free blacks had dropped steadily in Savannah over the past three decades, had fallen below 1 percent in Macon, Atlanta, and Athens, and had increased only slightly in Augusta. This decline can be explained only partially as a response to urban legislation prohibiting free blacks in certain urban occupations. More significantly, free blacks may have decided to leave Savannah and other Georgia towns in the hope of taking advantage of better opportunities in smaller towns or in agriculture.[35] And as Kent Leslie, Whittington B. Johnson, Adele Alexander, and others have argued, registers and census records cannot be considered wholly reliable when determining free black numbers since many free blacks, whose lives have been recorded in qualitative evidence, cannot be located in these quantitative ones.[36]

This fact, among others, suggests that a quick look at urban growth in Georgia can be deceiving. Georgia's urban population showed a steady increase throughout the antebellum era, increasing 44.3 percent between 1810 and 1820 and 86.3 percent between 1820 and 1830. The numbers for subsequent decades, which reflected the rise of the trade centers, continued to be impressive. Urban growth increased 76.0 percent between 1830 and 1840 and 58.1 percent between 1840 and 1850. During these decades most courthouse towns were all but economically defunct, attracting little new industry and few inhabitants. But the trade cities were beginning to flourish, especially with the arrival of the railroads, a reality reflected in the 93.5 percent increase in urban population between 1850 and 1860.[37]

Yet other than demonstrating that Georgia cities experienced increases in the number of their inhabitants over the antebellum years, these figures do not prove especially illustrative. Population growth may or may not be linked to urban development. Urban populations may increase, while productive relations may not. Artisanal opportunity was shaped far more by the latter factor than the former.

The manuscript returns of the 1820 Census of Manufactures confirm not only the nascent state of manufacturing in Georgia, but the subservience of town to country. In that year, 3 percent of all Georgians, or 3,427 individuals, were engaged in manufacturing. In fact, only one-third of all manufacturing occurred in the twenty-one largest cities, towns, and county seats in the state.[38] And wherever manufacturing did take place, whether in urban or rural Georgia, it was usually small-scale and performed in homes, barns, and workshops.

Thus the very use of the term "manufactures" becomes suspect. Federal census-takers themselves, appointed to enumerate Georgia manufactures, questioned its applicability on their returns. Upon attempting to tabulate Clarke County's manufactures, census-taker John R. Golding concluded, "I did not conceive from the printed instructions that I should make a return of the domestic workshops." Accordingly, Golding's paragraph-length report simply noted the existence of several small distilleries in the area.[39] When another census-taker discovered no manufactures in newly established Hall County, he decided to record every domestic workshop in this northern upcountry place but was quick to add, "Nearly one-third of the male inhabitants [2,511 white males] . . . are artificers or workmen of some kind or other, though not professionally, as agriculture is their principal occupation."[40]

Even Chatham County, home to Savannah, the largest city in the state, with its extensive trade relations with transatlantic ports, was unable to boast much about its manufacturing enterprises. Census-takers in 1820 published information on only seven establishments, adding that these were "all that could be procured."[41] In fact, the entire set of Georgia returns was prefaced by this disclaimer: "[T]he state of Georgia is chiefly agricultural. The towns [are] commercial and principally depending on northern importation and foreign intercourse for almost every article of manufacture." [42]

Nevertheless, these enumerators missed an important point. Production in Georgia was not linked to the rise of manufacturing that was beginning to characterize the economy of the Northeast. Instead, production in Georgia remained, for the most part, in the workshops of artisans, white and black, slave and free. Some goods were imported from the North and Europe, but most rural communities, towns, and even major cities in the state would rely on traditional forms of artisanal production through most of the antebellum era.

Because this society was indeed "chiefly agricultural," the majority of manufacturing enterprises identified by the census bureau promoted agricultural as opposed to commercial- and manufacturing-oriented production. Not surprisingly, ginning establishments and sawmills outnumbered all other manufacturing enterprises at this time. The manufacturing enumerated in the census then, no matter how limited, did in fact illustrate this society's ability to be self-sufficient; for local production generally fulfilled the most immediate needs of farmers and planters. In Washington County, for example, two potters originally from Edgefield County, South Carolina, made stoneware "equal to any of the Southern States." To sell their wares, one of the potters simply filled a wagon with pottery and drove through the country until all the earthenware was sold. [43] Few enterprises made any effort to produce for markets beyond the county and its surrounds, let alone beyond the borders of the state.

The varieties of manufacturing that census enumerators sought to document were dependent on settlement, geography, proximity to urban markets, and population. In the black-majority lowcountry, where large plantations prevailed and slave artisans performed most production-oriented tasks, large-scale manufacturing was nearly nonexistent. Liberty County contained four blacksmith shops, two sawmills, and one gristmill. Bryan County reported only one manufacturing enterprise: a rice-threshing operation powered by a steam engine under the operation of two men and two boys. [44] Even the presence of Savannah did not induce widespread investment in manufactures in lowcountry Chatham County. Though the published 1820 manufacturing census listed seven establishments, the manuscript returns listed nine:

1 Bakery
1 Candle and Soap-Making Business
2 Brick Manufactories
1 Blacksmith Shop
1 Tannery
1 Stone-cutting Establishment
1 Steam Saw Mill
1 Iron Foundry

These nine manufactories produced total goods valued at $50,500 a year.[45]

In comparison, fourteen Richmond County establishments were listed in the census:

4 Tailor Businesses
7 Saddleries
1 Chairmaking Company
1 Carriage-making Company
1 Nailery

They produced a total of $191,000 worth of products. Although Chatham County claimed a total population of 14,737 and Richmond County claimed only 8,608 (with urban populations in both places roughly half the county population), and although Chatham County vaunted the more commercially sophisticated of the two cities, it was Richmond County that could brag of the most productive manufacturing enterprises in the state, according to the census records. Yet all indications suggest that these "manufacturing" enterprises were little more than artisan workshops and that the Richmond County census enumerator, desperate for something to count, included traditional modes of artisanal production as "manufactories."[46]

Some conclusions can be made about this situation. That the number of Chatham County manufactures was low should not be surprising. The surrounding lowcountry was usually able to supply its own coarse manufacturing needs through the use of skilled slave labor. When this was impossible, planters chose to import superior manufactured goods from the north or abroad. The manufactories of Chatham County seem to have been destined not for lowcountry consumption but for port city consumption. The bakery produced barrels of navy bread and hard biscuits

Table 2. Market Value of Articles Annually Manufactured and Number
Employed in Manufacturing by County, 1820

County	Value of Articles Manufactured	No. Employed in Mfg.
Richmond County (Augusta)	$191,000	47
Morgan County (Madison)	65,039	138
Jones County (Clinton)	54,370	85
Chatham County (Savannah)	50,500	43
Washington County (Sandersville)	43,035	43
Hall County (Gainesville)	22,414	48
Elbert County (Elberton)	19,650	17
Pulaski County (Hawkinsville)	18,652	37
Wilkes County (Washington)	16,500	18
Lincoln County (Lincolnton)	9,300	15
Jasper County (Monticello)	8,500	9
Jefferson County (Louisville)	7,300	9
Laurens County (Dublin)	3,937	13
Warren County (Warrenton)	3,100	5
Liberty County (Darien)	1,000	NA
Franklin County (Carnesville)	1,000	86
Early County (Blakely)	950	3

Note: Some counties are missing from this list because census-takers failed to file reports for them or
the information provided was too vague to lend itself to classification above.
Source: Records of the 1820 Federal Census for Manufactures, Roll 19, Schedules for North Carolina, South Carolina, and Georgia, GDAH.

for docked vessels in need of provisions. The sawmill and iron foundry
supported ship-building and repairing along the harbor. The brickeries,
manufacturing over 110,000 tons of brick, and the stonecutting company
were involved in local construction, and their products were bought by
Savannah planters and merchants eager to demonstrate their opulence and
taste with showcase homes. And it would seem that the census enumerator
for Chatham County had enough "real" manufactories to count, because
he chose not to add artisan workshops to his records, unlike the Richmond
County enumerator.

Thus, manufactured goods produced in Richmond County, as enumerated by the census, were in all likelihood made in artisan workshops. In a
pattern established in the late eighteenth century, farmers from the South

Carolina and Georgia upcountry relied on Augusta for their supplies as well as for their cotton market. In 1820, the forenamed Richmond County "manufactories" produced clothes, saddles, harnesses, chairs, cabinets, and nails. These goods were all items that upcountry farmers were unwilling or unable—because of time and money constraints—to secure from larger and more distant places yet did not want to do without and did not want to waste time producing themselves.

Upcountry demand for local artisanal production was also reflected in other upcountry counties with smaller towns than Augusta. Because census-takers defined "manufactures" more broadly in these rural places and willingly included artisan workshops and individual artisans in their enumeration, an analysis of the returns indicates that a small artisan population, men who "style[d] themselves mechanics" as one enumerator noted, resided in nearly every upcountry county by 1820.[47]

Despite differences in settlement patterns, white and slave populations, and the size and function of county towns, census-takers discovered the same sorts of white artisans throughout the piedmont. Burke County, an older, black-majority county with a courthouse town populated by only 316 residents, managed to sustain:

1 Hatter
1 Cabinetmaker
1 Tanner
2 Saddlers
2 Painters
2 Stone Grinders
4 Tailors
4 Wagonmakers
5 Wheelwrights
6 Masons
21 Carpenters
22 Blacksmiths

Baldwin County, another black majority county, though somewhat younger than Burke and the home of the state capital, claimed similarly large numbers and a similar variety of artisans.[48]

Likewise, Morgan County, which opened for settlement with the advent of the 1805 lottery, was located in prime cotton-growing land with a countywide population of 13,520 and a black population of 6,057. Madison, the county seat, was inhabitated by 585 residents in 1820, and harbored the bulk of the impressive number of artisans and artisan shops in one of the fastest-growing cotton counties in the region:

48 blacksmith shops
37 carpenters
16 saw mills
13 carriage-makers
12 distilleries
11 shoemakers
8 hatters
6 bark mills
6 gin makers
5 gristmills
4 bricklayers
4 saddlers
3 brickmakers
3 cotton machines
3 wheelwrights
3 cabinetmakers
2 millwrights
1 tailor
1 tobacco maker
1 silversmith
1 cooper

Moreover, Morgan ranked second only to Richmond in market value of annual manufactures. The self-sufficiency suggested by this number of artisans was due both to Morgan County's burgeoning cotton economy and its fairly isolated location. Clinton and Milledgeville were the largest towns in the area, but a good two days' ride away. Jones County, which in many respects resembled Morgan County because it too was a relatively new, black-majority county, though on the edge of the Georgia border, ranked an impressive third in the state in market value of its annual manufactures. A surprised census-taker observed that Jones County manufactures were "in tolerable demand." [49]

These figures show that those artisans who were willing to follow the cultivation of the land across the piedmont were likely to find work in these relatively new and isolated places. And indeed, this story repeated itself again and again in other piedmont counties, including Twiggs, Laurens, and Pulaski to the southwest and Gwinnett and Jackson to the northwest. The census-takers' generalizations about the state of manufacturing in each of these counties underline the wisdom of artisan migration. For example, in the long settled headright counties of Warren and Franklin, manufactures were described as "in a declining state" and "not very flourishing." Even in Baldwin County, the location of the state capital, the enumerator concluded that manufactures were "declining . . . as usual."

It is difficult to judge the extent to which northern goods were displacing local manufactures, but the declining sales of saddles and other leather goods in Jasper County, a middle Georgia county opened to settlement with the 1805 land lottery, were described as "dull, owing to northern importations." [50] Excluding the apparently stable trade center of Richmond County, where manufacturing was described as "in good order and demand," the majority of promising reports came from the newer and more isolated counties. For example, manufactures in Pulaski County, in south middle Georgia, were "generally in great demand," and manufactures in Jackson County, in the foothills of the Appalachians far to the north, were also "generally flourishing and in demand." [51] This information suggests that older, better established towns with improved transportation links in the form of rivers, stage lines, canals, and eventually trains could import more manufactured goods from the North and Europe. In contrast, new, isolated towns were far more dependent on local artisanal production and were ideal locales for ambitious journeymen eager to establish themselves as master craftsmen with their own shops and eventually to become slaveholders and landholders themselves.

By 1840, twenty years later, manufacturing in the form of textile mills and iron foundries had come to join traditional artisanal production in rural Georgia. The foremost urban counties, Chatham, Richmond, Muscogee, Bibb, Baldwin, and Clarke, accounted for only two-fifths of the total capital, $2,899,565, invested in manufactures—now clearly defined as factory and mill production—statewide. The leading manufactures in number and in capital invested were the mill industry and the building industry, both traditional local services necessary in an agricultural economy. [52]

While these numbers suggest that urban development proceeded at a slack pace and that production in Georgia continued to be geared toward the local market in the countryside, the census also reveals a new degree of diversification in manufacturing. By 1840, nineteen textile manufactories produced cotton goods with the aid of 779 workers and a total capital investment of more than half a million dollars, putting the young industry in third place in invested capital in the state. The gold mining industry employed 405 men in 130 smelting houses and turned out $121,881 worth of the precious ore. A small iron industry also existed, with a statewide capital investment of $24,000 in fourteen furnaces worked by forty-one men. These furnaces were mostly in rural places, Jones County (5), Habersham County (1), Carroll County (4), and Cass County (2). Richmond County, with two furnaces, was the only urban county to lay claim to any iron-making in 1840.[53]

Other changes were afoot as well. Furniture-making, hat-making, saddle-making, and wagon-making, the skilled crafts listed most frequently on the census, were now being performed in small-scale manufactories that employed a handful of journeymen as well as in more traditional artisan shops. The production of carriages and wagons, though used extensively by the rural population, had become increasingly concentrated in towns. A third of all carriagemakers statewide were employed in the six aforementioned urban counties, which accounted for nearly three-quarters of the capital invested in this industry statewide and which turned out about half of the state's carriages and wagons. These trades produced luxury goods consumed almost exclusively by planters, the only class able to afford them.[54]

These changing numbers did not indicate, however, a significant transformation in the agricultural economy. Instead, nearly 94 percent of all white males fifteen and older were engaged in agricultural occupations in 1840. The 7,984 men engaged in manufacturing positions represented less than 4 percent of the adult white male population. While the actual number of white men in manufacturing had increased by 57 percent between 1820 and 1840, there was no significant change in the percentage of the adult white population engaged in manufacturing. Unlike the North, where manufacturing was making rapid strides and creating a growing wage-earning class of workers, manufacturing in Georgia remained relatively nascent by 1840.[55] The 1840 returns suggest that urban manufacturing, while at a more advanced state than twenty years earlier in terms of

Table 3. Leading Manufactures in Georgia, 1840

Number	Type of Manufacture	Number of Employees	Capital Invested	Value Produced
114	Flour- and gristmills	1,051	$1,491,973	$1,268,715
NA	Construction	2,274	NA	693,116
NA	Brickmaking	555	NA	148,655
19	Cotton goods	779	< 500,000	NA
130	Gold mining	405	NA	121,881
14	Iron-making	41	24,000	NA

Source: U.S. Bureau of the Census, "1840 Mines, Manufacturing, and Agricultural Census," GDAH.

capital invested and diversity of products, was still relatively young. Moreover, manufacturing was a rural phenomenon for the most part. Eighty percent of all men engaged in manufacturing lived and worked *outside* of urban Georgia.

Information on manufactures in 1850 is much less extensive than that available from the 1820 and 1840 federal censuses. Yet even these 1850 numbers indicate that rural production continued to challenge urban manufacturing. Of the five and a half million dollars invested in manufactures in Georgia in 1850, just over half (54 percent) was spent in the six counties with the largest urban populations. Only 36 percent of the 8,378 men engaged in manufacturing lived in these same six counties.[56]

By 1860, capital invested in statewide manufactures had leaped to almost 11 million dollars, a 52 percent increase over a decade earlier. Nearly two thousand establishments employed 9,511 men and 2,064 women. The annual value of Georgia's manufactured goods was just under 17 million dollars. Despite these noteworthy increases, the leading urban counties in the state were responsible for only 38 percent of the total amount of capital invested in manufacturing statewide.

Urban commitment to industry, as reflected in invested capital, slowly ebbed and flowed from urban county to urban county and from decade to decade in the late antebellum era. Yet cities were forced to diversify their economies with the expansion of the railroad throughout the state. After a period of prosperity in the 1820s and 1830s, Augusta, a marketing and distribution center, experienced hard times between 1837 and 1845.

Table 4. Manufacturing in Principal Urban Counties, 1850

County	Capital Invested	Number Employed	Annual Value of Manufactures
Richmond (Augusta)	$775,600	995	$1,020,651
Muscogee (Columbus)	713,217	719	738,580
Bibb (Macon)	138,920	453	533,200
Clarke (Athens)	320,350	498	345,220
Chatham (Savannah)	130,550	215	256,250
Baldwin (Milledgeville)	92,200	132	85,422

Table 5. Comparison of Capital Invested in Manufactures in Six Urban Counties, 1840–1860 (in Constant Dollars)

County	Capital Invested		
	1840	1850	1860
Richmond (Augusta)	$168,306	$749,600	$1,104,189
Muscogee (Columbus)	168,213	689,443	844,433
Bibb (Macon)	121,826	134,289	997,581
Clarke (Athens)	263,332	309,672	307,798
Chatham (Savannah)	285,510	89,030	153,246
Baldwin (Milledgeville)	90,203	89,803	150,204

Percentage Change in Capital Invested in Manufactures in Six Urban Counties, 1840–1860 (Based on Constant Dollars)

	1840–50	1850–60
Richmond (Augusta)	+78	+32
Muscogee (Chatham)	+76	+18
Bibb (Macon)	+10	+87
Clarke (Athens)	+15	−1
Chatham (Savannah)	−69	+41
Baldwin (Milledgeville)	0	+41

Calculation for constant dollars based on: Taylor Wholesale Price Indexes for Charleston, S.C.: 1731–1861, in *Historical Statistics,* Part I, 204.
Sources: 1840 Census of Manufactures; *Statistical View of the U.S.,* 215–18; Manufactures of the U.S. in 1860.

Augusta's decline was caused by national economic woes that were exacerbated by local disasters and competition posed by railroad transport.[57] City residents and the Georgia Railroad joined forces to combat the economic downturn in 1845 by selling stock in their newly formed cooperative venture, the Augusta Canal Company.

Investors believed that the construction of a canal to bring water into the city would entice new manufactures to Augusta and revive the city's dying economy. The Georgia Railroad and Banking Company recognized that the influx of new manufactures would require year-round railroad transport. With the completion of the railroad connection between Augusta and Chattanooga on the horizon, both groups of investors assumed that in a few short years they could count on the added markets of western Georgia, northern Alabama, and Tennessee.[58]

The canal and the citywide enthusiasm for new industry gave a much-needed spur to local manufacturing. By 1850 the city claimed fifty-six establishments, representing a capital investment of $702,500. Richmond County ranked first among the six leading urban counties in the amount of capital invested in 1850. A decade later, Richmond County manufacturing continued to lead the other urban counties in money invested, at over one million dollars.[59]

Still, the kinds of manufacturing sustained in Augusta and surrounding Richmond County had not changed that dramatically despite the attractions posed by the arrival of the canal and the railroad. Among the newly opened businesses were a cotton and woolen manufactory, employing eight men, and two steam engine manufactories, employing fifty men, designed to support the textile industry in the area.[60] And although the local textile industries employed the most men and women in manufacturing, it ranked second to the county's sixteen sawmills in capital investment and second to flour and meal in annual product value, both more traditional modes of production.[61]

Although Richmond County manufactories soon had access to more distant markets, the history of the county's textile industry suggests that this access did not essentially alter the prospects for new industry. At least two-thirds of the cotton goods annually produced by the Richmond County textile factories, which amounted to $315,419 in 1860, were sold within the state of Georgia, a market common to the majority of Georgia textile concerns in the state.[62] The remaining goods were not always shipped to the Mississippi Valley, however, but were often sent to New York brokers who, in an ironic twist, reshipped them to Georgia to be sold to planters at cheaper prices than those offered by the local mills.[63]

While Augusta's manufacturing sector was clearly growing if not exactly booming, Savannah's, in contrast, was floundering throughout most of the antebellum period. Unlike those in Augusta, city leaders in Savannah made little effort to promote industry in a city that thrived on commerce. Built on trade from its inception, Savannah had been one of the South's most enterprising cities at the end of the eighteenth century, but the port city's retail trade showed signs of decline by 1820, the result of upcountry cotton cultivation across the expanding state. This decline was hastened by the arrival of the railroad. With the completion of the Hamburg Railroad in 1833, connecting Augusta's hinterland to Charleston's market, Savannah was in danger of losing its river trade as well as its inland trade.

Savannah responded to this threat by building the Central Railroad, which reached Macon in 1843 and tapped into the most productive cotton-growing region of the state.[64] Savannah's population, at a virtual standstill between 1800 and 1830, tripled over the next three decades. By 1860, cotton exports shipped through Savannah by river and railroad surpassed $17 million.[65]

Manufacturing was not so readily transformed by Savannah's newfound carrying trade. The building industry remained the largest manufacturing concern in 1840 with the construction, by eighty-six employees, of thirty-eight homes valued at $86,500. Brickmaking was the second-largest industry, employing 207 men who produced bricks valued at $47,000. Other manufactories including a furnituremaking establishment that employed fourteen men and produced $25,000 worth of goods, a soap and candle manufactory that supported five workers and produced $6,000 worth of goods, and a carriage manufactory that employed four men and produced goods valued at a paltry $1,700. As in 1820, these manufactories were aimed exclusively at the local market.[66]

Although manufacturing in Savannah was not thriving in 1840, the completion of the Central Railroad in 1843 provided local efforts with an added stimulus—the promise of new markets. In 1848 census-taker Joseph Bancroft was proud to report on the transformation brought on by the railroad. He counted eighteen manufacturing establishments in the city, fourteen of them erected within the last ten years. In addition, Bancroft was impressed by many manufacturers' new willingness to use steam power. Together, these changes provided "evidence of a healthful state" in the urban economy.[67] Still, by 1850, only 215 hands were employed in local manufacturing, and annual production of manufactured goods in Chatham County was valued at just over a quarter of a million dollars, while Augusta and surrounding Richmond County goods were valued at over a million dollars, Columbus and surrounding Muscogee County at three-quarters of a million dollars, Macon and surrounding Bibb County at half a million dollars, and Athens and surrounding Clarke County at a third of a million dollars.[68]

In sharp contrast to Savannah, the inland transportation center of Macon boasted one of the most sophisticated urban economies in Georgia during the late antebellum years. Macon had spawned successful workshops and small manufactories since its inception. In the 1830s, several shoe manufactories, a hat manufactory, two saddle- and harnessmaking firms, two soap and candle manufactories, two large furniture manufactories, and a number of other wood-turning businesses supplied planters with necessities within a sixteen-county radius. Skilled smiths of all varieties also worked in the city, as did small-scale manufacturers of cotton gins.[69]

During the 1840s, three new manufacturing concerns attempted to compete for the middle Georgia market: the Ocmulgee Iron Foundry, the Fulton Foundry and Machine Shop, and the Macon Iron and Brass Foundry. This latter business had originated in 1839 as a "Blacksmith, Coppersmith, and Boiler Making Business" with a small and largely inadequate foundry.[70] It produced iron castings, spindles, and sawmill punches, suggesting the diversity of its clientele and explaining the attitude of many locals who predicted its failure.[71] That same year the three partners added a fourth, Robert Findlay, a Scotsman who had migrated to America and been apprenticed to a cabinetmaker in Philadelphia. Findlay must have recognized that his trade was becoming obsolete as more and more mass-produced furniture was available in even more distant markets, for he radically changed his career path by taking a job in a steam engine and locomotive works. When the Panic of 1837 dealt a death blow to his Philadelphia employer's firm, Findlay headed south to Macon to work on the Monroe Railroad at its Macon terminus.[72] In less than a year's time, however, he left the Monroe Railroad to set up his own millwright and machinist workshop in Macon, serving the plantations, mills, and factories of the area, before deciding to join the partnership in 1839.[73] Within a year, Findlay had bought out his partners' interests.[74]

The amount of capital investment needed for establishing antebellum foundries at this time in Georgia was fairly small. A foundry required a water or steam engine for power, sand for castings, and wooden molds, and since these essentials were relatively cheap and portable, most southern founders traveled from location to location as the market dictated. Findlay's Macon firm was one of the first to maintain a permanent location.[75] But his shop was not very impressive, described by natives as "a little iron foundry in an old wooden building." Begun with a tiny two-horsepower engine and small quantities of iron, the foundry grew over time, despite fellow townspeople's belief that Findlay's undertaking was foolish when castings from the North were so cheap.[76]

Over the next two decades, the sale of parts for gin gears, plowshares, and spindles—all local work capable of completion in any large blacksmith shop—proved the mainstay of Findlay's ironworks. The establishment of the Fulton Foundry in 1841 provided more competition, but it was never a true contender, folding in 1849. Meanwhile, a third foundry, the Ocmulgee Iron and Brass Foundry, was established in 1844. This company sold cotton gins in addition to the same goods produced by the other firms.[77] Findlay felt compelled to expand his business to compete with these new firms and did so by becoming an agent for New York millstones, New York waterwheels, South Carolina waterwheels, New York cotton packing presses, and Pennsylvania ornamental ironwork. Findlay also made a number of improvements on standard steam engines and built the largest cogwheel, 4,000 pounds, ever made in Georgia.[78] By the 1850s Findlay's market had grown into a regional one, and Findlay had great plans for employing 300 to 350 workmen. In 1852, he built $20,000 worth of buildings to house $70,000 worth of investments in machinery.[79]

Despite Findlay's ambitious undertakings, he was never able to luxuriate in his success. R. G. Dun and Company estimated his worth at $20,000 in 1850, and three years later at $30,000. The company, which evaluated business risks for potential investors, expressed concern upon analyzing Findlay's company that Findlay was "perhaps extending the business too much" after the erection of the new buildings. Following the Panic of 1857 the Dun reporters observed that "the pressure of last fall cramped them but their property is ample to carry them through."[80] This national depression left the ironworks in bad financial shape and Findlay himself died in 1859 without ever realizing his plan to employ over 300 workers. In fact, he had never had in his employ more than 70 men at any one time and never experienced the market expansion that he had wished for.[81]

Findlay's experience was symptomatic of the problems Georgia industrialists faced in the late antebellum era. Georgia leaders had learned in the 1830s and 1840s that the predominance of agriculture and Georgians' reliance on manufactured goods from the North had left them wide open to the debilitating effects of economic depressions, large and small. They had responded to these realizations by encouraging investment in the kinds of manufactures that would allow diversified production within the Georgia economy in the name of self-sufficiency. Accordingly, many leaders pushed hard for the construction of new textile mills and the support of old ones, for the development of manufactories like Findlay's to serve these mills, and for grist- and sawmills for use on plantations and farms. Their efforts were somewhat successful.

By 1850 Georgia ranked eighth in the country in textile production (though production levels when compared with those of the New England states were paltry).[82] Subsequent industrialists' efforts, however, were stunted by their desire to serve a limited regional market and by their dependence on the national economy. The minor depression of 1854 followed by the Panic of 1857 sent textile mills into financial ruin and left many other new industries (like Findlay's) badly weakened.[83]

In the late antebellum era boosters hailed Georgia as "the Empire State of the South." The state, in fact, boasted five major cities, Savannah, Augusta, Columbus, Atlanta, and Macon, as well as a number of secondary towns, including Athens and Milledgeville. By 1860, some 1,890 manufacturing establishments employed 11,575 workers producing goods valued at 7 million dollars. Urban growth and an increase and diversification in manufacturing were among the most prominent hallmarks of change in antebellum Georgia between 1820 and 1860. But the contributions of urban manufacturing to the state economy were indisputably dwarfed by those of the countryside, just as urban manufacturing's contributions to the broader marketplace in Georgia were all but nonexistent.

Despite the encouraging words of Georgia's boosters, despite the significant improvements in transportation, and despite new levels of capital investment in manufacturing, Georgians simply could not break the stronghold of the northern economy. No matter how hard entrepreneurs and investors worked to diversify the local economy and bring on the industrial revolution, they found themselves beaten back by circumstances beyond their control. Cheaply made, mass-produced northern goods had begun to flood Georgia's markets. The cost of making new manufactories competitive with their northern competitors simply proved too prohibitive to launch an all-out effort to transform the Georgia economy.

Thus, most Georgians preferred to continue their pursuit of agriculture, for it was familiar and profitable. Unlike the free family farmers of the North, the family farmers of the South could expand through the purchase of slave labor.[84] Within this antebellum plantation society, towns and cities grew in size and scope and manufacturing began to take root, but these developments were always in response to the demands of the countryside. In the end, Georgia cities and towns served the needs of the plantation economy and, bound by these confines, did not participate fully in the capitalist marketplace. While demand for artisanal skills, goods, and services spread across the state after 1820, there was no industrial revolution in antebellum Georgia. This reality held important implications for the kinds of work artisans performed and the kinds of opportunities available to them in the years leading up to the Civil War.

4 *"Thriving and Money-Making Men"*

In the late eighteenth and early nineteenth centuries master craftsmen had worked to transform themselves into planters. This status, however, was increasingly beyond their grasp by the mid–nineteenth century. The economic options of Georgia's white artisans had become constrained by the internal realities of plantation slavery and the external realities of the broader capitalist marketplace, which limited the prospects of local artisan producers and artisan manufacturers over the course of the antebellum era. Master craftsmen learned to accommodate themselves to their changing world in new ways. In the process, many came to discard their old planter ambitions and replace them with new ones but continued to consider themselves full participants in the white social and political order of the slave South.

The economic changes that these men encountered, though partially attributable to the broader economic processes that were fundamentally transforming production in the North, were basically peculiar to the South. At first few white artisans in the antebellum slave economy experienced the kind of debasement of their skills and the kind of division of labor that had become hallmarks of metropolitan industrialization in the North. In this other region of the nation, technological innovation, the availability of capital, and the rise of manufactories relegated many artisans, both masters and journeymen, to perpetual wage-earners, while a small number of affluent, entrepreneurial artisans, in trades like shoemaking and furnituremaking, turned their shops into the very manufactories and warehouses that employed this new wage-earning class. The class and political tensions produced by these changes in northern cities played a decisive role in the creation of a new working class.[1] In the South, master craftsmen dealt with a completely different set of tensions that were distinctive to the slave economy and the limited regional market. How white southern artisans adapted to these regional circumstances is the subject of this chapter.

While new commitment to manufactures had encouraged some urban development within the state, this urban development was generally modest. Moreover, it remained subservient to the all-powerful cotton economy. Therefore the kind of work available to white artisans continued, as in the late eighteenth century, to be shaped by the demands of plantation slavery. By and large, the plantation world respected and needed the skills of white master craftsmen. In turn, master craftsmen earned the bulk of their income from planters. This set of relations was encouraged by economic realities as well as political ones. Master craftsmen serviced much of the plantation economy and were instrumental in building and maintaining the kinds of industries—from railroads to textile mills—that permitted the continued competitiveness, or at least self-sufficiency, of the plantation system in the changing world economy.

Plantation slavery concentrated wealth among a small group of people. Accordingly, the wealthiest men in Georgia were generally planters.[2] Because of their disproportionate share of wealth, counted in land, cotton, and capital as well as in slaves, planters exerted substantial economic and political control over the rest of society. Master craftsmen, like all Georgians, white and black, were subservient to the dictates of the planter class.

Historians have long stressed the self-sufficient nature of the large plantation. They have demonstrated that there were very few artisanal tasks that slaves could not accomplish on these very large units.[3] A substantial body of evidence supports this conclusion. As one ex-slave, Mammy Lou, recalled about her youth on a large plantation near Columbus, "Where de mens worked was like a village. Dere was a shop for de blacksmiths and carpenters. Dere was harnessmakers, tanners, coopers and cobblers. Dere was a shop for makin' brooms and scourin' brushes, and baskets and chairs." [4]

Evidence that skilled plantation slaves performed the sorts of tasks that Mammy Lou described has long been used to explain the lack of white craftsmen and the lack of town development in the South. To some degree, this is a misguided or at least incomplete argument. [5] The presence of skilled slaves did permit a certain degree of plantation self-sufficiency, but planters also relied extensively on the knowledge and skills of white artisans to keep their plantations running efficiently. [6] Receipts for monies owed for a variety of artisanal work performed by white men appeared frequently in Georgia plantation records. [7]

Although planters may have preferred to run a self-sufficient plantation, most skilled plantation slaves, especially in the upcountry, possessed only rudimentary craft skills often acquired through practice or from each other. Their work bore little resemblance to that of trained master craftsmen. [8] As Mammy Lou noted, "Mars Jimmy got his [slave] millers to grind all de flour and corn," but the construction and running of the machinery for his sawmill and gin-house, she observed, was reserved for white artisans with mechanical experience. [9]

The receipts and records of David Barrow, a prominent Oglethorpe County planter, bear witness to the amount of plantation work performed by white craftsmen. While Barrow employed his own slave artisan, Daniel, at simpler types of mechanical work like screw-making and bolt-making, he relied on white blacksmiths, millwrights, and mechanics for critical jobs like "castings for my mills" and "plastered boilers." [10] For example, he instructed white mechanics to put a waterwheel together at his sawmill and put a white millwright in charge of his mill to maintain the machinery once it was operable. [11]

Howell Cobb's account books and receipts tell a similar story. The politician-planter employed a number of white craftsmen, including carpenters, blacksmiths, masons, and mechanics. [12] In 1849, Cobb contracted a white Athens carpenter, W. G. Yoakum, to build an eight-room house for $3,200. Cobb owned at least several slave carpenters but apparently preferred to hire this white craftsman to oversee the job, although he may have assigned his skilled slaves to assist Yoakum.[13] Likewise, Clarke County planter William A. Carr hired a white Athens area blacksmith in the late 1830s for a variety of farm tasks and Burke County planter Samuel Clark relied on white craftsmen for construction jobs, blacksmith work, and gin repairs on his two plantations, despite his 73 slaves.[14]

Planters' reliance on the skilled labor of white craftsmen as borne out in their account books is corroborated by the account books of white craftsmen themselves. The anonymous record of a Baldwin County blacksmith's dealings in the early 1820s lists charges for agricultural implements, the shoeing of horses, the making of staples and hinges, and "to minding [the] steel mill," among other entries, all indicating he served the plantations in the surrounding countryside.[15] White blacksmith John Castleberry's account books for 1854 through 1856 show similar transactions.[16] The account book of an anonymous white blacksmith in Sparta shows that even town blacksmiths performed agricultural work. Besides making the typical chains, spikes, buckles, locks, and bolts of his trade, he also mended wagons, harrows, and plows.[17]

Since the late eighteenth century, white artisans had depended on the service demands and consumption needs of planters for their incomes. But planters had never relied exclusively on the skills of local artisans, white or black, for all their wants. They acquired their goods from some amalgam of local, national, and European markets. Thus, Ambrose Baber's purchasing patterns were not unique in 1827. The planter made plans to furnish his new home in Macon with locally made tables but sent to Savannah for several dozen imported chairs and a sideboard.[18] By the 1820s and 1830s luxury goods that upcountry planters once bought locally were increasingly available from northern cities, particularly from New York. This transition from reliance on local production to imported goods fundamentally restricted artisanal demand in a number of important trades, including silvermaking, furnituremaking, shoemaking, clothing and clothmaking, and pottery and glassmaking. By the 1830s most planter families preferred northern silver and furniture over locally made goods. And by the 1840s even middling Georgians—professionals, shopkeepers, small planters, and slaveholding farmers—preferred imported goods. White Georgians conered these northernmade items fashionable. Moreover, they were inexpensive since they were mass-produced in large-scale northern manufactories.[19] As a result of this demand, many white master craftsmen turned themselves into merchants and retailers. Though they continued to call themselves artisans in newspaper advertisements, they were actually selling merchandise brought in from the North.[20]

Artisans in luxury trades like silversmithing and furnituremaking were most affected by these changes in consumer tastes and market availability. These changes were not peculiar to the South. Vermont artisans were experiencing the same effects of industrialization.[21] Though many master craftsmen attempted to diversify their skills to meet changing demands— some silversmiths, for example, learned to repair watches, clocks, instruments, and even guns—others readily turned themselves into merchant importers. For some, this transformation brought upward mobility, as was the case of Adolphus Brahe.

An Augusta watchmaker and jeweler, Brahe had lived and worked in Albany, New York, before moving to Augusta around 1840. He set up his own shop but quickly decided to become a dealer in New York-made watches, jewelry, and silver and plated ware. Brahe's new career brought him wealth. His returns from this venture allowed him to build an impressive two-and-a-half-story house, complete with columns, and a two-room slave house by 1852.[22]

The technological advent of electroplating, which all but destroyed demand for hand-wrought silver, compelled other Georgia silversmiths to make the same choices as Brahe. This reality held true for Savannah silversmiths with their wealthy lowcountry clientele as well as for upcountry silversmiths with their more commonplace patrons. So dramatic was the impact of this new technology that by 1841 Augusta possessed no traditional silversmiths. In fact seven jewelry stores, all importers of northern goods, had taken over the work of the traditional silver craftsman.[23] And only three silversmiths-turned-jewelers and watchmakers, all importers of northern goods, claimed the Athens market between 1850 and 1860.[24]

Planter tastes also extended to northern-made furniture by the 1830s and 1840s. In order to compete for a share of this market, local craftsmen pursued one of two options. They could work as local agents for northern firms, an arrangement that was best suited for Savannah craftsmen prior to the arrival of the railroads because of their port location, or they could buy premanufactured parts (more easily transported to upcountry towns) and assemble them locally.

Since planter desire for northern-made furniture had dampened demand in traditional cabinetmaking and chair-making shops, artisans who hoped to continue making their own furniture learned to cater to a new market, a rising middle class eager for cheaper, mass-produced pieces. When these families needed furniture, they went to the nearest large town with a manufactory. For example, the Hattons of Merriwether County, a comfortable farming family, made a daylong pilgrimage to Atlanta by railroad to buy their furniture in the 1850s.[25] Under these new conditions, however, a single master with several journeymen simply could not produce items as quickly or as cheaply as desired.[26]

By the late antebellum period one or two furniture manufactories had come to replace the traditional workshop in most towns. In Macon, for example, two firms had subsumed the business of most independent artisans by the late 1830s.[27] At least one of the manufacturers, Thomas Wood, was importing northern-made furniture as early as 1838. He later formed a partnership with the only other furniture manufacturer in town. The two men increased their own production but continued to import northern-made furniture and supplies.[28]

While planter tastes and market shifts dictated change in some traditional artisan trades, however, they did not affect all others. Wealthy planters and their families may have patronized the finest stores in New York and Charleston for house furnishings and clothes, but they also relied on nearby regional markets and even "made do" with local items, especially in the upcountry. Mrs. P. W. Booth, a wealthy Athens matron in the 1840s and 1850s, filled her account books with receipts from New York City stores. She also sent to Augusta for many other goods. At the same time, however, she relied heavily on the services of local artisans, hiring woodworkers, blacksmiths, painters, masons, shinglers, and bricklayers to spruce up her home as well as several local dressmakers, a hatmaker, and a corset-maker to clothe her.[29]

Market changes, then, did not obliterate all artisanal industry. Traditional crafts in particular, were still sought after, especially in the more rural and isolated upcountry, so that even the arrival of the railroad did not mean completely bad news to upcountry artisans. Instead the iron horse created a host of new opportunities for skilled artisans willing to pursue mechanical work.[30] By the mid-1840s foundries, machine shops, and repair facilities attracted scores of white mechanics to the major railroad centers of the state, and particularly to Atlanta and Macon. White mechanics at the machine works in Augusta produced the first state-made railroad cars in 1851.[31] The Central Railroad in Savannah employed carpenters and machinists to build engines and make passenger cars throughout the late antebellum era.[32]

The growth of the railroad industry in Georgia attracted northern mechanics and engineers, as well as native Georgians and other southerners, to these towns and cities.[33] In fact, promotional literature put out by railroad concerns hoped to draw northern mechanics southward by proclaiming "the country [is] fully ripe for the harvest."[34] And indeed, the industry did encourage a new form of mobility. William Morrill Wadley was a young New Hampshire man who arrived in Georgia in the mid-1830s. He began work for the Central Georgia Railroad as a blacksmith but was made a contractor in 1849, then chief engineer of the Western and Atlantic Railroad in 1852, and eventually superintendent of the Central. While such success stories were not commonplace, they did occur and encouraged other ambitious white mechanics, who lacked the capital and investors needed to open their own shops by the late antebellum period, to excel at their work and seek promotion in this new system of corporate structure.[35] The industry also generated a number of other labor needs. For example, artisans skilled in the construction trades were employed to build engine houses and machine shops.

The emergence of factories in Georgia, though limited in number compared to the Northeast, also necessitated the skilled labor of mechanics and machinists, though the numbers of men employed in this capacity are difficult to determine. The more than three dozen textile mills spread across the piedmont between 1840 and 1860 required the skills of master craftsmen and mechanics to build, maintain, and service buildings and equipment, though some mills seem to have relied on the original parts-makers in New England and Europe for repairs and replacements.

One historian has estimated that by 1860 one out of every ten adult white males in Georgia was skilled at a craft or trade.[36] Because artisans tended to locate their shops in urban places where consumer-traffic was likeliest, their numbers were higher in these places. In Augusta in 1841, artisans listed in the city directory represented fifteen percent of the adult white male population of 1840.[37] A third of these artisans practiced luxury trades. They produced goods for clients able to indulge in items other than necessities. A third worked in traditional trades, mostly clothing and

Table 6. Occupations of Artisans in Augusta, 1841 (Numbers in Parentheses Indicate Percentage of Adult White Male Population)

Luxury Trades	(4%)
Jewelers	8
Cabinetmakers	14
Carriagemakers	17
Printers	12
Bookbinder	1
	52

Traditional Trades	(5%)
Tailors	28
Dyer	1
Boot- and shoemakers	15
Tanners and saddlers	8
Butchers	3
Bakers	6
	61

Construction Trades	(3%)
Builders	3
Carpenters	27
Painters	7
	37

Metal and Smithing Trades	(2%)
Blacksmiths	11
Coopers	3
Gunsmiths	2
Coppersmith	1
Wheelwright	1
	18

Mechanic Trades	(1%)
Machinists	3
Tinner	1
Pattern-maker	1
Mechanic	1
Engineer	1
	7

Note: Percentages rounded to nearest whole number.
Source: Augusta City Directory, 1841; Manuscript Returns, U.S. Bureau of the Census, 1840.

Table 7. Occupations of Artisans in Athens and Clarke County, 1850 and 1860 (Numbers in Parentheses Indicate Percentage of Adult White Male Population)

	1850	1860
Elite Trades	(4%)	(3%)
Silversmiths	2	0
Jewelers/watchmakers	3	3
Cabinetmakers	4	9
Carriagemakers	25	20
Printers	18	8
	52	40
Traditional Trades	(5%)	(4%)
Tailors	13	9
Boot- and shoemakers	13	20
Tanners	2	6
Harness- and saddlemakers	5	5
Wagonmakers	10	0
Butchers	3	1
Bakers	2	3
Millers	14	13
Gardeners	1	2
	63	59
Construction Trades	(5%)	(6%)
Stonemasons	2	4
Brickmasons	5	8
Carpenters	62	59
Painters	5	8
	74	79
Smithing Trades	(2%)	(1%)
Blacksmiths	11	11
Coopers	3	1
Wheelwrights	5	2
Tinners	2	2
	21	16

Table 7. (Continued)

	1850	1860
New Trades	(1%)	(3%)
Papermakers	2	3
Founders	0	8
Machinists	3	6
Gap-Fitters	0	4
Mechanics (in Mills)	0	17
	5	38

Note: Percentages rounded to nearest whole number.
Source: Manuscript Returns, U.S. Bureau of the Census, 1850 and 1860, Schedule I.

footwear. The construction and smithing numbers were fairly small, not surprising since the national economy was in a depression and the local economy had ground to a halt. Unlike luxury tradesmen who were fairly immobile, blacksmiths and carpenters could move to locations where their work was needed. This may partially explain the number of craftsmen in the luxury trades during this economically stagnant period.[38]

A look at similar data for Athens and surrounding Clarke County shows that 17 percent of the adult white male population worked as craftsmen in 1850 and 1860. The actual number of artisans had grown by only 7 percent over the decade. Yet this figure is not particularly revealing, for it fails to distinguish between masters and journeymen. The percentage of luxury, traditional, construction, smithing, and mechanic trades compared to the adult white male population changed very little over the same period as well. These percentages resemble those for Augusta in 1841, with two exceptions. More construction occurred in Clarke County and more white men were employed in specialized mechanic trades. These differences can be explained by the lack of a national and local depression that discouraged construction and by the slight increase in manufacturing that had occurred in Athens between 1840 and 1860.[39] These data suggest that demand for artisan skills remained fairly constant through the late antebellum period. While changing consumer needs apparently did not alter the artisan population in these two large towns, the population did not increase dramatically either. It also stands to reason that the inroads made by mass production and importation in the plantation economy were beginning to trap some white artisans into perpetual wage-earning, journeyman status.

Historians have argued that the dominant political ideology of the South was a "country republican" ideal of personal independence for white men based on a system of black slavery. Most white male citizens believed that slavery made white male liberty possible. By the late antebellum period many southern politicians contended that slaves performed the role of a working class in the South, thereby leaving all whites free to live and work as independent producers. This situation, they stressed, was in sharp contrast to the North where growing numbers of dependent working men struggled for increasingly elusive economic and political equality. This ideology was attractive to white southern men because it helped mitigate the obvious class differences that separated planters from yeomen and artisans. One study of upcountry farmers in South Carolina has shown, for example, that while yeomen certainly did not share equally in the wealth procured from the slave system, they wanted to preserve it in order to ensure their own personal independence. Accordingly, yeomen expected the planter gentry to treat them with dignity and respect. Georgia master craftsmen seem to have shared these views. Many conceived of themselves as independent producers in the Jeffersonian tradition, regardless of their declining circumstances, and believed they too deserved the same treatment from planters that upcountry farmers received.[40]

In the face of the changing marketplace, some enterprising and flexible master craftsmen had transformed themselves into merchant-importers, often with the help of credit supplied by northern firms.[41] In contrast, other white craftsmen—including those craftsmen experiencing the pressures caused by mass production and importation—clung at all costs to this economic and personal independence awarded them by virtue of their race and gender. Thus John Riley Hopkins, a Gwinnnett County cabinetmaker, spent perhaps a third of every year turning out desks and chairs as well as bed and table parts on his workshop lathe but spent the bulk of his time on his farm (from which he secured most of his financial support).[42] Master mechanics who did not own enough property to farm and who supported themselves solely through their artisan skills also sought personal and economic independence. They generally expected and usually were granted the right to choose their own working hours, to negotiate and set their own wages, and to quit a job or project as they desired. These were the work relations of a preindustrial, Jeffersonian world of republican farmers and artisan producers. These expectations suggest that the plantation economy, in many respects, remained an exceedingly traditional society, despite its reliance on the broader market economy of the United States, Europe, Africa, and the West Indies.

Planters were seldom pleased with what they perceived to be the overly independent work habits of white artisans, but they were forced to adapt to them. Oliver Hillhouse Prince, the wealthy Macon planter and politician, complained to fellow planter John B. Lamar that work on his house was long overdue: "It seems to be the hardest thing in the world to get [the master builder and his craftsmen] to work, but I have pinned them down to the day and I shall endeavor not to let them fly off."[43] John Carter, a miller and merchant in the Macon area in the 1830s, recorded similar problems with stonecutters: "The last day of March I started to Allabama [*sic*] was gone fifteen days returned sick and found the hands who I had left to cut stone gone away."[44]

The fight to retain artisanal independence in the face of evolving market changes and some measure of competition from black artisans must have been a frustrating one in light of the degree of drunkenness that seemed to characterize the personal habits of white artisans. When the planter David Barrow tried to discuss his account with his brickmaker on June 4, 1858, he reported that the craftsman informed him "he was drinking whiskey and thought I could see him some other time."[45] Warren DuBose, a member of a moderately wealthy Washington, Georgia, family, told his manager not to employ DuBose's carpenter brother, for he was unreliable. "[H]e is the finest workman in the country – but a drunken scamp in whom there is no confidence."[46] One has to wonder to what extent the structural realities of the antebellum plantation world compelled some white artisans to drown their fears in drink.

Even Governor Joseph E. Brown was subjected to artisanal independence, though in this case it does not appear his employee was an alcoholic. The governor was so angered by his discovery of poor workmanship on his new home in Cherokee County that he took time away from his political duties to send several strong letters of accusation to the master builder. "I have your letter asking me to send you $300 and stating that you have finished my house," Brown began. As he found "the whole job . . . exceedingly rough," he felt bound to remind the builder of his contractual obligations. Brown then listed specific points of contention: the absence of locks, crooked doors, windows that failed to open, and weak and cracked mortar, pillars, and columns, to name the most worrisome construction problems. "I am astonished to hear you say the house is done," Brown concluded, and challenged builder Daniel Grambling to find "any three good workmen" to concur on the project's completion.[47]

Grambling must have sent an immediate reply to Brown's indignant letter. Although the contents of this reply remain unknown, the tone of Brown's response to it proves revealing, for the governor's tone grew even more defensive as he wrote at length about Grambling's irresponsibility. Ironically, the modern reader forgets that the uneasy and vulnerable sounding voice of the author of these letters belonged to one of the most powerful men in the state. It is the absent master builder, Daniel Grambling, who strikes the reader as the superior person in this battle.[48] While no extant artisan writings explain whether or not artisans chose to be unreliable in response to their treatment by certain clients, one can speculate that in the face of market forces and competition with skilled slave and free black artisans, factors that mitigated against white artisanal mobility, some white artisans did choose to display a measure of authority and independence that could be gained only through *not* doing a job well or on time.

Master craftsmen were not the only artisans who attempted to lead independent working lives, even if that effort incurred the wrath of their patrons. Wage-earning journeymen demanded their independence as well, although this tended to occur only in sections of the state where men with artisanal skills were more of a rarity. The letters that wealthy cotton factor Godfrey Barnsley, who lived in a remote, sparsely populated community in north Georgia, exchanged with his property managers and his son from 1835 to 1860 reiterate the typicality of rural white craftsmen setting the terms of their employment. "I cannot get people to work unless at higher wages than others will give them," Barnsley complained to overseer John Reid in 1842. "They have an idea that because I have paid liberally I must on all occasions."[49]

When Barnsley found an artisan with skills he admired and needed, he bent over backwards to accommodate him, as in the case of Ed Parsons, whom Barnsley hired in 1849.[50] Barnsley so wanted Parsons that he not only paid his travel costs from the North, but also paid off all Parsons's debts to speed his coming. While under Barnsley's employ, Parsons made extra money selling shoes on his work time. Disapproving neighbors had informed Barnsley of this practice, but Barnsley let him pursue this sideline, though his sentiments mirrored those of his neighbors.

After almost a year in Barnsley's employ, Parsons wrote to his employer that he planned to leave Woodlands to enter into a butchering partnership at the end of his contract. Until that time, he wanted several days off a week to pursue this new enterprise. Barnsley congratulated Parsons on his future venture, promised to patronize the business if his prices proved fair, and then proceeded to gently accuse him of working for him under false pretenses.[51] "Having permitted you to carry on a shoe trade which preoccupied considerable of your time," he admonished Parsons, "besides furnishing you with funds for the purpose of enabling you to discharge some debts which you owed in the North, I had certainly a right to expect you to be equally attentive during my absence as when I was at home." Nevertheless, Barnsley benignly agreed to Parsons's terms.[52]

In this respect, Georgia white artisans in the mid–nineteenth century continued to resemble Georgia white artisans in the late eighteenth century. Their lives remained circumscribed by the demands of the plantation economy. They still sought, and secured to some degree, a measure of equality from the planter class that revolved around their belief in their right to their independence. But in one singularly crucial respect, many of these men differed dramatically from earlier generations of Georgia artisans. Unlike their predecessors, these later master craftsmen no longer aspired to planter status because it was no longer attainable for them. This does not mean, however, that later generations of master craftsmen failed to accrue capital, property, and slaves like their late-eighteenth-century counterparts. For example, in 1840 in Augusta, three out of every four master craftsmen owned five or more slaves. In 1850 in Athens, half of all master craftsmen owned an average of 4.5 slaves apiece.[53]

Georgia artisans were frequent slaveholders. Indeed, a handful of Georgia artisans were quite wealthy on the eve of the Civil War and had followed many of the same steps to acquire this wealth as their artisan forefathers. What was different, however, was that prosperous white artisans generally did not lead rural lives in this later era. Successful master craftsmen in the antebellum era inhabited the towns and cities of Georgia where they invested their earnings in property, slaves, and even in manufacturing ventures. The most successful of these men—an admittedly tiny minority—actually transformed themselves into manufacturers.

The personal odysseys of several carpenters responsible for antebellum town building read like rags-to-riches stories and demonstrate the changing ambitions of successful master craftsmen in Georgia. These case histories, while not representative of all artisans in construction trades, suggest the kinds of opportunities available to them under the best of circumstances in the antebellum era.

Jett Thomas was one of the earliest master builders to leave his mark on upcountry building architecture. Born in 1776, he chose an unlikely career path for the son of a Spotsylvania, Virginia, planter.[54] About 1800 Jett joined his brother, Stephens, who had already settled in the village of Athens. The two brothers pooled resources to purchase one of the first town lots sold to the public by the university trustees.[55] Jett apparently worked in some capacity on the construction of the university buildings during this time, having already acquired some building experience. (He had built the Jackson County Jail for $797.)[56] Unlike his brother, who remained in Athens throughout his life, Jett moved on.

He next appeared in the records of Milledgeville, where he and fellow builder John Scott came to dominate the construction trade between 1805 and 1815. They were responsible for erecting the original state capital building, a long-term project that took more than five years to complete, and they built many local plain-style residences until Jett's death at age forty in 1817.[57] Jett Thomas's career demonstrates the value of arriving at a young upcountry town on the verge of growth. A number of master builders who followed plantation development as it moved across the state were also able to take advantage of these opportunities throughout the antebellum period.

Thomas's immediate Milledgeville successor was John Marlor, an Englishman born in 1798 whose whereabouts before his arrival in the capital remain unknown, although Marlor may have served an apprenticeship in Charleston before arriving in the upcountry (because his Georgia houses incorporated South Carolina lowcountry designs). The Englishman's career in Milledgeville spanned fifteen years, during which time he built public buildings, and merchant and planter houses. He attracted a number of protégés eager to duplicate his building genius and his monetary acumen.[58]

It is highly likely that during the 1820s Marlor employed as a young carpenter a man whose reputation as an innovator and a businessman would outlast his own. Daniel Pratt, the Alabama industrialist who established a thriving mill community named after himself, Prattville, was born in 1799 to a large New Hampshire family barely able to eke out a subsistence on a small farm. At sixteen Pratt was apprenticed to a carpenter, and at twenty he borrowed money for a ship's passage to Savannah. Pratt worked in the port city for over a year before deciding to venture into the upcountry. He arrived in Milledgeville in 1821 and spent the next ten years constructing elegant town residences, as well as more modest homes, before dramatically changing his occupation.[59]

Although he had made a local name for himself as a Milledgeville builder in the 1820s, Pratt must have recognized that such unbridled building could not last forever. Established planters had staked out the surrounding countryside, and slaves were now the majority of the Baldwin County population. These realities signaled a shift from promising young upcountry to mature plantation county, and, in fact, growth in Milledgeville was subsequently constricted by these changes. Weak transportation links to other towns and cities, along with an increase in the number of self-sufficient plantations, discouraged further endeavors in urban commerce, manufacturing, and industry.[60]

Such changes would have spelled an end to his career had he attempted to stay in Milledgeville much longer, and they probably explain Pratt's decision to leave the capital in 1831 and join Clinton manufacturer Samuel Griswold in the production of cotton gins. After two years with Griswold, Pratt packed his wagons with enough spare parts for fifty gins and took his wife and two slaves to Autauga County, Alabama. In this new county, not unlike the middle Georgia piedmont counties several decades earlier, he built and sold enough gins to enable him to buy more land and erect a sawmill, a gristmill, and a gin factory. The unqualified success of these ventures eventually allowed him to finance a cotton mill, a woolen mill, a foundry, a carriage factory, and a tinshop. Pratt, giving his own name to his self-sufficient enterprise, eventually employed several hundred people, and stood as a shining example of successful manufacturing to southern leaders interested in economic development. By 1858 Prattville was valued at more than $500,000.[61]

Pratt was not the only master builder to transform himself into an industrialist. Elam Alexander left North Carolina around 1820 and spent time in Augusta and Milledgeville before settling in Macon, a small town of about 800 when he arrived in 1826. By 1830, the fast-growing town boasted thirty-two stores patronized by the inhabitants of sixteen counties who traded their cotton here. Thirty to forty flatboats carried seventy to eighty tons of cotton each down the Ocmulgee to the ocean. Alexander's timing proved ideal.[62]

Calling himself a master mechanic, the brash young North Carolina farmer's son immediately acquired contracts to build stores, homes, and other buildings. By 1828 Alexander and several other builders were responsible for the construction of the new courthouse valued at $12,750. Alexander's reputation as a master builder was secured with the completion of this well-received building. Over the next two decades he built cottages, churches, and plantation houses as well as other public buildings.[63]

Alexander spent his later years promoting Macon's urban development. In 1840 he and a partner received the contract for the construction of the Central Railroad between Macon and the Oconee River. This position sparked his commitment to the railroad and ultimately landed him an appointment as a commissioner of the Southwestern Railroad. By 1847 he was elected its president, but his dreams were even greater. He believed that Macon would never regain its prominence as a trade center if the city did not usher in the telegraph, for he was convinced of the necessity of a timely connection to the market. Alexander decided to take matters into his own hands by buying $20,000 worth of telegraph stock to ensure its arrival in Macon. By the late 1840s Alexander had become a bona fide town leader and a leading capitalist. He served as president of the Washington and New Orleans Telegraph Company in 1849 and president of the Manufacturers' Bank of Macon in 1852.[64]

As late as the 1850s, when the bulk of Georgia's wealth was increasingly restricted to small numbers of large slaveholding planters and merchants, and journeyman artisans were more likely to suffer low wages and competition from either northern-made goods or in some cases from slave artisans and free black artisans, some Georgia towns continued to provide opportunities for skilled white builders. Carpenter John Wind, born in England in 1819, appeared in Thomas County around 1840. Over the course of the next decade, Wind worked as a watch- and clock-maker. He was not particularly successful in his trade and claimed only $300 worth of real estate in 1850.

Fortunately for Wind, the expansion of the cotton belt into this southwestern corner of Georgia in the 1850s brought farmers, planters, slaves, churches, stores, towns, and wealth to the county. This wealth was translated into local desire for distinctive public buildings and new homes befitting the county's new prosperity. Wind apparently recognized the implications of this new wealth, as well as the dearth of local builders, and decided to exchange his watchmaking tools for those of a master carpenter. He quickly established himself as the premier builder in the county, a position he held throughout the decade.[65]

Wind's life story along with those of Marlor, Pratt, and Alexander demonstrate that master builders sensitive to the nature of economic development in antebellum Georgia could parlay their knowledge and ability into comfortable livelihoods. This particular group of men did not establish themselves as planters, however, despite their impressive wealth, as had earlier generations of successful craftsmen. Instead, they were more likely to invest their capital in manufacturing enterprises. Master craftsmen in other trades often followed suit.

That antebellum Georgia contained opportunities for enterprising white artisans did not go unobserved by outsiders. The oft-quoted English traveler J. S. Buckingham was amazed to learn that a simple glazier from London had become "a prosperous master-builder" in Milledgeville. (Buckingham may have been writing of Marlor.)[66] While such opportunities did exist in Georgia, however, they proved rarer and rarer by the 1840s. The wealth, upward mobility, and entrée into the planter class that white artisans had once achieved comparatively easily became increasingly difficult to achieve during the changing conditions of the antebellum era. Nonetheless, some master craftsmen and journeymen were able to adapt fairly well to their new circumstances. The key ingredients to ensure this transition after 1830 rested on a combination of critical factors: family connections; access to capital (earned or borrowed); the ability to convert slavery to their needs; a high level of skill at their craft or trade; a sensitivity to changing markets; and the shrewdness to invest wisely in manufacturing.

Thomas Sansom, an Athens shoemaker, used his shop as a base for broader entrepreneurial activities. He sold tanned leather and shoes to the surrounding community between 1849 and 1852 and accepted payment in leather, sheepskins, shingles, corn, flour, peaches, hay, eggs, and chickens, as well as cash. Yet Sansom was more than a traditional artisan willing to barter goods. On several accounts he charged interest. The shoemaker also sold hogs, planks, shingles, and potatoes, probably the same items he had received as payment, in addition to footwear from his shoe shop. In 1850 he owned fifteen slaves, twelve men and three women, and his real estate was valued at $5,000.[67] He hired out at least two of these slaves who earned a respectable wage of $1.00 a day, as much or more than the average unskilled white laborer.[68] Sansom also hired at least one white journeyman to do piecework for him over a two-month period and paid him half in goods and half in cash.[69]

Thus Sansom as white master artisan was a curious amalgam. He employed a white journeyman at piecework and accepted customer payments in goods as any traditional artisan of the late eighteenth and early nineteenth century might have done throughout the nation. On the other hand, he charged interest on some accounts, sold goods outside his craft, owned skilled slaves, and hired them out. In many respects, the contents of Sansom's account books demonstrate the kinds of accommodations that antebellum white male artisans learned to make in their particular world.

Accommodation took other forms in other trades. Demand for locally made cotton gins, for example, gave white artisans with some mechanical talent the opportunity to turn themselves into local manufacturers. William H. Jones of Columbia County pursued this course in the 1830s. He purchased gin parts in New York City and New London, Connecticut, built cotton gins in Columbia County, and sold them in nearby counties as well as in the new cotton states west of Georgia.[70] Jones did not use skilled white labor in help him put his gins together. Instead, he taught his own slaves to do this work.[71]

E. R. Hodgson and his two younger brothers established a carriage- and wagonmaking shop in Athens during the early 1840s. The success of their venture compelled them to turn their business into a manufactory, aided by the labor of hired white journeymen and their own slaves. The Hodgsons also established a stable that hired out horses and buggies to the public, as well as a U.S. mail line that ran between Athens and Gainesville. Begun in 1840, the Hodgson business continued to grow through the

1850s. By 1860 the brothers shared $6,500 in real estate and $17,300 in personal estate.[72]

The Hodgson brothers were the sons of an English carriagemaker who brought his family to America in 1836.[73] After their arrival the brothers, all young adults, and their father worked as journeymen in Troy, New York, for more than a year before moving to Carlinville, Illinois, where they opened their own shop.[74] Their father soon died unexpectedly. Then a tornado destroyed their new workshops. The discouraged Hodgsons returned to Troy where the sons resumed work as journeymen. During that time, their neighbor and family friend John Bishop, a skilled landscape gardener from Ireland who had been invited to Athens to oversee the botanical garden of Franklin College, persuaded E.R., the oldest Hodgson brother, to move to Athens with him.[75]

Arriving in Athens in 1839, E.R. immediately found work in a wagon shop but did not work there as a journeyman for long. His earnest attitude captured the respect of two well-heeled Athens businessmen who gave him enough financial backing to set up his own shop in 1840. Hodgson immediately married Ann Bishop, John Bishop's sister, and then persuaded his brothers and mother to join him in Athens.

Initially, the young coachmakers owned absolutely no property and barely managed to scrape up the thirty-one cents to pay the annual poll tax during the early 1840s.[76] Their business soon picked up, however, and by 1848 they had bought a house and town lot valued at $3,200 and had paid taxes on two carriages, luxury items they maintained for their own personal use. At this point, a decade's worth of hard work had begun to pay off. The Hodgsons shared $8,000 in capital and $11,000 in capital investments in 1852. Two years later their taxable income had climbed to $32,950 and would continue to grow steadily over the next few years.[77]

E.R. owned seven slaves by 1850. While three of his slaves were women, two adults who probably washed, cooked, and cleaned for the extended Hodgson household, the four remaining adult slaves were males between the ages of 26 and 40 who probably worked in the shops; there was also a slave infant.[78] Ten years later, E.R. still owned seven slaves, though they were not the same seven.[79]

Together the Hodgson men shared a reputation for hard work and fair business. Their industry did not escape the sharp eyes of the representa-

tives of R. G. Dun and Company. The investigators sang the praises of
the Hodgson brothers during their fact-finding visits in 1847, 1849, and
1851. They described the Hodgsons as "thriving and money-making men,"
"men of high character," and "thrifty, prosperous, and . . . very clever
men," despite a cautionary note about Rob, who was "rather wild, [and
too] fond of brew and frolick." [80]

Nearly every farmer in northeastern Georgia and western South Carolina reportedly owned at least one Hodgson wagon by the time of the Civil
War. Beautifully crafted from seasoned hickory, the wagons lasted for
years and were so popular that the addition of colorfully painted designs
purportedly brought gypsies to Athens to buy them. [81] The Hodgson enterprise was unusual in that it manufactured the bulk of its goods. Almost all
other carriage-making shops in the state imported northern-made carriages and wagon parts at this time.

The Hodgsons had relied on their traditional artisanal skills to build a
flourishing business and they had succeeded admirably. They had used
their relationship as brothers to good advantage by combining skills and
capital in one business. They bought slaves and apparently put some of
them to work in their shops. They secured capital initially through Athens
acquaintances and then later through the R. G. Dun Company. They par-
layed this capital into a larger business and into other ventures that increased their profits. Like the aforementioned artisans, the Hodgsons embodied the new successful master craftsmen of the Old South.

Not all artisans, however, experienced the rise to success that characterized the career of the Hodgsons and others. Many master artisans began
their careers as poor and itinerant young journeymen traveling around the
countryside before settling in a place to practice their trade. Journeying
artisans in the building trades and in many other trades were an ordinary
part of the urban and especially the rural Georgia landscape by the 1830s.
Depending on their skills, journeying white artisans secured work from
established white artisans as well as from planters and farmers.

A Sparta blacksmith hired James Winay for half a year in 1821. Several
months after Winay had left his shop, the blacksmith employed another
white man, Kenneth Cooke, for nineteen days. [82] A Macon tailor's 1848
account book shows he hired a white journeyman for one month and paid
him $32 in wages. This was a low wage. The average skilled artisan earned
$1.54 a day at that time, compared to $0.76 for unskilled labor. The Ma-

con tailor had paid his journeyman approximately $1.14 a day.[83] Athens shoemaker Thomas Sansom hired Josiah Homes to do piecework from March 2, 1850, through May 25, 1850. Homes made seventy-eight shoes and seven half soles for Sansom during those two months and received in pay $18.29 worth of items, including a hat, tobacco, and shoe parts, and $19.87 in cash, before Homes went on his way.[84]

Planters employed white journeymen in much the same fashion as master craftsmen. Cotton factor and planter Godfrey Barnsley spent over twenty years building a mansion in the north Georgia hills.[85] This endeavor required a constant supply of talented white journeymen, who often found their way to Woodlands while on prescribed rounds in search of work. While working at Woodlands, these itinerants so enjoyed the stable situation and good pay they found at Barnsley's home that they wanted to come back on their next tour through the area. Some men even wrote Barnsley several months in advance to assure their job at his place. A bricklayer who had worked for Barnsley the previous summer sent him a letter in February to arrange employment at Woodlands for the upcoming season. As added incentive, he promised to bring "good brickmasons"–more white journeymen–if Barnsley agreed to hire him.[86] Mr. Willis, described by Barnsley as "a slippery character but a good workman" whom he valued for "his knowledge–his head–headwork is always more valuable than that of the hands," similarly requested and was granted work the following year after spending the previous summer employed at Woodlands.[87]

These letters and others like them indicate that white journeymen in Georgia were constantly on the move in search of new and better jobs. Sometimes they sought new and better careers. Joseph Watts, a carriage trimmer, worked in Madison, Augusta, and Athens between 1840 and 1846. He left Augusta for Athens in 1846.[88] Hired by the carriage-making Hodgsons, Watts stayed in their employ for less than four years. By 1850 the forty-five-year-old North Carolinian had moved to rural Union County in north Georgia where he worked his own small farm, perhaps purchased with the wages he had accrued as an itinerant carriage painter.[89]

In 1850 the Hodgsons employed five young white journeymen. A decade later none of them worked for the Hodgsons and not one of them had remained in Athens. In fact, only one out of the five still lived in the state, and he did not practice carriage-making. William Da Costa, a teenager when in the Hodgsons' employ, had transformed himself into a Columbus merchant with a personal estate valued at $10,000 at the tender age of twenty-three.[90]

These accounts suggest that young white artisans were traveling through the region in search of work. These men were reminiscent of Reuben King, the Connecticut tanner who supported his six-month-long circuitous journey from his hometown to Georgia by picking up a number of shoemaking jobs in Pennsylvania and Maryland in 1803. King's travels were not particularly unusual for journeymen at the beginning of the nineteenth century.[91] But within three or four decades, the accessibility of new kinds of jobs in factories and in cities, along with the decline of workshop production in many trades, made artisan tramping less common in the North.[92] This was not so in the plantation economy of the South. Artisan itinerancy, in fact, was suited to the needs of the countryside.

Useful insight into the peripatetic career of one artisan, William Price Talmage, an Athens blacksmith, comes from the journal he kept in which he described his life events. Such journals are exceedingly difficult to come by. While artisans' account books occasionally crop up in manuscript collections in archives around the South, actual journals, diaries, and letter collections by southern artisans are virtually nonexistent. Not only did many artisans lack the time and energy to record their life events and the stable circumstances in which to treasure them, but subsequent generations of family members often failed to appreciate the value of these firsthand accounts in a society where the lives of planters and their families were held in the highest esteem.

William Talmage's diary, which has been preserved, began on May 7, 1847, shortly before his thirty-fourth birthday.[93] Calling it "a Journal or Memorandum Book," the account was neither a true diary that detailed his daily experiences and emotions, nor an account book that tallied his receipts and expenditures. Indeed, Talmage's unpublished journal, which he kept until a few weeks before his death in 1877, was both an almanac and a personal log. It contained those events, according to Talmage, "which I may See Proppor [*sic*] to Note down through the Course of My life." He began his story with his twenty-first birthday.

On May 12, 1834, William Price Talmage turned twenty-one years of age, an event that marked the conclusion of his apprenticeship and the official arrival of his manhood.[94] Talmage chose this propitious occasion to leave the household of his father, who had trained him in the blacksmith trade. He also left his hometown of Franklin, New Jersey, a mining community that manufactured pig-iron. He spent the summer not as a newly minted journeyman, however, but as a farmhand for several villagers in the neighboring community of Rockaway.[95]

Following his stint as a farm laborer, Talmage traveled to Newark, probably to seek work. An industrial center of some twenty thousand residents supported by iron forges and furnaces, carriage-making, leather, hat-making and brewing trades and the newly formed New Jersey Railroad and Transcontinental Corporation, Newark seemed a promising place for journeyman blacksmiths to find employment.[96] He does not reveal what he did in Newark during his stay but he must have widened his political horizons. By Talmage's arrival, the city's workers, organized into some sixteen trade unions, had formed a Workingmen's Party in 1830 and were busy waging a battle for the right to a ten-hour day, the removal of property-holding qualifications to vote, and free schools.[97] Despite these workingmen's political struggles, or perhaps because of them, Talmage left Newark within a few months of his arrival.[98]

Shortly thereafter, he set out on foot for New York City, where he boarded a sailing vessel bound for Charleston, South Carolina.[99] The ship arrived in Charleston harbor, at which point Talmage took the railroad to Augusta, Georgia, and walked westward some sixty-five miles, often in the rain, to his brother's home in Athens, a university town on the Oconee River deep in the Georgia piedmont. Finding his older brother John "in good health," he "set in to work for him in his [blacksmith] Shop . . . till 23rd March 1836."[100]

At this time Athens was a small town, located in the northeastern corner of the Georgia cotton belt, with fewer than two thousand inhabitants. While the presence of the university had secured the town's existence, it did little for local economic development. The school lacked strong financial support from the state and rarely enrolled more than one hundred students in any one year.[101] Thus, Talmage found little more than a bustling village upon his arrival in 1834.

John Talmage, eighteen years older than William, owned a residence and the largest blacksmith shop in town. He produced "excellent work in that line and had no competition" according to a local resident.[102] A missionary as well as a blacksmith, John had arrived in Athens with his wife

Emily and his brother-in-law Abijah Conger, a carpenter by trade, by 1830. These two men and their families had served the Cherokees in northwest Georgia until the state ordered their departure.[103] Apparently John Talmage's missionary zeal did not prevent him from assuming the nature of acquisitiveness characteristic of antebellum southern white men. Shortly after the Trail of Tears, John owned—in addition to his Athens home, shop, and five slaves—nearly one thousand acres, much of it in newly created Cherokee County.[104]

Talmage relates virtually nothing about the months spent in his brother's employ, except that he made several visits to his cousin Aaron's farm in nearby Monroe County.[105] One can imagine, however, that Talmage received an important education of sorts during this period, one that included learning how to work with skilled slave laborers, since his brother must have used several of his slaves in his shop. He undoubtedly also learned about the social significance of the master-slave relationship, which permeated all aspects of southern life.

At the conclusion of these sixteen months, Talmage returned to New Jersey, traveling by stage to Augusta, his ticket presumably paid for with the wages he had collected from his brother. This time he journeyed to Elizabeth Town where he appears to have worked for three men in quick succession. At the conclusion of four and a half months, he purchased two lots "and built a shop on one of them." [106] Talmage probably secured this property from a group of New York City businessmen who had bought a large piece of land bordering the Staten Island Sound in anticipation of the arrival of the railroads. By 1835, they had plotted the tract, christened it "the new Manufacturing Town of Elizabeth Port," and laid it out into rectangular lots, which they offered up for sale.[107]

One can surmise, given his return to New Jersey, that Talmage preferred seeking his fortune in his native state rather than the Georgia countryside. To what extent his decision was a comment on the nature of work in the slave South and his attitude toward slavery can only be guessed at. It certainly suggests that Talmage had some serious doubts about making his home in Georgia. Unfortunately for Talmage, the economy ground to a halt shortly after he established his new business. Talmage must have secured his lots and shop through a mortgage that was called in during the Panic of 1837. Talmage was sanguine about his misfortune when he wrote about it ten years later, however, reporting only that he "settled up my business[,] went to see my Father and set out for Athens[,] Ga," where he arrived in August 1837. Once again he worked for his brother.[108]

After sixteen more months in John's shop, Talmage traveled to Mt. Pleasant, Georgia, where he entered into a business deal with John Graves. Mt. Pleasant was a plantation located in the northeastern corner of Newton County, south of Athens but north of the prime plantation districts that surrounded Milledgeville and Macon. The Mt. Pleasant property consisted of some 7,500 acres originally purchased by John Graves's father, a North Carolinian, in 1818. The land was ideally situated at the crossroads of the heavily traveled east-west stage coach route between Charleston and New Orleans and the north-south route that passed through Athens, Eatonton, and Milledgeville. Throughout the antebellum era the Graves family owned several dozen slaves, ran a general store at the crossroads, and operated a plantation, a flour mill, a sawmill, and a blacksmith shop.[109]

Plantations like Mt. Pleasant that developed small manufacturing enterprises to serve themselves and the local community gave Talmage the opportunity to hold steady employment and receive board for several weeks or months. Unfortunately, Talmage rarely encountered such opportunities, and they did not always work out, as in the case of the Graves family.

John Graves, a gin manufacturer, must have been eager to put the highly skilled blacksmith to work on making his acquaintance.[110] After six months' residence at Mt. Pleasant, however, Talmage traveled to nearby Monroe County to live with his cousin Aaron for the remainder of the year. The business relationship between Graves and Talmage apparently had gone sour. During this time, Talmage returned to Mt. Pleasant on four separate occasions, once to collect his tools and three times "to settle" with Graves, who "put off" paying Talmage the money owed him until the fourth visit.[111]

It is not clear why John Graves refused to pay Talmage given the family resources of the time. No extant records indicate family financial trouble. Perhaps Graves was simply unwilling to let a man of Talmage's expertise out of his employ. Most area blacksmiths lacked Talmage's sophisticated skills. Account books from a shop not far from Mt. Pleasant show that these smiths handled routine work only—the making of farm implements like shovels, plows, pails, hoops, hooks, hinges and blades, the sharpening of knives and axes, and the shoeing of horses.[112] Talmage's journal by contrast indicates that his skills required far more expertise; he was capable of making machine parts, mill irons, and barouche irons as well as repairing equipment in steam mills and sawmills.[113]

Throughout his stay with his cousin, Talmage made frequent trips around the countryside, traveling to the towns of Macon, Athens, and Monticello as well as to Butts County. He also continued to frequent Mt. Pleasant.[114] These trips through middle Georgia's cotton belt suggest that Talmage was searching for work, or knew of work to be had, on surrounding farms and plantations. The majority of counties that he journeyed through between 1838 and 1841, especially Butts, Walton, and Newton, were not prime plantation districts. Although many residents cultivated cotton, the populations of these counties were all small, well below 3,500, whites outnumbered slaves, and town development was minimal. Under these conditions, the services of a talented blacksmith with a knack for repairing machinery must have been especially welcome among middling farmers and planters eager to make improvements upon their property.[115]

Yet Talmage did not choose to continue his services as an itinerant blacksmith indefinitely. After a year's absence, he returned to Athens in the summer of 1840, working in his brother's shop now and then while boarding with other residents. After the New Year, Talmage once again began traveling through Walton and Newton Counties until the end of February. At this time, he undertook an ambitious and unusual tour that took him through the newest plantation lands to the southwest. This tour would change his life by making it possible for him to own a shop of his own.

Why Talmage chose to make this trek is unclear. Perhaps the work available to him in Athens and the surrounding piedmont had not been sufficient to support his bid to be an independent artisan. Perhaps he was growing discouraged at his inability to shed his lowly status as a nonslaveholding journeyman. After all, he had been working for wages for seven years and still owned no property, land or human, besides his horse and tools. Unable to find suitable work in New Jersey as a journeyman, he had traveled south to Georgia, relying upon his brother and relatives for work. He had accrued enough cash to return to New Jersey to open his own shop at the age of twenty-four only to lose it in the Panic of 1837. He had returned to Georgia, and once again frequently depended on his relatives for work and board over the following four years. By 1841, Talmage was twenty-eight years old. The last seven years had been trying ones. He may have decided to head to the newest settlements in western Georgia and central Alabama based on word-of-mouth reports about opportunities for skilled artisans. Regardless of his motivation, Talmage embarked upon the six-month tour on March 1, 1841. The money he earned on this tour enabled him to buy a shop of his own and secure the status of master craftsman shortly after the trek's conclusion.

The idea that artisans participated in a tramping tour through plantation lands is foreign to one's notions about the nature of work in the antebellum South. Yet since the 1820s, planters and farmers in northern and western Georgia and Alabama had depended upon itinerant wheelwrights, blacksmiths, and millwrights to build and maintain their mills and gins. Some of these men owned slaves, but few were willing to spend valuable capital to purchase an artisan whose abilities would be put to use only on occasion. Moreover, the sorts of skills that these rural farmers and planters sought often demanded specialized training. While many slave blacksmiths could shoe horses and make farm utensils, a limited number of upcountry slaves had experience building and repairing equipment for steam mills and sawmills. Under these circumstances, itinerant white artisans could find plenty of work in the newest lands of the cottonbelt.[116]

Talmage began his journey from the home of George Boyd near Mt. Pleasant. He traveled by horse in a southwestward direction through middle Georgia to McDonough and on to La Grange, where he crossed Georgia's western border, the Chattahoochee River, into Alabama, over rolling hills overshadowed by distant mountains.[117] After passing through Dadeville and Nixburg, Talmage made his first prolonged stop at the plantation of Joseph Billups, owner of twenty-nine slaves and one of the earliest and most prominent white settlers in Coosa County.[118] Talmage stayed at Billups's home for four days, and though he does not state this in his journal, probably worked on Billups's gins and mills. He then proceeded south to Wetumpka in Montgomery County.

Talmage traveled from trading center to trading center. This route must have been deliberate. Talmage was probably assessing the need for a blacksmith shop in each of these places even as he sought information about temporary work opportunities in mills and manufactories. He had departed Dadeville, a bustling lumber town in the Alabama forest, to make his way to Wetumpka, a shipping point for cotton situated alongside the shoals of the Coosa River at the foothills of the Appalachians.[119] His next stop, Mt. Meigs, was a center for merchant trade.[120]

It was just outside Mt. Meigs, at the plantation of Nicholas Marks, that Talmage located his next long-term job. He stated in his journal, "I found [Marks] at his Mill place [and] applide [*sic*] to him for A Job at his Steam Mill." He proceeded to work for Marks for the next six weeks at $3.00 per day and "board and washing and my horse board," a remarkably high wage for that period.[121]

Talmage's new employer was one of the earliest white landowners in Montgomery County. He had emigrated to Alabama from Oglethorpe County, Georgia, with a small retinue of relations, all Georgians, in the 1820s.[122] The five families with whom he traveled, although of modest wealth, managed to purchase some of the richest land in Alabama, just outside the town of Montgomery, from the land office at Cahaba for $1.25 an acre.[123] Long considered infertile, the prairie lands they purchased turned out to be rich, fertile loam, making Nicholas Marks and the other families quite wealthy.[124] By 1830, Marks owned several thousand acres of prime land and 62 slaves.[125]

During Talmage's employment at Marks's mill, he also spent a fair amount of time visiting with other craftsmen who lived in the area. He was an overnight guest at the home of George Stubblefield, a millwright on the Cabahatchee River, a dinner guest at the home of Mr. Fountain, a carriage maker, and a dinner guest at the home of Mr. Merrit, a blacksmith, all nonslaveholders.[126] It seems likely that Talmage used these visits to gather information about the possibilities for relocating to this rich plantation district. His wages while under Marks's employ were high. He may have been considering setting up a shop of his own in the area and sought the advice of fellow craftsmen. He may also have observed that these artisans, while they had been able to acquire homes and shops of their own, had been unable to acquire land and slaves.

This may explain why Talmage chose to move on at the end of six weeks. He returned to the Billups plantation to make tools and perform "plantation work" until the beginning of May. He then headed north to Robert Jemison's mill, and after a false start chasing down his runaway horse, "set in to work" for Jemison for the next two months. Here he received wages of $3.50 a day along with board, washing, and fodder for his horse, a $.50 increase over the wages he had received from Marks. Both Marks and Jemison must have appreciated Talmage's skills in a region that typically lacked such highly skilled craftsmen. Under these circumstances, Talmage could command high wages.

Jemison was a wealthy planter, lawyer, state legislator, and entrepreneur, originally from Georgia, who owned an array of business concerns in the Tuscaloosa area, including a stagecoach line that carried the mail, a lumber mill, a gristmill, a sawmill, and a turnpike and bridge company.[127] Jemison also owned one of eight forges that operated in Talladega County at this time. Jemison's iron mill, located on Cheaha Creek, which is probably where Talmage worked, produced farm implements and cooking utensils for his own use and that of neighboring plantations.[128]

Talmage spent 39 days working for Jemison, which should have secured him about $136.50 in wages. He had worked approximately 32 days for Marks, securing him another $96.00. At the conclusion of his time at Jemison's mill, Talmage had pocketed at least $232.00. This princely sum did not include wages from the work he had performed for Billups and others along the way. Talmage must have felt pleased with his earnings for he headed back to the Georgia border into Paulding County, bypassing some Alabama gold mines by ten miles, where he might have ventured to find work had he sought more cash. He then spent the next two months journeying through his old stomping grounds, Gwinnett, Clarke, Walton, Newton, and Monroe Counties—perhaps he was considering relocation to one of these places—before finally winding up at his cousin's home, where he stayed until early October to make Aaron a "set of Barouch irons."[129]

Talmage's journey had taken him through prime cotton-growing regions in Georgia and Alabama as well as through newly settled agricultural communities. His return home took him back through the Alabama and Georgia piedmont where planters and farmers were cultivating cotton and corn equally, sometimes with and sometimes without slaves. This route, or parts of it, may have been a well-known circuit for itinerant blacksmiths. A Paulding County blacksmith's account books indicate that he too traveled through Troup, Meriwether, and Talladega Counties, all places on Talmage's journey, to do business.[130]

Historians have sometimes assumed that the existence of slave labor in the plantation South made free labor inviable. These scholars have reasoned that because slave labor was the predominant form of labor in the antebellum South, free labor had to have been of marginal value and therefore virtually nonexistent. Slave owners had invested significant amounts of capital in the purchase and maintenance of their chattel and had no desire to shell out wages for free laborers when slave laborers were already paid for and readily available. Talmage's experience and that of other artisan itinerants suggests a far more complicated scenario. For Talmage's journey through western Georgia and Alabama reveals that time, place, and degree of settlement played major roles in determining whether planters preferred slave labor over free labor. It is clear that planters eager to establish plantations in the fertile soil of central Georgia and Alabama used their slaves to chop trees, clear land, and erect fences and barns when establishing their new plantations. But these same planters also preferred to hire skilled mechanics to set up, run, and repair the sawmills and cotton gins, often fueled by steam engines, as well as foundries and machine shops that made their plantations self-sufficient. While a self-sufficient plantation was the ultimate goal of many planters, particularly when they lived in relatively remote areas, it was not necessarily a logical decision to buy an expensive skilled slave when the majority of work required on the new land was agricultural in nature.

Talmage presumably gained a great deal of experience from his tramping tour. Though he would use the proceeds from his journey to set up his own shop in Athens, one wonders whether this was his intention when he began his trip. Was he seeking new markets in which to set up shop? Did he harbor planter ambitions himself? His journal provides no definitive answer. It is clear, however, that—excepting this six-month period—Talmage depended heavily upon his brother and cousin, both slaveholders, for work and board. The power of kinship, especially for a northern-born man in a new place, may have compelled him to settle near his relatives, who offered him their financial support and their connections as well as their friendship, rather than risk potential poverty in the newer plantation lands to the west.[131]

Thus, shortly after Talmage's return from his tramping tour, he purchased a town lot and built his own blacksmith shop in Athens. A few months later, on March 17, 1842, he married Elizabeth Royal at the Methodist Church. His new status as master craftsman and married man marked an end to his jaunts. His journal took a new turn, recording weather, comets, the pelican he shot, stuffed, and gave to the university museum, and scattered local and national events, rather than the places he had visited and the men he had met along the way.[132]

William Talmage was an enterprising man, and while he may have missed the physical independence that characterized his itinerant years, the Athens blacksmith spent the next decade diligently working in his shop and carefully investing his capital.[133] During that time, Athens developed into a modest transportation and manufacturing center, despite its small population. The Athens branch of the Georgia Railroad, the only connection to Augusta and the outside world in all of northeast Georgia, was completed in 1841. As a result, Athens became an important trade center patronized by farmers and village storekeepers from as far away as North and South Carolina.[134] The arrival of the railroad also encouraged some local manufacturing, including the establishment of three textile mills on the Oconee River, two of which, along with the railroad station, were little more than a stone's throw from Talmage's shop.[135] Talmage benefited from these developments. His shop's growing success enabled him to enter into a series of business ventures that turned him into a wealthy man.

His wealth grew slowly at first. By 1846 he owned one slave, a town lot valued at $600, and capital and stock totaling $400.[136] Six years later, however, his property holdings were valued at $7,800, and he owned five slaves as well as $5,000 worth of stock in the Pioneer Paper Manufacturing Company.[137] Talmage had secured the controlling share of the company in 1848, a development he underscored in his journal. His investment proved to be a wise one because very little paper was manufactured in the antebellum South. Accordingly, his company gained a near monopoly on an extensive southern market for folded writing paper, wrapping paper, paper bags, and newsprint folio.[138]

Talmage also purchased shares in the Athens Steam Company.[139] The manufactory advertised that it could make goods as cheaply as in the North. It turned out doors, sashes, blinds, cast iron and brass, machine parts, circular saws, pumps, gearing, steam engines, boilers, and iron fences, items which were quite familiar to Talmage.[140] By 1860, his property was valued at $33,300 and his investments were growing. Despite his wealth, Talmage continued to maintain his blacksmith shop and continued to consider himself first and foremost a blacksmith by trade.[141]

Talmage made clear throughout the first section of the journal that his identity as an artisan was important to him. This is substantiated by the artisan community he created around him. After working at Nicholas Marks's mill all day, Talmage would spend his evenings with his new artisan acquaintances. His father-in-law, John Royal, was a saddler. Royal also ran a boarding house full of artisans. It was here that Talmage rented a room from Royal following his Alabama trek, and here that he made Elizabeth's acquaintance while enjoying the fellowship of other craftsmen like himself.[142]

Athens supported a substantial population of white artisans; they comprised almost one-third of the adult white male population in the town by 1850. Moreover, one out of every two master craftsmen owned an average of 6.5 slaves apiece.[143] Talmage himself became a slaveholder, though he was somewhat elusive on this subject in his journal. In fact, he did not use the words "slave" or "slavery" throughout this first section. By examining the events he chose to relate in these pages, however, one begins to see how much significance the social world of slavery, and the status conferred by slaveholding, held for him.

Talmage's first entries dealing with slaves record events that broke with social expectations about the nature of slavery. Thus, he related that he attended a public hanging of a "negro" on October 30, 1840.[144] Three months later, he reported that the wealthy planter John A. Cobb's "negroes" had been sold.[145] Both instances represented challenges to the social order of the South as he understood it. A slave who committed a heinous act against whites, for which he was hanged, challenged widely held notions that slaves were childlike dependents content with their lot. Likewise, John A. Cobb's fall from grace, in the public form of a sheriff's sale of sixty-one of his slaves to pay off his heavy debts, also challenged widely held notions about the invulnerability of the planter aristocracy. These two entries alone indicate the extent to which Talmage had internalized the values of southern society.

But the way in which Talmage listed the growth of his household in his journal is just as suggestive. Talmage became a father and a slave owner several times over during the 1840s. Throughout this period he listed the births and deaths of his children and the purchases of his slaves interchangeably, demonstrating the degree to which he derived his authority as a white male from his household.[146] Thus, an entry on the birth and death of his firstborn children, twin daughters, recorded on March 24, 1843, was followed by an entry listing the purchase of George from Thomas Gresham for $450 on August 3, 1843. This pattern continued over the next four years. An entry listing the birth of another daughter was followed by an entry on the purchase of a second slave named Robert, followed by an entry listing the death of this daughter, followed by Robert's death by drowning, followed by the birth of another daughter, followed by the purchase of John, whom he returned because "he was not sound in boddy [*sic*]." [147] These entries comprise the entire sum of the experiences he chose to record during this four-year span—the births of four children, the tragic losses of three of them, the purchase of three slaves, the death of one, and the return of another. By 1847 Talmage's accommodation to the slave South was complete. He fully understood the meaning of slaveholding, which ensured increased productive relations in his household, just as he understood the significance of the births of his children, which ensured the perpetuation of his lineage.

Many journeymen artisans in the Northeast were forced into unskilled work in response to the transition to capitalism in the early nineteenth century. William Price Talmage, who found he could not make his living in New Jersey, went south in response to this dearth of opportunities. Talmage's case, as well as the aforementioned ones, suggests that white artisans in the South created economic opportunities for themselves within the confines of their structural circumstances—the needs of the local market within the slave society. White artisans like Talmage could achieve upward mobility through the application of whatever resources they commanded, whether family connections, degree of skill, access to capital, use of slave labor, or investment in manufactures.

Yet few white artisans commanded this set of resources upon embarking on their careers. A period of itinerancy offered skilled young men like Talmage the opportunity to accrue some of them. By seeking work across the spreading plantation countryside, artisans could retain their personal and economic independence, save part of their wages to put toward a shop of their own, and assess the market possibilities of each town they moved through. Journeymen may have found this course of action preferable to wage employment in the Northeast or in the older towns and cities of the Southeast where the presence of skilled blacks, slave and free, devalued their efforts.

White journeymen's periods of itinerancy in Georgia were often intended as a means to an end. Talmage, along with other white journeymen like Watts and Da Costa, saved enough of their wages to set themselves up in more permanent positions. Although Georgia's wealth was tied to the planter class in the antebellum period, and although the rising costs of land and slaves made entry into the planter ranks exceedingly difficult by the late 1830s, other comfortable livelihoods remained available for some skilled white men. The spread of the cotton economy, which brought with it a measure of urban development, as well as improved transportation and industry, provided some white artisans with opportunities for upward mobility.

Talmage's rise to prosperity, his slaveowning, and his later alliance with manufacturers and planters epitomized the kinds of opportunities artisans might hope to make for themselves by the late antebellum era. While they could not always aspire to planter status, as they had in the early republic, they could learn to marry their craft traditions with the maturing plantation society around them. By seeking work across the spreading plantation countryside, artisans could retain their personal and economic independence, save part of their wages to put toward a shop of their own, and assess the market possibilities of each town they passed through. Journeymen artisans may have found this course of action preferable to wage employment in older towns and cities where the presence of skilled urban blacks challenged traditional journeymen working conditions.

The majority of skilled slaves in Georgia worked on plantations in the countryside, but a small number also worked in Georgia's towns and cities. Though their numbers were never overwhelming—an estimated one out of every ten adult urban male slaves was skilled in the antebellum era according to Robert Fogel—they formed an important segment of the urban workforce. Free black artisans formed another significant segment. As many as half of all adult free black men in these urban places possessed marketable artisanal skills. White journeymen and unskilled whites formed the final segment of the workforce in urban Georgia. This diverse workforce, slave and free, black and white, provided employers with a number of labor arrangements, depending on availability and cost.[148]

The presence of a large urban black population affected the nature of work relations for skilled laborers, white and black, in these cities. By

1840, nearly one out of every two residents in Savannah, Augusta, and Macon was black. Most of these urban blacks were slaves. Free blacks represented one out of every ten blacks in Savannah and less than one out of every twenty in most other Georgia towns.[149]

Urban slaves, whether hired out on a daily, monthly, or yearly basis, lived lives of relative freedom. While some slaves traveled to and from their jobs with passes in hand, reminders of their bondage, they often were given permission to seek their own employers. Furthermore, many urban masters allowed their slaves to make their own decisions about lodging and boarding arrangements. In Savannah, for example, 60 percent of all slaves lived away from their owners.[150]

Urban slave artisans not only experienced the freedom of finding work and a place to live, they also experienced the freedom to spend their leisure time much as they desired. Though whites enacted state and urban laws—such as curfews for blacks and ordinances against Negro gatherings—in an attempt to restrict these freedoms, these prohibitions frequently went unenforced.[151]

A traveler who passed through Savannah's market in the early 1840s was amazed at the uninhibited, cosmopolitan, and omnipresent nature of the black community. "Such a collection you will seldom expect anywhere . . . [they] are there making their purchases for Sunday, and such a confusion of sounds and tongues as one can scarcely imagine."[152] In Augusta slaves gathered in the grog shops during race week where, according to white reports, they gambled and drank themselves into a stupor until after midnight.[153] And even in small-town Athens, slaves eagerly awaited the university's commencement day, "when poorer whites and blacks flocked to the university gates for the celebration—with fried fish and red lemonade on every corner."[154]

The quasi-independence of urban slaves had important implications for skilled bondsmen. Urban slavery, in all its diversity and complexity, provided skilled slaves with a strong community network that could be relied on to share news of jobs or places to stay. The urban slave community was also intimately tied to the urban free black community. Again, this expanded network allowed slaves and free blacks to look out for each others' interests.[155]

Slave owners feared the long-term effects of this independence and

Table 8. Urban Black Populations in Georgia, 1840–1860

1840	Slaves	Free Blacks
Savannah	4,692	632
Augusta	2,989	148
Macon	1,606	25
Columbus	1,069	32
Milledgeville	917	40
Urban population	11,273	877
As percentage of state population	4	32

1850	Slaves	Free Blacks
Savannah	6,231	686
Augusta*	4,718	243
Macon	2,353	38
Columbus	2,258	52
Milledgeville	1,020	19
Atlanta	493	19
Urban population	17,073	1,057
As percentage of state population	5	36

1860	Slaves	Free Blacks
Savannah	7,712	705
Augusta	3,663	386
Macon	2,829	22
Columbus	3,547	141
Milledgeville	837	39
Atlanta	1,914	25
Athens	1,892	1
Urban population	22,394	1,319
As percentage of state population	5	38

*Figures for 1850 were unavailable. The U.S. Census Bureau relied on 1852 figures provided by Augusta census-takers.
Sources: Compendium of the Sixth Census, 40–46; *Seventh Census of the U.S.,* 366; *Population of the U.S. in 1860,* 74.

attempted to guard against it. Before John B. Lamar, a Macon planter, sent a slave to find his way to Lamar's sister's house in Athens, he lectured him against getting a "big head" upon making the transition from "a rustic life into the gay world." Lamar intoned that symptoms of a big head included "thinking himself more knowing than his owners, and a desire to act as he pleases." [156] Lamar's speech, which he apparently gave to all slaves he sent into town to work, was not always effective. "That interesting representative of colored life, Alfred has become disgusted with rural life and turned his face toward the polished mony [*sic*] circles of Athens," complained Lamar to a friend when Alfred ran away on the railroad. [157]

Masters disciplined skilled urban slaves by threatening to send them back to the countryside. Sometimes they carried out their threats. When Maryann Cobb, the wife of planter-politician Howell Cobb, received an offer from a rural planter to hire her slave carpenter Gilbert, she accepted it. Although she had wanted to put Gilbert to work in Athens, she found him too "self willed and spoilled [*sic*]." [158] Godfrey Barnsley was delighted in 1859 when a Savannah acquaintance decided to send his slave carpenter to Woodlands in north Georgia. "Carpenters are in great demand here," the acquaintance informed Barnsley by letter. Woodson, the slave carpenter from Savannah, proved no bargain for Barnsley. The "drinking and discontented" slave—"a bad influence on the place"—brought liquor to Barnsley's other slaves throughout his year-long stay. In all probability Woodson's master sent him to the remote Woodlands estate in an effort to discipline and perhaps even rehabilitate him. [159]

How slave artisans behaved, and whether or not they posed a threat to the institution of slavery, however, was far less important to employers than their ability to work and the cost of that work. Moreover, while some employers had traditionally refrained from combining black and white labor, this practice was becoming a far more common sight by the late antebellum period as employers increasingly adapted their labor needs to the available workforce.

In 1836 the Milledgeville *Federal Union* described an incident it deemed noteworthy. Ten white mechanics and twenty black mechanics had been observed building a boat together on the banks of the Flint River under the guidance of Macon resident Mr. Butts. The editor concluded, "The scene to us was novel and sublime." [160] But in city, town, and countryside elsewhere, skilled labor was clearly integrated, proving neither novel nor sublime. Skilled laborers, whether free or slave, white or black, were in demand, and employers often hired according to availability and not race. In southwest Georgia, builder John Wind hired white carpenters to work alongside black carpenters.[161] Robert Findlay's Macon iron foundry employed skilled whites and skilled blacks, slave and free.[162] An overseer of a Savannah brickyard undergoing construction listed the races of the carpenters he employed. His entries show that white and black mechanics worked together at the same tasks in his establishment.[163] When Joseph Watts sought a carriage trimmer position with the Hodgsons, he gave the name of Jefferson Holbrook, "a yellow boy," probably a mulatto free black, as a job reference.[164] The Yoakums, a family of carpenters in Athens, boarded six young carpenters in their household in 1850, one of whom was a free black carpenter who worked with the white family and the other five white journeymen.[165]

The rough parity created by working together was reinforced by the wages employers were willing to pay skilled whites and blacks. A master carpenter in Savannah who built tenements and renovated existing structures owned a crew of seven or eight slaves. After evaluating a job, he either sent out "hands to do the work" on their own, or he joined them himself. He charged seventy-five cents a day for the labor of his semiskilled boys (the nominal rate for white unskilled labor was $0.83), expected as much as $2.75 a day for his best slave carpenters (the nominal rate for white artisans was $1.98), and charged $3.00 a day, only twenty-five cents more, for his own work.[166]

Some employers demonstrated a preference for one form of skilled labor over another. Experience showed the carriage-making Hodgson brothers that hiring slave artisans, for example, substantially reduced wage costs. A white artisan offered his services to the Hodgsons for no less than $2.50 per day in 1849, though the nominal rate for artisans in the South Atlantic states was $1.54.[167] That same year the Hodgsons were invited to hire an experienced slave carriage-maker for $150 a year, plus board and clothing (estimated at about $69 per year). Hiring a slave artisan, at a total of $219 a year, was far less expensive than the white artisan, at approximately $780 (a year's worth of wages at $2.50 per day for a white artisan working six days a week, not including room and board).[168] Not surprisingly, extant Hodgson letters indicate that the brothers searched just as widely for skilled slave labor as for skilled white labor.[169]

Master artisans accommodated their labor needs to their available labor market. As already indicated, master craftsmen contracted apprentices, employed white journeymen and free black journeymen, hired slave artisans by the day, month, or year, and bought their own slaves to fill their labor demands. Master artisans' ability to adapt their labor needs to the labor supply was a critical factor in their success.

Athens carpenter Abijah Conger owned no slaves. He hired no white journeymen and no skilled blacks. Yet Conger found a way to adapt his labor needs to available sources.[170] In 1840 he signed an indenture entrusting him with the training of two young slaves. In this indenture, Conger promised: "to take Ned and Sanders both colored boys, belonging to the said Mrs. Thomas for three years from the date above and feed and cloath the said Ned and Sanders as apprintices [*sic*] and teach them in the art and occupation of house carpentry [and] to watch over their morals and behaviors as much as though they were wholly his." [171] Clearly, the clever carpenter had found a way to adapt traditional craft practices to the slave economy.

Master artisans who hired skilled hands were able to tailor their labor needs to the available market. When skilled slaves proved cheaper than skilled whites, employers hired them. Thus journeymen who wished to avoid competition with blacks altogether needed to pursue luxury trades or mechanized industry by the late antebellum period. As free laborers in a slave society, journeymen's labor was desirable only in relation to the numbers of blacks able to perform the same skills and the comparative costs of wages.

Master craftsmen were among those employers who made these labor choices. Their decisions affected the kinds of work opportunities available to journeymen. This situation produced significant social tensions, for it cast master craftsmen who owned or hired urban blacks against journeymen who competed with urban blacks for work from master craftsmen. Yet these tensions were mediated by white journeymen's expectations of upward mobility. Journeymen anticipated that someday they would be master craftsmen too. They would have a business and some capital and would be faced with the same kinds of labor choices as their current employers. As master craftsmen had demonstrated throughout the antebellum period, the ability to accommodate themselves to the slave economy and to the marketplace provided them with the best path to wealth and success. White journeymen attempted to follow suit.

Mechanics like Talmage who migrated to the antebellum South encountered a society fundamentally different from the free labor economies of the North and Europe they had left behind. Accordingly, these men often had to redefine their work lives, their ambitions and goals, and even their values and ideologies. This ability to adapt their skills and thinking to this new world could transform poor men into modestly comfortable if not wealthy ones. These rags-to-riches stories were clearly dependent on a host of critical factors, in particular, being in the right place at the right time in respect to demand for their skills and to lack of competition from other mechanics, black and white, slave and free.

The spread of the plantation economy and the rise and fall of the market towns and commercial centers accompanying that spread dictated in large measure the kinds of opportunities artisans in a variety of trades encountered. Mechanics willing to adapt their skills, engage in merchandising, or be mobile were at a distinct advantage.

The success stories of those artisans turned entrepreneurs and planters underline another reality about the antebellum South. This was an exceedingly dynamic world where free labor and slave labor were in constant negotiation in respect to place, time, and context. Migrant artisans understood that while the antebellum South could not give all white men a leg up on the social ladder, a bit of skill mixed with some luck often offered better prospects for their future, even in a slave labor economy, than the industrializing world they had left behind. Thus, mechanics' skills in this changing society could often become a means to a more lucrative end. By the mid–nineteenth century this more lucrative end almost always centered on the acquisition of slaves as well as new land and sometimes new businesses. By contrast, artisans whose skills were not in consistent demand were destined to modest if not impecunious lives, regardless of their talent or ambition.

5 *Politics in a Slaveholders' Republic*

White artisans in Georgia in the mid–nineteenth century dealt with divisive if not explosive issues peculiar to their situation as free laborers in a slave labor society. This was not a new phenomenon for these men. Like earlier generations of master craftsmen who had worked to transform themselves into planters, they did not view their situation as paradoxical. Since the 1790s many had been able to reconcile their status as free laborers with their status as both southerners and slaveholders.

Identifying each of the separate strands that contributed to white male artisans' ability to find a place for themselves in their slaveholding world is not an easy task. It is made more complex by the changing nature of southern politics and party politics during this volatile period. Artisan issues never fit neatly into any one political camp. Instead, artisans moved between and also outside of state and national parties to adhere to their mixed bag of economic and political principles. These beliefs included manufacturing as progress, upward mobility, democratic equality, property rights that extended to slavery, and the dignity of free labor, arguments that at face value seem wholly contradictory.[1]

Georgia artisans' collective identity and political consciousness had been at its strongest during the 1790s when mechanics in Augusta and Savannah had used the principles of artisanal republicanism to help organize themselves as a class.[2] The nature of this particular artisan republicanism had been predicated upon a set of important economic transformations, including the existence of staple-crop economies, the availability of inexpensive land, and minimal competition from other urban artisans (white and black, slave and free).[3]

By the turn of the century, the artisan leadership that had launched these mechanic societies had begun to abate. The popularity of the Democratic-Republican Party, along with statewide interest in national issues, served to unify many Georgians across class, occupational, and geographic lines. By the War of 1812, planters, merchants, and mechanics had often joined forces to support the domestic and foreign policies of the Democratic-Republican government in the face of growing political opposition from abroad.[4]

But changes in the artisan class itself also help explain the decline of a distinctive artisanal republicanism, for many artisan leaders had transformed themselves into local politicians and successful businessmen by the 1800s. While building mechanic communities to support their political ambitions, these same mechanic leaders had managed to accrue substantial wealth and thereby transform themselves into planters.

By the 1820s and 1830s, however, younger generations of white artisans found themselves more often than not consistently closed off from the political and economic worlds that their predecessors had found open to them. In response to the maturation of the cotton economy, extensive settlement of the upcountry and middle Georgia, competition from growing numbers of migrant white journeymen, skilled slaves, and free black artisans in some trades, and the flood of low-priced, northern-made goods into even the most youthful of urban markets, white mechanics' opportunities for political leadership as well as economic opportunity had begun to wane in comparison to the earlier era.[5] Given these circumstances most white artisans, particularly journeymen, found their ambitions increasingly thwarted.

Fewer master craftsmen became well off over time. Even fewer were able to transform themselves into planters and politicians. Some wage-earning artisans tacitly accepted this situation, continuing to work as journeymen at unreliable jobs in the largest cities and towns in Georgia. Others, masters and journeymen alike, chose to travel westward to the newest settlements on the cotton frontier, where they hoped to set up shops or at the very least find work as itinerants.

Artisans' dwindling economic opportunities discouraged a class identity—even a temporary one. Artisan organization and political activity became sporadic as planters gained more and more control over state and local politics as well as the economy. Few Georgians were empathetic to artisans' changed circumstances.[6] Instead of acknowledging the factors that had undercut artisan prospects, public opinion generally castigated impoverished master craftsmen and wage-earning journeymen as ne'er-do-wells whose lack of industry, temperance, and ambition explained their misfortune.[7] An anonymous Georgia author opined in 1832:

> If the sums spent by tradesmen at gambling houses, grog-shops, and other places of amusement, were invested in Lyceums, books, chemical and philosophical apparatus—and that the tradesmen instead of idling away their time . . . would soon become one of the most respectable and influential classes of people among us . . . its attractions would be such . . . as to reclaim the young apprentice and young journeyman from the haunts of vice, and thereby, by making them intelligent and useful, cause them to be a blessing to their friends and the pride and support of their country, instead of being a curse to them all, as is too often the case.[8]

The failure of the Manual Labor School Movement during the late 1820s and early 1830s also reflects the new disenchantment of southern white society with the dignity of labor and laboring men.[9] Designed to combine mechanical and agricultural employment with academic studies, the mission of these Protestant schools was "to encourage health, economy, industry, and add a sense of dignity to labor."[10] This mission was imperative, claimed one supporter, because young men needed to learn "the ordinary affairs of life, [including] their liability to be deceived and frauded by crafty and unprincipled workmen."[11] Although these schools were adopted by the three leading religious denominations (Baptists, Methodists, and Presbyterians) of Georgia, the manual labor component of the curriculum was abandoned within a few years.

This lack of respect for laboring men encouraged an already growing division between masters and journeymen. While masters came to identify themselves and be identified with the urban middle class of shopkeepers and merchants and professionals in the South, journeymen were far less likely to find such a comfortable niche for themselves. Although William Thomson, a Scottish wool-carder and spinner, observed that journeymen mechanics in Georgia and the Carolinas earned good wages, lived respectably in boarding houses, and were treated well by their employers (presumably master craftsmen) when compared to British tradesmen, he advised his fellow countrymen against seeking work in the South, where "if a man is poor, there are *150* ways in which he will feel it." [12] While journeymen a generation earlier had acquired shops, land, slaves, and social respect in a relatively short time, journeymen by the 1830s could no longer expect this degree of economic and social mobility. Indeed, journeyman status was no longer a temporary situation for some young men bearing the skills and tools of their trade. Instead, they could anticipate an entire career spent as wage-earning workingmen employed by contractors, manufacturers, and merchant importers in urban Georgia or as itinerant workingmen tramping through the countryside.

Master craftsmen themselves contributed to the growing disrespect for journeymen. In seeking to preserve their respectability and status, they often formed exclusive new mechanics' societies that bore little resemblance to their forerunners in the early republic.[13] The Mechanics' Society of Augusta (MSA) was revived in 1823 following a meeting of the mechanics of the city. The charter granted to the organization by the Georgia General Assembly noted only that the MSA was vested with all legal rights entitled to corporations.[14] No part of the charter referred to pride in craft, mechanics' consciousness or the importance of political equality. Unlike the charter members of the original MSA, the majority of the new MSA mechanics were well established before their involvement in this organization. They practiced elite trades, which they tended to manage from afar as importers and employers, occasionally held community positions, and owned substantial property, including slaves.

The MSA charter listed twenty-five names. Information was located on twenty-two of these mechanics. Mechanic occupations were found for ten of them; they included builder, upholsterer, carpenter, saddler, tinner, brickmaker, carriagemaker, and shoemaker. Yet a number of these men were not traditional craftsmen but retailers, wholesalers, and entrepreneurs. George Jackson owned a tin manufactory that sold northern tinware. Moses Roff Jr. was a partner in a shoe manufactory that purchased goods from the North. Cosby Dickinson, an upholsterer by trade, owned and operated several hotels. MSA president G. B. Marshall owned a coachmaking establishment, whose daily management he turned over to others, and was a partner in a brick-making manufactory. Examples of participation in local leadership positions include Cosby Dickinson, justice of the peace; John Cresswell, officer of the Masons' Society; and William Jackson, adjutant for the 10th Regiment of the Georgia Militia.

Fifteen of the twenty-five members owned slaves at some time between 1820 and 1830. Only six members owned more than one hundred upcountry acres by 1820. Most chose business pursuits over farming. For example, five members invested in local bank shares in the late 1820s and early 1830s, two held positions as commissioners for the Richmond Manufacturing Company organized in 1832, and one was a charter member of the Mechanics Bank of Augusta in 1833.[15]

> Distribution of Slave Ownership:
> Owned fewer than 5 slaves: 3
> Owned 5 to 9 slaves: 5
> Owned 10 to 19 slaves: 4
> Owned more than 20 slaves: 3

This evidence supports the contention that the new MSA appears to have been designed to bring its members the status and respectability traditionally awarded master craftsmen, even as the members' interests grew more and more entrepreneurial in nature. In fact, no evidence indicates that these men were committed to mutual aid or collective political activism of any kind.[16]

Similarly the Athens Mechanics' Mutual Aid Association (AMMAA), established in 1836 by five well-known Athens businessmen, apparently pursued the same philosophy as the MSA, despite its name. Created to "diffus[e] . . . useful knowledge among us of a nature not only to make us better mechanics but more useful and enlightened citizens," the AMMAA held debates that exempted from discussion all religious and political topics. It also established a mechanic library.[17] Membership was exclusive, requiring a character assessment, a two-thirds vote of approval, and an initiation fee of one dollar; membership was maintained by paying fifty cents dues per month and exhibiting respectful conduct.[18] Like the revived MSA the AMMAA allegedly upheld the dignity of its members while erecting a strict social barrier between themselves and journeymen who could ill afford the high cost of dues or the spare time for self-improvement by participating in debates and reading in the library. For example, the Hodgson brothers who opened a carriage-making shop in Athens in 1840 could not afford the 31-cent poll tax let alone the AMMAA dues.[19]

The Newton County Mechanics' Society was also organized by master mechanics to the exclusion of journeymen. Located in the cotton belt of middle Georgia, it represented the one group of organized mechanics in Georgia with a clear political agenda by the late antebellum era. Several weeks before the Whig Party's state convention in 1840, thirty-three artisans met in Covington, the county seat of Newton County, to pledge their allegiance to the Whig presidential ticket as a mechanics' society. Despite their disclaimer that they were "by profession Mechanics and . . . our business in life may be regarded by the aristocracy as too humble and lowly," these men were solid middle-class citizens who owned shops, businesses, land, and slaves.[20] Proclaiming themselves freemen, they condemned Martin Van Buren and the Democratic Party for their support of the Tariff of 1828, calling them would-be abolishers of democratic franchisement and "enemies of the South on the subject of slavery."[21] The Whig ticket, they felt by comparison, offered them a candidate sympathetic both to the South's interests and to their own contributions to society as industrious, hard-working master mechanics.[22]

The national two-party system had operated in America since the founding of the new nation, despite founding fathers' fears of such a system. The two-party system gave stability and coherence to political ideologies and platforms in a new nation fragmented by its great size, various economies, and diverse populations. The two-party system began to resemble its modern form after the War of 1812 when Americans divided over intense political differences. Under the leadership of Andrew Jackson, the Democratic Party advocated a more egalitarian and participatory democracy. In contrast, the developing Whig Party pressed for a strong centralized government and economy. The Democrats drew their support from southern planters, farmers from all over the country, and workers and immigrants in urban centers. The Whigs not only drew some support from these sectors but from the commercial classes as well.

By 1840, citizens were voting in unprecedented numbers and the Democratic Party was in its ascendancy. In fact, it was the nation's majority party from the 1830s to the Civil War. The unwillingness of the Democratic Party to take a stance on slavery, however, led to a major political realignment in the 1850s, which launched the Republican Party that brought Abraham Lincoln to Washington and precipitated secession and the Civil War.

The influence of the national two-party system was not felt heavily in Georgia until the 1830s. For the first decades of the nineteenth century, Georgia politics often revolved around personal factions unique to sections of the state. By the 1830s, however, these local parties were giving way to the national ones and more and more Georgians began labeling themselves Democrats or Whigs, though their party allegiances would reflect their local interests as much as national ones.

Despite the influence of this national system, mechanics' interests in Georgia rarely fit neatly into either party. The Democratic Party, which replaced the state's Union Party in the 1830s, paid little attention to mechanics given its anticommerce, proagrarian platform. When on occasion it did court the mechanic vote, it did so by emphasizing journeymen mechanics' exclusion from the middle class (and by association, from the master mechanic class).[23] In comparison the Whig Party, which replaced the States Rights Party in Georgia by the 1830s, took a proprietary interest in middle-class master mechanics as early as 1828. The party of upward mobility and economic expansion, Georgia Whigs considered mechanics an important ingredient in establishing a balanced economy in the South that would place the region beyond the North's reach.[24] Thus, the developing party system reflected the growing division between masters-turned-businessmen and journeymen-turned-workingmen.

The widening distance that master mechanics placed between themselves and journeymen was honored in the political sphere not only in terms of party developments. From 1820 through 1840, the state legislature passed nine laws that gave master carpenters and masons the right of first lien in a succession of towns stretching from Savannah to Decatur. As a result, a large group of master craftsmen received protective legislation that privileged their debts over other creditors. These acts, reflecting no partisanship since they were passed by Troup and Clark, States Rights and Union, and Whig and Democratic governments alike, earned local and state politicians the good will and future votes of a stable segment of the elite artisan population. They also privileged the interests of masters over journeymen since no such protective legislation was passed to secure journeymen's rights to their wages.[25]

Indeed, white journeymen had more to fear than unpaid wages. As one citizen declared in a letter to the editor in the *Southern Banner* in 1838, master craftsmen clearly were undermining white workingmen's interests. The polls offered white workingmen their sole opportunity to force the legislature to pass laws that would give preference to white labor over slave labor.[26] Yet this citizen overestimated the political power of these workingmen, whose very livelihoods depended upon the hiring decisions of the master craftsmen who employed them. Despite the growing democratization of the state government, despite some interest by the Democratic Party in securing their allegiance, wage-earners could not express their grievances as long as they were dependent upon masters who had the choice of hiring slave and free labor alike.

While northern mechanics challenged their employers and the political system with strikes, unions, and workingmen's parties in the 1820s and 1830s, the master mechanics of Georgia worked to preserve their status as master craftsmen. They were generally apolitical, choosing instead to build elite organizations that reflected their inherent conservatism and their belief in meritocracy. They often pursued occupational lines that bore little resemblance to the traditional work of master craftsmen but used their mechanic societies to secure social respect. Most important, they implicitly relegated journeymen to a sort of second-class citizenship as free laborers in a slave labor society. This reality shaped the nature of party politics in Georgia through the late antebellum era.

The Whig Party was in the ascendancy by 1843 in Georgia. Plummeting cotton prices following the Panic of 1837 prompted many Georgians to rethink their position on manufactures in the South. Georgia Whigs, like national Whigs, were enthusiastic proponents of manufacturing and economic growth. Disappointed by the decline of their agricultural economy, many Georgians found comfort in the alternative commercial economy promoted by the Whigs and subsequently joined their party.[27]

This had not always been the case. Georgia was the world's leading cotton producer in 1826, but when a six-year slump in cotton prices combined with the imposition of the Tariff, a handful of future Whigs turned to industry as a solution to the ups and downs of the cotton market and national politics.[28] This did not earn them the approval of either the Clark party (predecessor to the Democratic party) or the Troup party (predecessor to the Whig party). Even Governor John Forsyth, a Troup man himself, believed that manufacturing was dangerous and that the initiation of industry within the state would "enrich a few villages and small incorporated companies, and ruin states and communities." To Forsyth and the majority of Georgia's agriculturally minded citizens, industry was a "wretched system, which uses man as a mere machine."[29] The system of agriculture, they believed, was infinitely superior to the system of manufacturing.

This prevailing opinion forced the five investors of the brand-new Athens Manufacturing Company to issue a reconciliatory statement addressing their seemingly antiagricultural and antisouthern undertaking. At the textile factory's groundbreaking in 1829, antitariff agitator Judge Augustin S. Clayton, one of the Athens Manufacturing Company investors, explained, "The agricultural character of the South has been compelled . . . to partake of that manufacturing spirit which seems to have been forced down upon the nation at the expense of every individual . . . [The Athens Manufacturing Company's] project is certainly not to give countenance to a system which they have always denounced; but it is to be regarded as a measure of *unquestionable defense,* [leaving] no alternative than to strike for *commercial freedom.*[30]

This line of reasoning, which convinced some Georgians of the wisdom of introducing manufacturing in the South, was shaped by current political and economic circumstances. It did not last long. Thus, in the middle of agitation over the Tariff and the depression in cotton prices in 1828, the promanufacturing editor of the *Savannah Mercury* could confidently critique Georgia's agricultural society, "How long will the people of Georgia be blind to their own interests? Millions of dollars are now invested in plantations and lands for growing cotton . . . and yet we content ourselves with wriggling along in the old way, exhausting our spirits in unavailing complaints against the Tariff, every day growing poorer when the road to prosperity and wealth lies plain and direct before us [in manufacturing]."[31]

The press for the development of manufacturing to bolster agriculture ebbed and flowed. The state boasted two new plants in 1828, which grew to fourteen within several years, followed by little development at all.[32]

In the late 1830s Georgia Whig leaders joined the national Whig party in its promotion of commercial expansion and business dynamism.[33] Georgia Whigs had begun to hail improved agricultural and industrial development as a means to a balanced economy. When agriculture and industry truly complemented each other, they argued, all southerners could rest assured that the economy would be self-sufficient, that slavery would continue, and that the region would secure its own political survival.[34] They continued to adopt this position through the 1840s. Meanwhile, the depressed state of the economy during the early through mid-forties continued to attract Georgians to the Whig agenda.[35]

Many Georgians, whether or not they called themselves Whigs, came to see the value of the Whig program during these hard times. Town leaders, manufacturers, and planters began to pursue manufacturing ventures in new numbers. Their press toward manufacturing was reinforced by the realization that the growth of manufacturing ultimately promoted southern independence. Accordingly, by the late 1840s, growing numbers of investors poured money into the railroads, large textile mills, and a handful of complete manufacturing towns like Etowah and Griswoldville, to the delight of Whig leaders.[36] The Crisis of 1850 added more political incentive to the manufacturing movement, however small, and secured a clear-cut victory for the Whig party within the state. But by 1852, the party was on the decline. The national party's strong antislavery wing offended many Georgians, and the recent rise of cotton prices lessened interest in manufacturing. These two factors ground the Whig machine to a standstill. By 1856 most Georgia Whigs had joined the Democratic party.[37]

As early as 1828 the predecessors to the Whig party (the Troup party followed by the States Rights party) had taken a proprietary interest in mechanics. In the 1830s the Whig party pundits urged artisans to read the latest newspapers and periodicals devoted to the artisan trades and to study the latest innovations and inventions.[38] In the 1840s Whig newspapers were likening mechanics to their so-called artisan forefathers Benjamin Franklin and Jesus Christ.[39] By the 1850s such esteem was expressed more tangibly. The newest engine in the Augusta firehouse in 1853 was named "The Mechanic."[40]

Seeing itself as the party of upward mobility and commercial expansion, as the party that recognized the contribution of every occupation to the economy, and as the party that encouraged the preservation of an enlightened republican government, the Whigs viewed all men in all classes as important allies who must be promoted and courted.[41] Therefore, the Whigs liked to brag that their party and its principles could be embraced by all men, not just by "aristocrats" as the Democrats claimed.

Following a Whig victory in Richmond County in 1837, the editor of the Whig *Augusta Chronicle* proudly noted that men of all classes voted the ticket, "the merchant, mechanic, and farmer, all lent a helping hand to victory."[42] The Whig party was in a strong position before the 1840 presidential election because Democrat Martin Van Buren had fallen out of favor and the benign Whig standard-bearer, William Harrison, had drummed up widespread support. Georgians attended the Whig convention in Macon in record numbers. Afterwards, the Whigs once again boasted of the diversity of their party's supporters. People bound for the convention formed crowds forty miles outside the city. Newspaper reports described a hitherto unimaginable phenomenon—Whig supporters "wending their way hither, by every possible conveyance, and combining all classes of citizens—planters, mechanics, laborers, merchants, doctors, and lawyers—all uniting in the great struggle to perpetuate American liberty."[43]

Whigs considered mechanics important to the Whig formula because mechanic labor contributed to a balanced economy, especially in the agricultural South. "There is no situation more enviable than that of the American Mechanic," proclaimed the editor of the *Southern Whig* in 1841. By 1846 the editor had begun to praise the mechanic's importance with a specifically southern slant. He urged Georgians to recognize the capacity of the mechanic to liberate the region from the North. "The encouragement of the mechanic arts alone can affect our emancipation from Northern thralldom, and render our country what it was intended to become, the garden-spot of the World."[44]

Thus for Whig leaders, advocating free labor *within* the context of a slave labor economy was a carefully reasoned piece of the Whig platform. Whigs in the state legislature argued likewise. Agriculture, they believed, was bound to prosper *if* mechanics stepped up production to insulate the state from the vagaries of the market. "The day is not far distant when Georgia will assure the high rank nature designed for her to hold in the confederacy," reported the Committee of Manufacturers of the Whig-dominated Georgia legislature in 1847. The committee emphasized the pivotal role of mechanics in this process. "That day will have dawned when her resources shall begin to be fully developed—when an improved agriculture should have resurrected her fields—an invigorated commerce bear her productions to every clime, and the mechanic arts, from innumerable workshops, roll out upon her people, the uncounted streams of wealth." [45]

The promotion of mechanics proved a useful means of critiquing the old agricultural society and the people who perpetuated it. Accordingly, Whig newspapers in Savannah, Macon, and Augusta attacked planters for not supporting the wealth-producing work of free laborers. "No community can ever grow where it is thought more respectable to be a gentle loafer than to get an honest living by the labor of one's own hands," warned the editor of the *Savannah Republican*.[46]

This appreciation of the mechanic extended to legislative acts, like the aforementioned liens, that attempted to obviate mechanics' economic difficulties. Before the rise of the Whigs, Georgia cities had responded to free laborers' economic grievances halfheartedly. The state attempted to defuse the issue by establishing a system of lien laws that legally protected certain groups of mechanics from employers who failed to pay wages. These laws, first passed in 1834, gave an artisan's bill priority over his customer's other bills in all contractual relationships. Any aggrieved artisan had the right to file a claim within three months of not receiving overdue monies and was entitled to pursue a legal suit within twelve months of the claim. Masons and carpenters were the first group of artisans to receive this protection in 1834.

State legislatures during the 1840s, usually Whig-dominated, expanded these laws to include employer-employee wage relations. Under these rules, employers were obliged to give payment of employee wages priority over all other debts. These new lien laws were enacted for steamboat employees on various rivers in 1841, employees of all steam sawmills in 1842, millwrights and builders of machines used in gold-mining in 1845, and machinists in 1852.[47] These occupations represented the kinds of skills that Whigs believed would promote the economic development of the state. The legislature also passed a bill in 1845 that exempted all journeymen mechanics and laborers from garnishment of their wages.[48] Thus the Whig

Party in Georgia, in its desire for southern economic dependence from the North, became an important ally of free laborers.

By contrast, the relationship between the Democratic party and white mechanics in Georgia proved more elusive. The party rarely championed the role of mechanics in southern society openly because the party tended to attract anticommercial agrarians. Yet clearly there was room for mechanics in the Democratic party's agriculturally oriented principles provided mechanics were willing to support the agricultural system as producers. Heir to Jeffersonian democracy, the state's Democratic party had just as much reason to expect some artisan support as the state's Whig party.[49]

Thus, when the Democratic party did on occasion attempt to pursue the mechanic vote, it took a very different tack from that of the Whigs. Democrats chose to emphasize mechanics' exclusion from the middle class. In 1845, Democratic papers in Milledgeville and Monroe argued that townspeople must do their part to encourage the "growth of a class of artisans and mechanics to strengthen their communities."[50]

The state party claimed that most mechanics were impoverished, not because of the slave economy, but because of the encroachment of the railroads. The new transportation system had introduced mass-produced northern- and European-made goods to southern markets at cheaper prices and thereby put mechanics out of work. And there was some truth to this claim. This argument obviously appealed to the traditional craftsman in the upcountry who was surrounded by yeoman farmers who advanced the Democratic platform and were firm in their belief that the iron horse was a monster. It might or might not attract the vote of the urban mechanic who earned his livelihood from the repair of mechanical parts. But it definitely would not attract the vote of the mechanic turned manufacturer who was eager to expand his market and relied on the importation of mass-produced goods for his livelihood.[51]

The principles of master craftsmen did not always fit precisely into either party throughout the 1840s and 1850s. In some instances, mechanics found themselves with one foot in each political camp. In other instances, they found that their political ideas could not be adapted to either party. The difficulty of finding a party that reflected mechanic politics was apparent in 1848 when Athens blacksmith William Talmage, the New Jersey-born shop-owner, slaveholder, and future investor in local manufactures following his long period of itinerancy, was interested enough in the political positions of both parties to take off several days from his shop, board a train headed to a state Democratic party meeting at Stone Mountain on August 14, and then travel to Atlanta a month later to attend the state meeting of the Whig party.[52]

There is some evidence that democratic principles transcended party when the reputations of white mechanics were on the line. When Whig party member Captain William B. Davis, candidate for a Richmond County assembly seat in 1830, discovered that a painter and glazier by the same name also resided in Richmond County, he went to great pains to distinguish himself from the artisan. His actions prompted his opponents to claim that he was too aristocratic to deserve the respect of the valued mechanic population. Voters of all classes, not the least of whom were mechanics, put aside their political differences to vote against Davis in the election. He lost and was subsequently unable to secure elective office until Reconstruction.[53]

In 1840, several weeks before the Whigs' state convention in Macon, thirty-three Newton County mechanics met to pledge their united allegiance to the Whig party and to decide upon their delegates. These mechanics believed that the current national government was at war with their private interests since Martin Van Buren's reelection campaign, in their eyes, was as unprincipled as Van Buren himself. The men hoped that others would heed their opinions.

"We are by profession Mechanics and though our business in life, may be regarded by the aristocracy of the country, as too humble and lowly for our voices to be uttered in discontent, yet we *proclaim ourselves freemen.*" As freemen, they argued, they had every right to advocate their political position. "No matter in whatsoever degree our occupations may be estimated, we have rights equal to the most pampered aristocrat, and having rights, will dare assert them."[54] Their use of this language suggests that these mechanics found themselves in a political quandary. The principles that they espoused were leveling, egalitarian ones, more suitable to the principles of the Jacksonian Democrats than the Whigs to whom they professed their support.[55]

The following statement explains their choice. As "working not speaking men . . . driven to necessity," these mechanics labelled Van Buren and his cronies aristocrats, Federalists, supporters of the Tariff of 1828, would-be abolishers of democratic franchisement, advocates of a large standing army, and "enemies of the South on the subject of slavery." In contrast, they believed Harrison and Tyler would "bring back the government to its original simplicity, purity, and economy" and prove "favorable to a freeman's pay for his labor." The meeting concluded with the unanimous decision that each of the mechanics present would attend the Whig Convention in Macon rather than simply sending a representative.[56]

Their lack of faith in Van Buren's stand on southern issues and his aristocratic notions of representation prompted the Newton County mechanics' commitment to the Whigs. Yet even in defending their choice, they continued to support the democratic principle of limited government—a position enshrined by the Jeffersonian republicans as well as the more recent Democratic party.

The economic status of these Newton County mechanics suggests that these men were committed to these principles—particularly to equality and fair labor—not out of economic necessity but out of deep-rooted belief, for they appear to have been financially comfortable master craftsmen on the whole. At least sixteen of these men were slaveholders in 1840, averaging 4.5 slaves each.[57] Furthermore, the majority of them represented the higher echelon of mechanic trades and wealth. They were solid middle-class citizens despite the disclaimers about their "lowly and humble" status in 1840. Occupational information (available only in 1850) shows that thirteen of these men had continued to work at artisanal labor:

4 carpenters
2 blacksmiths
2 carriagemakers
1 tailor
1 wagoner
1 cabinetmaker
1 manufacturist
1 silversmith

Thus, at least half of these mechanics were slaveholders who worked mostly at traditional trades that sustained the local plantation economy. Seven of the men who had called themselves mechanics in 1840 were landholding and slaveholding farmers in 1850, indicating their upward mobility. Six men held no real estate in 1850, while the remaining fourteen averaged an impressive $1,325 worth of holdings apiece. Most of them were native southerners: thirteen were born in South Carolina or Georgia, three in North Carolina and one in Kentucky. Of the three nonsoutherners, one man came from Connecticut and two from Ireland.

Eleven of the twenty men were town dwellers. At least several of these men were respected community leaders. John Royall, probably a carpenter or master builder since he built the Newton Academy in 1825, had been a state assemblyman in 1836. Frances McCurdy was sheriff in 1844. All were men of moderate wealth. The political positions of Royall and McCurdy were impressive and indicate that the mechanics of this cotton-growing community were held in high esteem.[58]

Despite their moderate wealth and status, these mechanics championed the right to "a freeman's pay for his labor." Yet it is highly unlikely that the majority of these men worked for wages. Indeed, most of them were master craftsmen with employees, slave and free, of their own. In touting "a freeman's pay," they saw no conflict between free labor and slave labor. Presumably the two were compatible as long as free laborers could expect to own or hire slaves themselves.[59]

White mechanics in other places also revealed their allegiance to these kinds of principles. In 1842 two Richmond County representatives in the state legislature proposed to divide Augusta's local government into a city council and a board of aldermen. Voters for the latter would be limited to men with real estate worth at least $1,000 and who paid a city tax of at least $25.[60] "A Mechanic" responded to news of this bill by penning a derisive letter printed in the Whig *Augusta Chronicle*. In it he likened the proposed board of aldermen to a "House of Lords" and called upon mechanics and other Augusta citizens, "as freemen, and strenuous supporters of political liberty and equality," to recognize this "dangerous encroachment upon their civil and political prerogatives."[61]

The bill grew out of a petition presented to the two legislators signed by eighty-nine Augustans, thirty-five of whom were not property-owners. Within several days of its publication, the letter evoked explanatory rejoinders from the two representatives. William Miller, a Whig, apologized profusely for his involvement, promised perpetual remorse, and swore he was not "anti-mechanic." Charles Jenkins, also a Whig, refused to alter his support for the proposed law. Miller's change of heart won him reelection. Jenkins was not so fortunate. Democrats and Whigs united across party lines to prevent his return to office, and the bill was eventually repealed.[62]

Mechanics did not always advance democratic principles, however. The Athens Mechanics Mutual Aid Association (AMMAA) had been established in 1836 by businessmen. Four of the five trustees for the AMMAA, shoemaker Right Rogers, confectioner A. Brydie, cabinetmaker Samuel Frost, and printer John Reynolds, not only pursued their own trades but also ran an auctioneering house together through the 1830s. Frost was elected town commissioner in 1838. Brydie opened the very popular Temperance Coffee House in 1842. Thus, the AMMAA presumably served the trustees' business and political interests at least as well as their moral and intellectual ones.[63]

Soon after the formation of the AMMAA in 1836, the group asked the *Southern Banner* to print the AMMAA Constitution because it felt citizens who were not mechanics were unclear about the organization's purpose. "[A]n impression exists in the minds of some, that it is a trades combination to regulate the prices of work," stated the editor. "This idea they [the AMMAA members] utterly repudiate." The AMMAA felt obliged to prove the members' master mechanic respectability and political authority, even as northern mechanics were challenging their employers and the political system with strikes, unions, and labor parties. "Their object is mutual improvement and they hope through the facilities afforded by the Association to become better mechanics and more useful citizens," assured the editor on the mechanics' behalf.[64]

To this end, the AMMAA members pledged to share their inventions (the organization promised to give all member-inventors a token amount of money for their articles), to bestow their patronage upon each other, and to purchase a library.[65] The organization met once a month in 1836 and 1837 to discuss any topics desired, though they exempted political and religious ones. This rule did not stop the members from debating the merits of capital punishment, imprisonment for debt, and labor-saving machinery. It took the AMMAA seven years to establish its library but the organization finally managed to open one in a room above Dr. Alexander's Drug Store by 1844. "Newspapers and periodicals from all over the U.S." were available free to members and for a fee to nonmembers.[66]

The organization adopted certain strictures in addition to these self-improvement measures that indicate AMMAA membership was intended for established master craftsmen. AMMAA men were required to pay one dollar for admission to the organization and fifty cents per month for ongoing membership. These charges would have effectively eliminated most apprentices and young journeymen from seeking admission to the organization. The AMMAA set other entrance requirements as well, "No person shall be received as a regular member who is not of good moral character and a practical mechanic." The AMMAA even reserved the right to expel members for immoral conduct.[67]

This association, with its successful businessmen leaders, its fees, and its conduct rules, preserved the status of master craftsmen. By holding discussions and establishing a library in a university town, the AMMAA was upholding the value that members placed on learning and knowledge. This underlining emphasis on hierarchy and status, on meritocracy and conservatism, was more reminiscent of Whig party principles, and devoid of any Jeffersonian, let alone Democratic, party tradition.

Yet all indications suggest that the AMMAA voted for Democratic party candidates at election time. Planter-politician Howell Cobb, a Democrat, assiduously courted the elitist AMMAA with gifts of *The American State Papers* and *The Congressional Debates,* as well as other periodicals and books, for the Mechanics' Library during the 1840s.[68] Cobb's electioneering tactics paid off in 1850. Athens resident William Hull wrote to Cobb following his election. "We did a glorious day's work here," Hull gloated, "every mechanic in town came up in solid column." [69]

Mechanics' organizations, whether in the form of mechanics' societies, manual labor schools, trade unions, or mechanic conventions, were as fragmented as mechanics' politics and principles by the 1840s. Each of these types of organizations remained in a rudimentary state throughout the antebellum period. Nearly all were short-lived. The already discussed AMMAA fell into hiatus after 1837 and was not resumed until the early 1840s. Apparently it was unable to attract enough mechanic interest during the hard times of the depression when the monthly fees may have proved too daunting for some.[70] The Newton County Mechanics met only once in preparation for the Whig Convention in 1840.[71] The Augusta Mechanics Society reformed in the mid-1830s, fell apart, and then reformed again in the mid-1840s, only to break apart yet again. The Macon Mechanics Society formed for a few brief years around 1850, only to fade into oblivion. These societies were far less sophisticated than their counterparts in Augusta and Savannah in the 1790s.

One issue drew sustained mechanic interest and even protest throughout much of the antebellum era—the employment of state penitentiary inmates at artisanal work. At the state prison in Milledgeville prisoners were forced to learn a trade in the prison workshops. Inmates made objects like furniture, slave shoes, buckets, bricks, and wagons, and acquired the skills of shoemakers, brickmakers, carpenters, painters, and blacksmiths in the process. The state maintained a penitentiary store outside the prison walls, where these goods were sold to the public, and also put these skilled inmates to work on the renovation of state property.[72]

Not surprisingly, Milledgeville's resident artisans were the first mechanics to protest these arrangements. The prison store goods decreased the market for their own goods, they argued, and reliance on inmate labor for construction work deprived local carpenters of jobs. Improvements on the governor's mansion from 1838 to 1840 were made by twelve carpenters imported from New Haven and New York along with inmate labor. Apparently no local artisans were employed in the lengthy project.[73] Initially, local mechanics received very little support for their position. "The objection that the Penitentiary injures Milledgeville by keeping away mechanics, ought not to avail anything," stated the less than sympathetic *Statesman and Patriot* in 1829. "If mechanics will do good work, on as good terms as those in the institution, they will find encouragement."[74]

Local artisans did not agree. Using republican rhetoric, they claimed that their basic rights as citizens had been usurped by this state policy. These artisans were unwilling to accept a situation that they judged inherently unfair. They clung to their republican defenses by championing equal rights. As one historian has argued, this confrontation was essentially a clash between precapitalist and capitalist traditions.[75]

Once again, however, the effects of the depression in the early 1840s ground mechanic interest in these issues to a halt. Artisans did not resume their arguments against artisan inmates until 1845. That year, the Augusta Mechanics' Society, supported by several other mechanics' societies, sent a petition to the penitentiary to protest skilled prison labor. The petition argued that the state was responsible for releasing "a corps of graduate villains, half skilled and half depraved, in most instances, to perform according to their ability, who will work at reduced prices."[76] The legislature addressed this grievance by sending it to the Committee on the Penitentiary. The committee recommended the abolishment of inmate hard labor to "relieve that large and respectable class of our citizens, the mechanical profession, from competition with penitentiary labor, and that contact with degraded mechanics, which to some extent must occur, so long as we continue annually to turn them out to earn their bread by the trade which serves as a badge of their disgrace." [77]

Despite the committee's conclusion, the elimination of this system did not happen. This protest indicates, however, that mechanics placed great value in preserving the dignity of their work, and by extension, their own worth in this society, although economic motivation was clearly just as significant. A disproportionate number of the prison inmates were marginal southerners—usually immigrants and unskilled or semiskilled wage-earning urban dwellers without property of any kind—by the last two decades of the antebellum years.[78] The mechanics' protest represented established mechanics' efforts to disassociate themselves from a growing group of free laborers with little or no attachment to the traditional values of this slaveholding republic. Thus, the petitions were meant to promote the property-holding master craftsman and his work and to establish his separateness from this new class of prison rabble. Again, however, mechanic protest against prison labor was sporadic and ultimately unsuccessful.

Likewise, trade unions were virtually absent from antebellum Georgia, unlike the border states, and Virginia and Louisiana, where trade union activity actually prevailed. Other than the Augusta butchers who petitioned the state to reduce stall rent in 1829, the brief organization of the Augusta Typographical Society in 1836 (partially in response to national issues and partially to protest the use of black labor in printing shops), and a strike of Central Railroad carpenters and mechanics in Savannah in 1853, white mechanics in Georgia rarely expressed their political and economic grievances as a single entity, let alone through individual trade union activity.[79]

Mechanics' conventions were the most popular form of mechanic organization in the state by the late antebellum era. Yet even the convention movement was short-lived; in addition, the conventions occurred only once a year. Moreover, mechanics' impetus for attending them was not always to share political ideas and economic injustices. These meetings were arranged to coincide with agricultural fairs. White mechanics appreciated the opportunity to demonstrate the latest machines likely to appeal to commercially minded planters and farmers as much as they appreciated the opportunity to attend their own mechanic meetings at these gatherings.

Nevertheless, a mechanics' convention movement in Georgia did occur between 1846 and 1853.[80] It originated with the formation of the Southern Central Agricultural Society. This organization sponsored its first state fair at Stone Mountain in 1846, complete with freak shows, P. T. Barnum acts, and premiums for farmers' tools and artisans' crafts. Mechanics from around the state met there as well.[81] Over the next few years the state fair grew more mechanic- and manufacturing-oriented. By 1848 few agricultural items were even exhibited. Instead, ironworks sent samples of their bar and band iron in use on the railroad and examples of their castings, cotton mills demonstrated the quality of the cloth and yarn produced by their spindles, and coachmakers, furnituremakers and other artisans exhibited their luxury goods. It is clear that profit-minded men had come to recognize that the fair was an ideal place in which to market their new machines and improved devices for that sector of the agricultural community that could afford them – the several thousand wealthy planters and farmers from around the state interested in commercial agriculture.[82]

Besides mechanics' overwhelming recognition of the economic benefits of their participation, they did come to recognize some political benefits as well. By 1851 mechanics had separated themselves from the agricultural branch of the state fair. Though they continued to meet and exhibit with the state's agriculturalists, they now put together their own organization, the State Mechanics' Institute, and chose to conduct separate mechanics' conventions during the evenings of the fair "so as not to interfere with the attendance on the Agricultural Exhibit."[83]

The initiative for the separate Mechanics' Institute seems to have come from Macon mechanic-manufacturers. Their motivation appears to have been twofold. First, these men wanted to bring the annual state fair to Macon to promote their city's modern manufacturing facilities. The Macon mechanic-manufacturers needed the statewide support of mechanics to convince the agriculturalists to move the fair. Thus, the brand-new Mechanics' Institute offered them an ideal lobbying opportunity.

And second, because Macon mechanic-manufacturers experienced a constant need for highly skilled machinists and mechanics and relied heavily on well-paid northern men to fill these jobs, they hoped to organize the state's mechanics in support of an actual Mechanics' Institute (hence the organization's name).[84] Such an institute would produce an indigenous class of white machinists and mechanics, claimed the Macon men. It would create a valuable labor pool for mechanic employers who could then lower wages with the increased labor supply. The actual establishment of the institute never occurred. Like most mechanic-backed organizational efforts, the institute lacked the support of the entire mechanic community and the broader planter community as well. In a society that viewed mechanic work with disdain, there could be little support for educational institutions dedicated to their professional training.[85]

The fair's agriculturalist leaders were more impressed by the offer from Macon city leaders to pay for the fair and the offer from Robert Findlay to build and operate a steam engine to power the mechanical exhibit, than the statewide support of the mechanics, persuading the agriculturalists to move the fair to Macon. In 1851 mechanics, farmers, and planters from across the state gathered in the cotton-belt city to study new steam engines, fertilizers, cotton gins, and other innovations that improved agricultural productivity. Supported by mechanic-manufacturers like Mark Cooper of the Etowah Iron Works, Robert Findlay of Findlay's Iron Works, and Samuel Griswold, the Jones County gin manufacturer, the state fair was held in Macon a second time in 1852.[86] The heyday of the state fair and the Mechanics' Institute had passed by 1853, however, the year Augusta served as site of the state fair. Macon mechanic support—the real impetus behind the annual Mechanics' Institute meetings—declined with the move of the fair, and statewide mechanic interest followed suit.[87]

Mechanic organization in all its forms had proved sporadic over the course of the antebellum period. White mechanic leaders had organized mechanic societies and conventions to meet immediate political or economic needs. Under these conditions artisan organization, let alone an artisanal political consciousness, simply could not be sustained.

In the end, the key reason that white artisans could sustain any measure of class consciousness over the course of the antebellum period rested on the divisive issue of skilled black labor. White mechanics felt their status and their pocketbooks jeopardized by competition with skilled black labor. By the 1840s the existence of skilled blacks concerned nonmechanic southerners as well. Periodically critics had blamed the poverty of the town-dwelling white wage-earner on competition from black mechanics. "I am aware and so must every other inhabitant of the city be," wrote an Augusta man in 1828, "of the difficulty with which every poor mechanic has to encounter, in order to obtain a daily support for himself and his family, and why? Because there are so many slaves in the city who pretend to be mechanics, and who hire their own time from their owners and re-duce the price of jobs so low that it is almost impossible for an honest mechanic to gain a sufficiency to subsist on."[88] A Macon man expressed similar sentiments about the competition between white and black skilled labor in his town in a letter to a friend in 1836.[89] Athens temperance pam-phleteer John Jacobs Flournoy argued in 1838 that employing black me-chanics only served "to cheapen their [white mechanics'] wages at a rate that amounts to a moral and physical impossibility for them . . . to live here and support their families."[90] Expressions like these grew more frequent toward the end of the antebellum period.

During the depressed agricultural years of the early 1840s, some plan-ters sent their slaves into the cities and towns to find work, just as the rail-road was beginning to bring cheap northern-produced goods to local ur-ban markets. Job opportunities for some mechanics were squeezed by this set of events, and while mechanics could not put a halt to capitalism's in-roads, they could protest competition with black mechanics, especially as they watched the numbers of urban blacks rise around them.[91]

In Columbus, for example, the population of urban slaves climbed 111 percent between 1840 and 1850 as cotton planters in the surrounding counties of the newest black belt hired out their bondsmen in the nearby town. In Augusta, an old town with a well-farmed hinterland, and Macon, a stable town supported by the middle Georgia plantation region, the slave populations increased by about 50 percent in a decade's time. Meanwhile, Savannah's slave population grew by 32 percent.[92]

Under this set of economic and demographic constraints, urban white mechanics were inclined to criticize the presence of skilled blacks in the trades. During the late 1840s and early 1850s, as they had throughout the nineteenth century, mechanics in the larger towns of Georgia ob-jected to black competition individually and in groups. They did not forgo their traditional arguments—their assertions of their respectability and the

Table 9. Urban Slave
Population Growth in
Percentages from 1840
to 1850

Savannah	32.8
Augusta	57.8
Macon	46.5
Columbus	111.2
Milledgeville	11.2

dignity of their work—in favor of more strident protest language. Nor did their level of organization reach new heights. Yet they aired their grievances against the competition they experienced with black mechanics with great urgency.

At least one historian has viewed mechanics' opposition to skilled blacks as evidence of growing political power among Georgian artisans. However, a developing sense of class conflict does not seem to have driven mechanics' protests. A heterogeneous group of men of diverse skills, residences, and ambitions, white mechanics in antebellum Georgia rarely joined forces except when immediate economic circumstances compelled them to prioritize their interests as a class over their interests as white male citizens in the slaveholding republic. But these were brief moments, even at the tail end of the antebellum period.[93]

Since Georgia's colonial era, state and local leaders had at least in theory attempted to curb the freedom of skilled blacks to give preference to skilled whites, especially in towns, and this tradition continued through the antebellum period. The majority of the local ordinances and laws enacted did not explicitly challenge local slaveholders' and employers' reliance on black mechanics. Usually town governments preferred to answer white mechanics' complaints by setting up a tax system whereby only slaves and free blacks whose owners or guardians had registered them with the city and had paid the required fee were free to live in the city and hire themselves out. Obviously these laws did more toward the policing of the urban black population than toward alleviating black competition in the mechanic trades.[94]

In 1845 the state legislature passed a law prohibiting black mechanics and masons–slave or free–"from making contracts for the Erection of any Building, or for the repair of any building." [95] This measure was one of appeasement only. Owners of slave mechanics and slave masons could still expect to hire out their property; they would simply have to make these arrangements themselves instead of leaving them up to their slaves. This law most seriously affected free black contractors who could no longer expect to work independently, but must reduce themselves to the status of wage-earners under the authority of white employers.

The issue of black mechanic competition did not die down with the passage of this law. Four years later, for example, Macon mechanics organized the Mechanics' Society of Macon (MSM). Its members planned to promote the use of machinery and to improve local architecture. They also hoped to establish a public library through a fund drive. In addition to these worthy goals, the MSM discouraged the hiring of black mechanics because they worked for less pay than white mechanics and deprived them of work. [96]

This ambivalence about black mechanics became a statewide issue in 1851 when four hundred delegates from mechanics' societies across the state, along with two thousand more supporters, assembled near Atlanta on the propitious occasion of the Fourth of July for the first meeting of the Georgia Mechanics' Convention. [97] After quickly dispensing with several issues unanimously agreed upon, the delegates raised before the gathering the issue of black mechanics. The hitherto calm meeting took an animated turn as attendees listed a series of societal ills caused by the "pernicious influence" of black mechanics on the slave population as a whole. "A few urban negro mechanics can do more practical injury to the institution of slavery . . . than all the ultra abolitionists of the country." Mechanic labor, they contended, promoted "mental development" among black men by encouraging them to learn to read and write. This knowledge would ultimately induce the "dissipation and depravity" of the black race. To avoid the overthrow of slavery as an institution, the delegates argued, Negro men must not be trained in the mechanic arts.

The convention-goers then launched a second attack against black mechanics. The delegates blamed the region's lack of manufacturing and continued dependence on northern goods on the existence of black mechanic labor. "[It] is a source of great dissatisfaction to the Mechanic interest– prejudicial to southern youths engaged in industrial pursuits–and it is believed to be inexpedient, unwise, and injurious to all classes of the community." The group claimed that the use of Negro mechanics created a shortage of white mechanics because few native men were interested in an occupation degraded by the presence of black labor. "Educated young men of the South can seldom be found who will engage in pursuits which will lead them into professional competition with persons of inferior morals and intellect." Following this discussion, the delegates passed a resolution against training Negro mechanics in the trades. Some opposition was raised against it but was "rejected by an overwhelming vote."

In their preamble to this resolution, the delegates had identified themselves "as Mechanics and Southern Men by birth or by adoption, and as slaveholders." With this statement, they indicated they were aligning themselves with all slaveowning southerners. Their first argument against training skilled black labor was based on the threat they believed these men posed to slavery.

The second argument in the resolution indicates that the mechanics were theoretically willing to eliminate slave labor from the mechanic trades— at an obvious cost to those slaveholding mechanics among them who depended on the work of their skilled slaves and at the risk of alienating nonmechanic slaveholders as well. The enthusiasm for this resolution shows the fear of competition from black artisans, slave and free, who undercut the value of skilled white men's work. Thus these white mechanics found themselves negotiating difficult terrain. They sought to eliminate competition from skilled Negro mechanics at the same time that they demonstrated their commitment to slavery.[98]

The *Rome Southerner* was incensed by the declarations against black mechanics made at the convention under the guise of dignifying the trades. The editor "called upon slaveholders to look to their rights, as this action was taken to mean an attack upon them, for if driven from one field, they will drive them [slaves] from all." The diatribe ended with this pronouncement on the mechanics' position on black mechanics, "We denounce it as part of a general system of attack upon Southern institutions and rights."[99]

Two years later, in the *Columbus Times,* "Virgil" claimed that the statewide mechanics' movement offered the "strongest evidences of the success of the *abolitionists.*" Mechanics' protests against black mechanic labor "would not have entered mechanics' heads without abolitionists' far-reaching influence." If Georgians were not careful, "Virgil" warned ominously, abolitionists' "inroads" would spread from mechanics to others.[100] This criticism seemed to have brought a halt to most white mechanics' protests against skilled black labor throughout the state. Henceforth white mechanics found themselves working to preserve their place in this slave-holding society rather than voicing their grievances.

At the insistence of master craftsmen and planters alike, white mechan-ics had been divided into two classes—masters and journeymen, slave-holders and nonslaveholders—over the course of the antebellum era. At the same time they found themselves debating each other and slaveholders and planters over white skilled wage-earners' competition with skilled free blacks and slaves.

This reality was truest in Savannah where these conflicts reached new heights by the 1850s and were exacerbated by a growing foreign popu-lation. In theory, political participation should have offered mechanics an opportunity to defend their concerns, profit from a collective political voice, and distance themselves from their black competition. In practice, white mechanics in Savannah, like white mechanics throughout Georgia, understood that the politics of slavery contributed both to their increas-ingly divergent economic interests as white mechanics and to their lim-ited opportunities for political expression. These truths served to moderate their differences with the prevailing social order and exacerbate their dif-ferences with each other.

While mechanics comprised about 10 percent of the white male work-ing population in Georgia by 1860, their numbers were even more signifi-cant in the city of Savannah.[101] By 1850, 31 percent of the 3,100 white male inhabitants listed in the U.S. census with an occupation were skilled me-chanics or artisans.[102] These men resided in the largest export center south of Charleston. In the late antebellum period, the now flourishing city had nearly doubled its population, from 11,212 residents in 1840 to 22,292 in 1860, the majority of whom were white.

As the main shipping point for all the state's foreign exports, Savannah, although it had undergone earlier hard times, prospered in the shadow of King Cotton at midcentury. Because of its primacy as a commercial and transport center, the city still attracted many planters, factors, agents, merchants, and shopkeepers, as well as mechanics and laborers.[103] The businesses that developed within its borders supported these functions. Banking, insurance, steamboat, canal, and railroad companies, along with

Table 10. Population of Savannah, 1840–1860

Year	White (%)	Free Black (%)	Slave (%)	Total
1840	5,888 (52)	632 (6)	4,692 (42)	11,212
1850	8,395 (55)	686 (5)	6,231 (40)	15,312
1860	13,875 (62)	705 (3)	7,712 (35)	22,292

Note: Percentages rounded to nearest whole number.
Sources: Enumeration of the Inhabitants and Statistics of the U.S., Sixth Census; The Seventh Census of the U.S., 1850; Population of the U.S. in 1860.

cotton presses, brick-making establishments, steam rice-mills, sawmills, planing mills, and iron foundries predominated. Workshop and factory production, by contrast, was of secondary importance.[104]

With the renewed growth of the port of Savannah, merchants with their business connections in New York and London firms came to displace increasing numbers of master craftsmen in many traditional trades, from silversmithing and furniture-making to shoe-making. The city's elite and planters in the surrounding lowcountry had long preferred the imported styles artisans had copied and merchants had offered for sale.[105] By the 1830s and 1840s, less well-heeled Savannahians as well as the elite could afford textiles, glassware, silver, and furniture mass-produced elsewhere. Savannah master craftsmen with enough capital or credit transformed themselves into merchants and retailers; others became local agents for northern firms.[106]

David B. Nichols's experience was quite typical of this transformation from artisan to merchant. Born in Danbury, Connecticut, in 1791, Nichols first advertised his abilities as a watchmaker and repairer in Savannah in 1817. Over the next forty years, he sold gold and silver watches, jewelry, and plateware purchased from New York and Paris in his Savannah shop. By the 1830s, he owned slaves, hired an employee to manage the store in his absence, and invested in the Central Railroad and Banking Company of Georgia. At his death, his estate was valued at a respectable $30,000.[107]

But most Savannah artisans were far less fortunate than Nichols by the late antebellum period. In many cases, their lives were circumscribed by the ever-present search for work. Of the twenty-four cabinetmakers listed as Savannah residents in the 1850 U.S. Census, only five remained residents of the city ten years later, according to the 1860 census. And only one of these five men owned a shop of his own at that time, able to do so presumably because he had come to assume the occupation of undertaker as well as cabinetmaker in a city where yellow fever and other diseases proved fatal to a number of residents each fall. Of the nineteen cabinet-makers who left Savannah sometime between 1850 or 1860 only one, Robert N. Adams, a native Georgian, could be found elsewhere; he had relocated to the state capital of Milledgeville.[108]

As the case of the cabinetmakers suggests, artisanal opportunities in Savannah in the late antebellum era were mercurial at best. But the traditional crafts were not the only occupations in flux. Even mechanics with engineering and machinery knowledge more often than not found themselves facing hard times despite the eagerness with which the city embraced steam engines, presses, and the iron horse. English-born William Harris Garland, a blacksmith and engineer, began his career as a wage-earning craftsman in 1832. By 1835, he had secured employment on a steamship that plied the waters of the Savannah River, leaving behind his wife in Charleston, and his mother and several other relatives in Beaufort. Garland spent most of the next thirty-five years in similar fashion, signing on for wage-work that rarely lasted more than a few weeks or months at a time. Although he managed to settle in Savannah from 1846 to 1853, working alternately as a mechanic for the railroad and as a blacksmith, he spent the remainder of the antebellum years as an impoverished itinerant, barely able to support himself, let alone his wife and child or extended family.[109]

The circumstances that pinned Garland and other mechanics like him to such poverty in a city experiencing rising prosperity turned on an important set of realities over which these men had little control. White mechanics sought work in a lowcountry economy based on staple-crop production and a slave labor force. This regional emphasis on staple crops had produced urban centers like Charleston and Darien as well as Savannah, where the marketing and transportation sectors of the economy flourished, while the manufacturing and industrial sectors did not.[110]

This structural situation had a profound impact on local demand for mechanics across their diverse trades and skills. The maturation of the staple economy had encouraged new measures of mechanical proficiency, which in turn had produced tools, equipment, and machinery for agricultural households, plantations, sawmills, and gins in the region. But by the late antebellum era, much of this material (like the consumer goods artisans had once crafted) was mass-produced in northern industries and shipped cheaply to southern ports. Mechanics were needed to install and repair this machinery but not to produce it, which placed important limits on demand for their skills.[111]

White mechanics like Garland were caught between a rock and a hard place within this economy. Their work enabled Savannahians to incorporate some important and innovative developments in antebellum technology into the local economy. Yet with the exception of the railroad, steam, and sawmill industries, residents were slow to embrace these developments in comparison to other regional economies. Garland's multiple skills as a boilermaker and steam engine operator and repairer and a blacksmith certainly were useful in an urban center like Savannah.[112] But in the wake of the national depressions of the late 1830s and early 1840s, Savannah was filled with mechanics from other parts of the country and Europe eager to receive wages for servicing the steamboats, trains, and sawmills that made commercial exchange possible. Garland had to compete for engineering work with other itinerant white mechanics like himself. He may even have competed with a few slave and free black mechanics as well.

Both free and slave labor contributed to the commercial success and economic growth Savannah experienced throughout the late antebellum era. Skilled and unskilled slave labor, like free labor, was utilized in virtually every sector of the city economy. Slaves represented roughly four out of every ten city dwellers during the twenty-five years that preceded the Civil War. Although many Savannah slaves were employed as domestic servants in a city known for its lavish entertainment and conspicuous consumption, many others worked as laborers, skilled workers and artisans. Slaves in the work force were either hired out by their owner or allowed to hire out their own time. This latter arrangement was clearly the most desirable from the slaves' vantage point for it ensured them the greatest number of personal freedoms, including the opportunity to live away from their masters and to choose their own employers.[113] Plantation owners throughout lowcountry Georgia and Savannah residents were quick to hire out their skilled slaves in the city, especially during slow parts of the agricultural year. The planter George Kollock, for example, who owned seventy-six slaves, hired out eight of his skilled bondsmen to a Savannah brickyard, and allowed his slave carpenter to hire out his own time in 1846.[114]

Many slaves were hired out to large firms, especially those invested in transportation development and maintenance, such as the Central Railroad, which had established a line between Savannah and Macon, and for a time the Brunswick and Altamaha Canal Company.[115] The steam rice-mills generally employed slave labor while the iron foundries generally employed whites. The sawmills employed both whites and blacks, although the laborers at one of the largest sawmills, the Savannah Steam Saw Mill, were largely slaves.[116] White carpenters and builders also used a combination of their own slave hands and hired slaves to meet their contracts.[117]

While skilled and unskilled slave laborers were especially visible throughout most sectors of the Savannah economy, skilled and unskilled free blacks also played an important, if less immediately obvious, role in the city workforce. While some historians have suggested that urban free blacks in the slave South were restricted to principally unskilled jobs, evidence from the 1848 Savannah Register of Free Persons of Color as well as the 1860 U.S. Census suggests a more complicated picture. Although few free blacks enumerated for the register and the census worked in luxury trades—the 1848 register, for example, listed only one free black cabinetmaker—significant numbers were clustered in skilled crafts in general. The 1848 register contained occupations for 94 free black men. Sixty-two (or 66 percent) identified themselves as craftsmen, not quite half of whom were carpenters, and roughly 40 percent were evenly divided among the occupations of coopering, bricklaying, masonry, and tailoring.[118] The 1860 U.S. Census contained occupations for 179 free black men. Sixty-eight (or 38 percent) identified themselves as craftsmen, about a quarter of whom worked as carpenters and another quarter as brickmakers.[119]

As these statistics suggest, in certain key occupations in Savannah, white journeyman artisans and mechanics and apprentices worked side by side with slave and free black artisans. Although white mechanics often fought the presence of black labor in their trades, such close contact must have forged some significant personal relationships across racial barriers despite the inherent competition.[120] That such bonds existed is apparent in the case of Henry Forsyth, a white journeyman employed in the cabinet-making workshop of Isaac Morrell. Forsyth persuaded Morrell's slave George to locate Morrell's key to his cashbox. Together, Forsyth and George apparently absconded with its contents of $118, George taking $87 and Forsyth the remaining $31. The two headed to Augusta where they were captured and Forsyth tried. That they split the money in this fashion and that George chose to flee with Forsyth rather than head northward alone toward freedom suggests that their relationship may have hinged more on friendship and mutual advantage, given their shared experience as skilled workers in their employer's shop, than on an imposed racial hierarchy in which whites assumed and acted upon their alleged racial privilege.[121]

As scholars Betty Wood and Timothy J. Lockley have amply demonstrated, white Savannah nonslaveholders and slaves and free blacks frequently formed relationships across the color line to engage in informal economies of trade deemed illegal by the city council. Most Savannahians knew that poor whites, including wage-earning mechanics, bought goods that slaves had stolen from their masters. The Chatham County Grand Jury often condemned the practice of white persons buying cotton, iron, and other pilfered articles from slaves.[122] Most Savannahians also knew that nonslaveholding whites ran dram shops in the rougher wards frequented by white workingmen as well as slaves and free blacks, despite local law forbidding it. Fearful that such practices were encouraging cross-racial bonds between nonslaveholding whites and blacks, the city elite formed the Savannah River Anti-Slave Traffick Association in November 1846 to restrict this trade. The city's slaveowners believed nonslaveholding whites were encouraging slaves to steal liquor from their masters as recompense "for the fruits of their own labors" and regarded slaveowners and overseers as "unjust oppressors."[123]

Why men like Henry Forsyth, the journeyman cabinetmaker, felt they had little to lose in associating with slaves and partaking in criminal activity is obvious. What is perhaps less clear is why men like William Garland, the impoverished blacksmith and engineer, did not. Yet a closer look at Garland's circumstances highlights another way in which Savannah mechanics were divided. Though he could in no way afford to own or hire slaves himself, Garland's Beaufort kin asked him to look after several slaves they had sent to Savannah to hire themselves out. Garland's duties on behalf of these slaves were manifold, and included securing their travel passes and bailing them out of jail or harm's way if they went astray.[124] His charges were those of a quasi-master and slaveholder, while Henry Forsyth, in contrast, probably never benefited in any such fashion from this alleged privilege of whiteness.

Importation, mass production, growing numbers of migrant white mechanics, the availability of slave and free black skilled labor, and the nature of the slave economy offer sound structural explanations for the lack of upward mobility that white mechanics like Forsyth encountered in the late antebellum period. These explanations also help explain why nonslaveholding white workingmen cooperated with slave and free black laborers both inside and outside the workshop. Such cooperation, however, quickly earned white mechanics the enmity of "respectable whites." By the end of the antebellum era, itinerant wage-earning white mechanics in particular had earned a bad reputation for themselves.[125] Instead of acknowledging the multiple factors that undercut white mechanics' opportunities and encouraged their relationships with blacks, prospective employers and whites in general castigated impoverished wage-earners as "ne'er-do-wells" whose lack of industry, temperance, and ambition lay at the root of their misfortune. This lack of respect for these new laboring men only exacerbated the growing distance between masters turned merchants and journeymen wage-earners. While many successful master craftsmen came to label themselves and be identified with the urban middle class of shopkeepers, merchants, and professionals, journeymen, especially migrant ones, were viewed as part of an untrustworthy, even dangerous population.

These differences were exacerbated by the increasingly ethnic composition—largely Irish—of the urban population in the oldest cities in Georgia. By 1848, two out of every five adult white males in Savannah were foreign immigrants. By 1860, half of Savannah's adult white population was foreign-born. More than a third of these new inhabitants worked as laborers, while slightly less than a third were skilled men who worked for the railroad and in the construction trades.[126] Only about 7 percent of these immigrants were slaveholders.[127] In Augusta, where white wage-earners outnumbered merchants and professionals by 1850, immigrants comprised more than a third of all laborers by 1860.[128]

Smaller inland urban centers like Macon and Athens did not experience such a dramatic influx of foreign immigrants. In Macon, a manufacturing town desperate for skilled machinists and mechanics, foreign-born male household heads numbered 20 percent of all male household heads by

1860. Only thirty-seven of these immigrants (18 percent) were laborers, eighty-three (42 percent) were skilled men, and the remaining seventy-nine (40 percent) were professionals or proprietors. Moreover, two-thirds of all white male household heads in Macon were southern-born (almost half from Georgia), while one out of ten white male household heads was northern-born.[129] In upcountry Athens and surrounding Clarke County, skilled foreigners comprised less than 10 percent of the population in 1850 and skilled northern-born men about 10 percent, leaving skilled native southerners the overwhelming majority of the mechanic population, a reality that mirrored the nativity patterns of the white population as a whole. These percentages remained virtually unchanged a decade later.[130] To the west, in the fledgling city of Atlanta, a full 90 percent of the white male population (which was the majority population by far) was southern-born between 1850 and 1860.[131]

In contrast to the interior of Georgia, the presence of so many immigrants in Savannah and Augusta added a new twist to the question of free labor's place in a slave labor society. The presence of this foreign-born population had the effect of bringing the issue of free labor in this slave labor society into sharper relief for the residents in these two key cities.[132]

The majority of immigrants who made Georgia their new home in the late antebellum era worked at semiskilled and unskilled labor. Unlike the artisanal class, these men lacked the skills and the connections to establish shops and achieve much upward mobility. Their low incomes prevented them from participating in the slave economy as slave owners or slave hirers. By contrast, one in three Augusta master craftsmen owned an average of five slaves apiece in 1840, and nearly one in two Athens master craftsmen owned an average of 6.5 slaves apiece in 1850. The economic and cultural differences that separated established craftsmen from unskilled and semiskilled immigrant wage-earners, not the least of which was this participation in the slave labor economy, compelled these craftsmen to make virtually no effort to include immigrant wage-earners in their organizations and societies, let alone in their political and social perspectives.[133]

Nowhere was this reality truer than in Savannah, where free white immigrants in the 1840s and 1850s had an especially significant impact on the nature of work. By 1860, about half of the adult white male population was foreign-born; the vast majority of these immigrants were Irish. Only a small proportion of Irish men actually worked as mechanics and artisans;

the majority of Irish men and women were congregated in unskilled labor.[134] Native white southerners' lack of respect for these Irish, and the presence of only a few Irish in the skilled workforce, only reinforced their opinion that poor white wage-earners and would-be mechanics, because they allegedly lacked a strong work ethic and moral character, brought their difficulties upon themselves.

A strong collective identity might have enabled wage-earning mechanics to combat these stereotypes and to air their grievances before the public, especially in a city as large as Savannah. But job competition with black artisans along with prevailing ethnic and class stereotypes made securing a collective voice exceedingly difficult. Since the eighteenth century, white artisans in Savannah had periodically petitioned city council to outlaw skilled blacks in certain trades and had met with moderate success. By the 1840s, all Savannah slaves, except house servants, employed by anyone other than their owner were required to wear badges purchased from the city. Slave cabinetmakers, caulkers, bricklayers, blacksmiths, tailors, barbers, and butchers paid $10.56 a year, while slave coopers, painters, sawyers, pilots, fishermen, boatmen, and grass cutters paid $8.56 for these required badges. Slaves with badges could work where they wished; slaves caught working without badges received 39 lashes, unless the slave's owner paid a fine.[135]

The intent of the badges, from the white mechanics' point of view, was to discourage slaves from practicing artisanal trades, given the high cost of the badge. But this strategy backfired, for by 1860 as many as half the adult male slaves in Savannah had bought badges or had badges purchased for them, with revenue from badge costs totaling almost $10,000.[136] Although these badges were intended in part to limit slave entrée into certain crafts and reflected City Council's desire to appease the white mechanics, the fact that so many slaves or their owners paid for these badges indicates not only that the impact of this legislation in terms of restricting black labor was nominal at best but also that slave artisanal labor was ubiquitous.

White slaveholding society was exceedingly ambivalent about the place of white skilled workers in the South. This ambivalence was omnipresent. On one hand, white slaveholders fearful about how white workers would cast their ballots recognized that they must maintain a distinction between the kinds of work nonslaveholding whites performed and the kinds of work slaves and free blacks performed. Not to respect such distinctions might open the door to serious class differences. On the other hand, it was not in their best interests as slaveholders to strictly limit the kinds of work slaves were allowed to do.

The maturation of Georgia's cotton economy and the penetration of the market had altered the number and kinds of opportunities available to whites in Georgia by the 1850s. Wealth was increasingly concentrated in the hands of a small group of elite planters, merchants, and manufacturers. While some 50,000 farms were spread throughout the state in 1860, only 3,500 of them included more than five hundred improved acres. Twenty percent of all household heads owned 90 percent of the state's slaves, while nearly two-thirds of white households owned none.[137] This changing world affected all Georgians but was probably felt most intensely by newly arrived wage-earners, especially foreigners, in the largest Georgia cities.[138]

Throughout the antebellum era the slave economy had remained open enough to allow a bit of social mobility. Most master mechanics had owned slaves or anticipated owning slaves and therefore considered themselves members of the slaveholding class. While all white men, mechanics or otherwise, did not share equally in the wealth available in this slaveholding republic, they did share in the benefits of the slave system. Many native white men anticipated buying slaves or at least hiring slave labor at some point during their lives, regardless of diminishing economic opportunities. This expectation of their participation in the slave economy, regardless of reality, reinforced their sense of themselves as southerners and slaveholders in this society.[139]

This was less true for newly arrived mechanics with limited skills, little capital, and few connections, especially by the 1850s. From the early republic through the 1850s, the division between nonslaveholding and slaveholding mechanics was never overt enough to split the mechanic community into two *organized* classes of poor wage-earners and comfortable businessmen. The expectations of upward mobility—mobility that included participation in the slave economy as slaveholders—had always intervened, even during the political tensions of the late antebellum era.

Newly arrived mechanics who were not master craftsmen, who were simply wage-earners, especially immigrants, experienced little hope of inclusion among the slaveholding class by the late 1850s, especially as slave prices soared. Although master mechanics had managed to avert class division and broader social division throughout the first half of the century, these realities suggest that with or without the interruption of the Civil War, a growing class of white wage-earners, many of whom were immigrants in the largest Georgia cities, eventually might have challenged the use of skilled black mechanics in a more sustained and strenuous fashion. That these men would have actually opposed slavery, however, remains unlikely.

White artisans in Georgia between 1789 and 1860, like their counterparts in the largest cities of the North and Europe, constructed a series of collective social and political identities for themselves as craftsmen. Because they lived in an agricultural slave labor economy their identities, however, differed fundamentally from their skilled brethren elsewhere. These identities experienced continual alteration as subsequent generations of artisans responded to the changing structural realities of the slaveholding economy.

Southern historians as a whole have paid little attention to white artisans. Yet they may need to cast their net a little more widely. The dynamic developments of the Georgia economy over the course of the antebellum period not only shaped the way artisans constructed their identities but the kinds of political debates they formulated and the nature of their social relations as well. The spread of cotton across Georgia allowed many men, including artisans, to transform themselves into planters and businessmen. This relatively fluid society, dictated by place and time, produced a host of self-made men reminiscent of Margaret Mitchell's fictional character Gerald O'Hara.

Southern white men's shared belief that their political and social independence rested on black slaves' dependence, along with their belief that the availability of ample economic opportunity leveled many social inequalities, served to unite white men, at least in theory, across their many differences. This system of beliefs served to diffuse potentially explosive class differences throughout the antebellum era and proved a powerful antidote to sustained outbreaks of social and political tension between whites. Artisans in Georgia, in their bid to be self-made men, not only embraced this belief system but rejected a uniform class-conscious identity for themselves. Like artisans in free labor economies, artisans in Georgia constructed multiple social and political identities for themselves, in this case as craftsmen, southerners, and slaveholders, throughout the antebellum era.

Notes

Introduction

1. I have used the terms *artisan, craftsman,* and *mechanic* interchangeably throughout this book. However, the term *artisan* was most popular in the seventeenth and eighteenth centuries, the term *craftsman* from the eighteenth century onward, and the term *mechanic* from the late eighteenth century through the first half of the nineteenth century. The term *mechanic* was used almost exclusively in Georgia throughout the period covered here. For a brief history of this usage see Thomas J. Schlereth, "Artisans and Craftsmen," 37.

2. Daniel R. Hundley, *Social Relations in Our Southern States,* 120.

3. Carl Bridenbaugh, *The Colonial Craftsman,* 15. This position originates from assumptions made about the colonial South. See Jean B. Russo, "Self-Sufficiency and Local Exchange," 389–93, for an excellent review of this work.

4. Marcus Wilson Jernegan, *Laboring and Dependent Classes;* Richard B. Morris, *Government and Labor;* David W. Galenson, "White Servitude," 40–41.

5. Charles G. Steffan, *Mechanics of Baltimore,* and Tina Sheller, "Artisans in Baltimore Politics."

6. Jean B. Russo, *Free Workers;* Christine Daniels, "'Wanted: A Blacksmith,'" 743–67.

7. Richard Walsh, *Charleston's Sons of Liberty;* Johanna Miller Lewis, *Artisans in the North Carolina Backcountry.*

8. Ulrich B. Phillips, ed. *Plantation and Frontier,* vol. 2 of *A Documentary History of American Industrial Society,* John R. Commons et al., eds., 347–79; Catherine W. Bishir, "Proper Good Nice and Workmanlike Manner," 48–129.

9. Richard B. Morris, "Labor Militancy in the Old South," pp. 32–36; Herbert Aptheker, *The Labor Movement in the South during Slavery.*

10. Fred Siegel, "Artisans and Immigrants," 221–30; Ira Berlin and Herbert G. Gutman, "Natives and Immigrants," 1175–1200; Michael P. Johnson and James L. Roark, *Black Masters.*

1. Planters in the Making

1. Virginia Steele Wood and Ralph Van Wood, eds., *Journal,* 1–2.

2. To find similarities between the lower South and the development of western frontiers, see Richard C. Wade, *Urban Frontier;* David G. McComb, *Houston.* Joyce Chaplin develops this theme throughout *Anxious Pursuit.*

3. Trevor R. Reese, ed., *Clamorous Malcontents;* Harvey H. Jackson and Phinizy Spalding, *Forty Years of Diversity;* Harold E. Davis, *The Fledgling Province.*

4. Kenneth Coleman, ed., *History of Georgia,* 54.

5. Harvey H. Jackson, "Georgia Whiggery: The Origins and Effects of a Many-Faceted Movement," in *Forty Years of Diversity,* ed. Jackson and Spalding, 251–73.

6. Sylvia R. Frey, *Water from the Rock,* 219–42.

7. Betty Wood, *Slavery in Colonial Georgia,* 131–34.

8. Wood, *Slavery in Colonial Georgia,* 131–34.

9. Wood, *Slavery in Colonial Georgia,* 133, 135, 199.

10. *Return of the Whole Number of Persons Within the Several Districts of the United States.*

11. Lewis Cecil Gray, *History of Agriculture,* vol. 2, 682–86.

12. Donald B. Dodd and Wynelle S. Dodd, *Historical Statistics,* 18–21.

13. Rachel N. Klein, *Unification of a Slave State.*

14. Dodd and Dodd, *Historical Statistics,* 18–21.

15. Dodd and Dodd, *Historical Statistics,* 19, 20.

16. Advertisements from the *Augusta Chronicle* (hereafter *AC*), Sept. 3, 1792; Feb. 16, 1793; the *Augusta Herald,* May 5, 1820; and the *Georgia State Gazette,* Jan. 24, 1789.

17. *AC,* Oct. 19, 1799.

18. George Barton Cutten, *Silversmiths of Georgia,* 96–97.

19. Will M. Theus, *Savannah Furniture, 1735–1825,* 43–69.

20. Eighteen were European-born, eleven New England-born, eight mid-Atlantic-born, and the remaining six Maryland- and Carolina-born. Based on quantification of biographies in Cutten, *Silversmiths of Georgia.*

21. *AC,* Oct. 19, 1799.

22. Wood and Wood, eds., *Journal,* 56. King also mentioned the deaths of the following artisans who resided in his village as well as their nativities: Robert Shankin, a bricklayer from Ireland, William Roberts, a blacksmith, and Gill, a carpenter from New Jersey, as well as Thomas McFall, a carpenter from Connecticut, 95, 97, 109, 110.

23. Mrs. Paschal M. Strong Jr., "Glimpses of Savannah," 28.

24. Wood and Wood, eds., *Journal,* 1–19.

25. *AC,* Dec. 19, 1798.

26. Robert Scott Davis Jr., "The Georgia Buhr Stone Industry."

27. For discussions of preindustrial staple regions and their attendant urban systems see Joseph A. Ernst and H. Roy Merrens, "Camden's turrets," 572–74; Carville A. Earle and Ronald Hoffman, "Staple Crops and Urban Development," 7–9, 64–67.

28. Douglass C. North, *Economic Growth of the United States*, 17; *Second Census of the United States.*

29. John C. Fitzpatrick, ed., *Diaries of George Washington*, vol. 4, 178; J. B. Dunlop, "A Scotsman Visits Georgia," 261; John Mellish, *Travels in the United States of America*, vol. 1, 27.

30. Earle and Hoffman, "Staple Crops and Urban Development," 64–67.

31. Jacob M. Price, "Economic Function," 123–86.

32. Strong, "Glimpses of Savannah," 26–35; Dunlop, "A Scotsman Visits Georgia," 259–65.

33. *Second Census of the United States*, 4N.

34. Betty Wood, *Slavery in Colonial Georgia, passim.*

35. Allan Kulikoff, "Uprooted Peoples," 143–71; Donald Wax, "New Negroes Are Always in Demand," 207–9, 216–18.

36. Allen R. Pred, *Urban Growth and the Circulation of Information*, 128–31. Also see Elizabeth Fox-Genovese, *Within the Plantation Household*, ch. 1; Eugene D. Genovese, *Political Economy of Slavery*, ch. 7; Roberta Balstad Miller, *City and Hinterland*, 5–7, 151–59.

37. Strong, "Glimpses of Savannah," 26–35; Dunlop, "A Scotsman Visits Georgia," 260–61; Lee Soltow and Aubrey C. Land, "Housing and Social Standing in Georgia, 1798," 448–58; Earle and Hoffman, "Staple Crops and Urban Development," 66.

38. Phinizy Spalding, *Oglethorpe in America*, 22–23; Edward J. Cashin, *Colonial Augusta*, 42–43, 117–19; Charles Colcock Jones Jr., *Memorial History of Augusta*, 25.

39. Naturalist William Bartram, who visited Augusta during his trek through the southeast in the 1770s, predicted the town would be a major city some day. "The site of Augusta is perhaps the most delightful and eligible of any for a city in Georgia. . . . [T]hus seated at the head of navigation . . . [it] commands the trade and commerce of vast fruitful regions above it, and from every side to a great distance; and I do not hesitate to pronounce as my opinion, will very soon become the metropolis of Georgia." Mark Van Doren, ed., *Travels of William Bartram*, 53.

40. George Rockingham Gilmer, *Sketches of the First Settlers*, 5–9; Cashin, *Colonial Augusta*, 121–23; Jones, *Memorial History of Augusta*, 132–34.

41. Dodd and Dodd, *Historical Statistics*, 18–21.

42. Jones, *Memorial History of Augusta*, 140.

43. Ibid., 148; James C. Bonner, *History of Georgia Agriculture*, 32.

44. Population figure for 1790 is the estimate of Edward J. Cashin, in *The Story of Augusta,* i. Richmond County census records for 1790 are no longer extant. *Second Census of the United States,* 2N.

45. Quoted in John Donald Wade, *Longstreet,* 17. In a decision reached by the Richmond County Superior Court in 1800, the grand jury declared that cotton was now the principal staple of Georgia (Jones, *Memorial History of Augusta,* 165).

46. Jones, *Memorial History of Augusta,* 144–48.

47. Bruce Laurie, *Artisans into Workers,* 36, 50.

48. Percentages derived from tabulation of artisans identified in Augusta and Savannah in the research files, Museum of Early Southern Decorative Arts, Winston-Salem, N.C. (hereafter MESDA Research Files), Chatham County and Richmond County, between 1790 and 1820.

49. Jones, *Memorial History of Augusta,* 145.

50. MESDA Research Files, Richmond County; *AC,* Oct. 8, 1813.

51. See Philip D. Morgan, "Black Society in the Lowcountry," 140–41; Kulikoff, "Uprooted Peoples," 162–63; and Julia Floyd Smith, *Slavery and Rice Culture, passim.*

52. *Second Census of the United States,* 2.

53. *AC,* Feb. 18, 1792; *Georgia State Gazette,* Dec. 2, 1786; Telamon Cuyler Collection, Richmond County, box 36, Hargrett Library, University of Georgia; A. B. Longstreet, *Georgia Scenes,* 97–105.

54. *Georgia Gazette,* Apr. 9, 1796; *Columbian Museum,* Feb. 14, 1800; Strong, "Glimpses of Savannah," 28–29; David R. Goldfield, "The Business of Health Planning in the Old South," 561–62.

55. Wood and Wood, eds., *Journal,* 95, 97, 109, 110.

56. *Columbian Museum,* June 21, 1796.

57. Wood and Wood, eds., *Journal,* 77.

58. Theus, *Savannah Furniture,* 45–46.

59. Advertisement of John Andrews, tailor and habit-maker, *AC,* Nov. 30, 1799.

60. *Columbian Museum,* Nov. 11, 1796.

61. Ibid.

62. *Columbia Museum and Savannah Gazette,* Sept. 26, 1818.

63. *Georgia Gazette,* Aug. 18, 1796.

64. Ibid.

65. Wood and Wood, eds., *Journal,* 54.

66. *AC,* May 5, 1798; Apr. 28, 1799; Feb. 2, 1801.

67. This is best evidenced by examining the MESDA Research Files for Chatham and Richmond Counties between 1790 and 1820. The files are based largely on the newspaper advertisements and announcements of craftsmen.

68. U. B. Phillips, "Economic Cost of Slaveholding," 266.

69. George R. Gilmer, *Sketches of the First Settlers,* 202–3; *Georgia Express,* Nov. 18, 1809.

70. *Georgia Express,* Nov. 18, 1809.

71. Tench Coxe, ed. *A Statement of the Arts and Manufactures of the United States of America for the Year 1810,* 148–53. The 1810 Census of Manufactures accidentally omitted, and therefore underestimated, many Georgia manufactories worthy of inclusion. See Meyer H. Fishbein, *The Censuses of Manufactures, 1810–1890,* Refer. Inform. Paper no. 50.

72. For example, see the *AC,* Oct. 6, 1797, Nov. 17, 1798, and July 15, 1800.

73. *AC,* Feb. 18, 1814; Davis, "The Georgia Buhr Stone Industry."

74. Cutten, *Silversmiths of Georgia,* 68.

75. Cutten, *Silversmiths of Georgia,* 85–88, 99–100.

76. Theus, *Savannah Furniture,* 64.

77. Theus, *Savannah Furniture,* 57–58.

78. *Columbian Museum,* Jan. 1, 1797, and Mar. 21, 1797.

79. For example, see *Columbian Museum,* Dec. 1, 1797; *AC,* Feb. 14, 1798.

80. Numbers calculated from the MESDA Research Files, Chatham County, 1790–1820.

81. From MESDA Research Files, Richmond County, 1790–1820.

82. Chatham County Tax List, 1799, microfilm, Georgia Department of Archives and History (hereafter GDAH), Atlanta.

83. Based on a comparison of taxpaying artisans listed in the Chatham County Tax Digests of 1798 and 1799, both available on microfilm, GDAH.

84. Fox-Genovese, *Within the Plantation Household,* 57–58, 64.

85. For examples of newly arrived artisans in diverse trades who placed advertisements seeking apprentices, see the *Columbian Museum,* May 13, 1796, and Aug. 2, 1796, and the *AC,* May 13, 1797, Dec. 16, 1797, May 8, 1801, Aug. 27, 1803, May 14, 1808, May 23, 1817, and Feb. 8, 1821. Robert Saunders makes this point in "Modernization and the Free Peoples of Richmond," 244–45.

86. *Columbian Museum,* May 19, 1797.

87. *AC,* May 2, 1797; Chatham County Tax Digest, 1806; *AC,* July 27, 1799.

88. See want ads placed in the *AC,* Sept. 13, 1811, the *Georgia Express,* Aug. 27, 1808, and the *AC,* Oct. 4, 1817, Mar. 7, 1820, and Sept. 21, 1825.

89. I am stretching Stephanie McCurry's argument that yeoman farmers recognized their inclusion in the southern order based on their conception of a republicanism that enabled them to view themselves as "masters" over the women–dependents–in their household. Nonslaveholding white male artisans included among their dependents not only women and children but apprentices and jour-

neymen in the tradition of both European and American craftsmen. Stephanie McCurry, "The Two Faces of Republicanism," 1245–64.

90. Phillips, "Economic Cost of Slaveholding," 257–75.

91. Cutten, *Silversmiths of Georgia,* 96.

92. Cutten, *Silversmiths of Georgia,* 100–101.

93. Records of the 1820 Census of Manufactures, schedules for North Carolina, South Carolina, Georgia, roll 19, Chatham County, microfilm, GDAH.

94. Examples include *Georgia Gazette,* Apr. 16, 1789, Apr. 23, 1789, Dec. 3, 1789, July 8, 1790, July 15, 1790, Aug. 26, 1790, and Mar. 20, 1800; *AC,* July 11, 1789; Oct. 23, 1790; *Columbian Museum,* Feb. 7, 1797.

95. On skilled runaways in a low-country economy similar to Georgia's, see Philip Morgan, "Black Society in the Lowcountry," 100, 140–41.

96. Robert William Fogel, *Without Consent or Contract,* ch. 2; *Aggregate Amount of Persons within the United States in the Year 1810,* 80.

97. *AC,* Mar. 9 and Aug. 30, 1794. Advertisements seeking skilled slaves in the *AC* between 1790 and 1800 were limited to July 17, 1790, Dec. 10, 1791, May 13, 1794, Dec. 30, 1797.

98. *AC,* Apr. 4, 1789, Mar. 25, 1793, July 7, 1805.

99. The Augusta miller Hugh Magee offered a $40 reward for the return of two of his runaway slaves who he suspected were heading "to the Indian country." *AC,* Nov. 15, 1800.

100. Kulikoff, "Uprooted Peoples," 143–71.

101. *Second Census of the United States,* 2N, 4N; *Aggregate Amount of Persons within the United States,* 80.

102. Register of Free Persons of Color, Chatham County, 1817, microfilm, GDAH, Atlanta; Register of Free Persons of Color in Savannah, 1819, microfilm, GDAH.

103. Whittington B. Johnson, "Free Blacks in Antebellum Savannah," 420–27.

104. Edward B. Sweat, "The Free Negro in Ante-bellum Georgia," 252; Ira Berlin, *Slaves without Masters,* 93–94; Ralph B. Flanders, "The Free Negro in Antebellum Georgia," 256.

105. Records of Savannah, minutes of the City Council, Dec. 27, 1809, Aug. 11, 1817, GDAH.

106. Whittington B. Johnson, "Free Blacks in Savannah," 420.

107. Morgan, "Black Society in the Lowcountry," 123; Ben Gates, "Mutual Aid or Monopoly."

108. MESDA Research Files, Richmond County; Richmond County Tax Digest, 1807, microfilm, GDAH.

109. U.S. Manuscript Census Returns, Chatham County, Georgia, 1820.

110. *AC,* Jan. 18, 1800.

111. Dearmond owned six slaves at his death, three of them women, each with one child. Therefore, he must have hired slave carpenters. William Dearmond, Inventory and Appraisement, Jan. 24, 1800, Richmond County Estate Records, Inventories and Appraisements, 1799–1813, book A, p. 22, microfilm, GDAH.

112. Richmond County Tax Digests, 1794–1797; Chatham County Tax Digests, 1802–1805; Richmond County Tax Digests, 1809; microfilm, GDAH.

113. Richmond County Tax Digests, 1809; Chatham County Estate and Probate Records, 1812; GDAH.

114. Wood and Wood, eds., *Journal,* 24–26, 33.

115. Wood and Wood, eds., *Journal,* 29.

116. Wood and Wood, eds., *Journal,* 35, 36, 41, 44, 48, 50, 52, 61, 62, 65, 66, 68, 69, 80, 89, 91, 92, 97, 101, 102, 118.

117. Wood and Wood, eds., *Journal,* 35–36, 61, 66–68, 73, 80–81, 89.

118. Wood and Wood, eds., *Journal,* 40.

119. Wood and Wood, eds., *Journal,* 75, 91, 98.

120. Wood and Wood, eds., *Journal,* 98.

121. Wood and Wood, eds., *Journal,* 98.

122. See McCurry, "The Two Faces of Republicanism."

123. Richmond County Tax Digests, 1794–1797, 1818; Ruth Blair, *Early Tax Digests,* 56.

124. Richmond County Tax Digests, 1808, 1818, GDAH.

125. Ibid.; Blair, *Early Tax Digests,* 54; MESDA Research File, Chatham County.

126. Richmond County Tax Digests, 1809.

127. *AC,* Mar. 6, 1790; *Index to the Headright and Bounty Grants of Georgia, 1756–1909* (Vidalia, Ga.: Georgia Genealogical Reprints, 1970) (hereafter *IHRBG*), 8; William Allen Will, Oct. 7, 1795, Richmond County Wills, 1798–1839, microfilm, GDAH.

128. *AC,* Aug. 8, 1801.

129. Richmond County Tax Digest, 1818.

130. MESDA Research Files, Richmond County; Richmond County Tax Digests, 1809, 1818; and U.S. Bureau of the Census, Manuscript Returns, Richmond County, 1830, microfilm, GDAH.

131. MESDA Research Files, Richmond County; Richmond County Tax Digests, 1818; U.S. Manuscript Census Returns, Richmond County, Georgia, 1830.

132. *Georgia State Gazette,* July 19, 1788; U.S. Manuscript Census Returns, 1820.

133. *Columbian Museum,* June 14, 1796; *IHRBG,* 703.

134. MESDA Research Files, Richmond County and Chatham County; Blair, *Early Tax Digests,* 307, 137, 115, 112, 131, 280, 308, and 210.

135. *IHRBG,* 416.

2. Artisanal Politics

1. On the "differentness" of a slaveholding economy, see Allan Kulikoff, "Transition to Capitalism," 121–44; Genovese, *Political Economy of Slavery;* Elizabeth Fox-Genovese and Eugene D. Genovese, *Fruits of Merchant Capital.*

2. Jean B. Russo, "Self-Sufficiency and Local Exchange," 389–93; Lewis C. Gray, *History of Agriculture,* vol. 1, 500; Carl Bridenbaugh, *The Colonial Craftsman,* 15; Marcus Wilson Jernegan, *Laboring and Dependent Classes;* Richard B. Morris, *Government and Labor;* David W. Galenson, "White Servitude," 40–41. Few books explore the role of the mechanic in the slave South between 1763 and 1815. See Richard Walsh, *Charleston's Sons of Liberty;* Charles G. Steffan, *Mechanics of Baltimore;* and Johanna Miller Lewis, *Artisans in the North Carolina Backcountry.*

3. Alan Dawley, *Class and Community;* Paul G. Faler, *Mechanics and Manufacturers in the Early Industrial Revolution;* Susan E. Hirsch, *Roots of the American Working Class;* Bruce Laurie, *Working People of Philadelphia;* Howard B. Rock, *Artisans of the New Republic;* Sean Wilentz, *Chants Democratic;* Steffan, *Mechanics of Baltimore;* Steven J. Ross, *Workers on the Edge;* Laurie, *Artisans into Workers;* Ronald Schultz, *Republic of Labor.*

4. Important work has begun to appear on artisanal experience in the upper South. See Jean B. Russo, *Free Workers;* Johanna Miller Lewis, "Women Artisans," 214–26; Christine Daniels, "'Wanted: A Blacksmith,'" 743–67.

5. This framework had its origins among European craftsmen who settled in America during the colonial era. These colonial craftsmen contended that small independent producers working with their hands were more virtuous than men making money from the labor of others. This belief shaped the nature of the colonial challenge to the mother country. Artisan patriots embraced a republicanism that enshrined liberty and natural rights in the face of an increasingly oppressive indigenous elite as well as a tyrannical mother country. See Schultz, *Republic of Labor,* ch. 2.

6. Charles Olton, *Artisans for Independence;* Gary B. Nash, *The Urban Crucible.*

7. Alfred Young, "Mechanics and Jeffersonians," 247–76; David Montgomery, "Working Classes and the Pre-Industrial American City," 3–22; Alfred Young, *Democratic-Republicans of New York;* Eric Foner, *Tom Paine and Revolutionary America;* Rock, *Artisans of the New Republic;* Laurie, *Working People of Philadelphia;* Gary J. Kornblith, "From Artisans to Businessmen"; Wilentz, *Chants Democratic;* Steffan, *Mechanics of Baltimore;* Schultz, *Republic of Labor.*

8. Reported in the *AC,* Feb. 13, 1790.

9. Artisans in colonial Georgia did not challenge the authority of the planter elite although evidence suggests that relations between artisans and those in power were

characterized by underlying social tensions. See Harold E. Davis, *The Fledgling Province,* 153–54, 253; Betty Wood, *Slavery in Colonial Georgia,* 199.

10. For studies that emphasize the shared values of white men in a republican political culture founded on the division of race during the antebellum era, see J. Mills Thornton III, *Politics and Power;* J. William Harris, *Plain Folk and Gentry;* Lacy K. Ford, *Origins of Southern Radicalism;* Stephanie McCurry, *Masters of Small Worlds.*

11. The *AC* published announcements and reports of MSA meetings as well as occasional election results from 1791 to 1804. The first recorded meeting was described in the *AC,* on May 7, 1791, the last on July 28, 1804.

12. Although Jones provides no details, he notes in his *Memorial History of Augusta,* 158, that this law caused a significant stir in Augusta.

13. *AC,* Dec. 26, 1789; Jan. 9, 1790; Jones, *Memorial History of Augusta,* 158; George R. Lamplugh, *Politics on the Periphery,* 96.

14. Executive Department Minutes, Jan. 8, 1790, on microfilm, GDAH.

15. Occupations and property-holdings could be identified for thirty-three of the fifty-five petitioners using the 1794–1795, 1795, and 1798 Richmond County Ordinary Tax Digests, local court records, newspaper sources, and county histories.

16. Lamplugh, *Politics on the Periphery,* 26–28, 42–77; J. G. A. Pocock, "The Classical Theory of Deference," 516–23.

17. Executive Department Minutes, Jan 9–12, 1790, GDAH; both Lamplugh, *Politics on the Periphery,* 96, and Kirk Wood, "From Town to City," 8–11, note the peculiarity of this election.

18. *AC,* Jan. 16, 1790.

19. *AC,* Jan. 23, 1790.

20. *AC,* Jan. 23, 1790.

21. *AC,* Mar. 6, 1790.

22. Lamplugh, *Politics on the Periphery,* 96.

23. Lamplugh, *Politics on the Periphery,* pp. 200–202; U. B. Phillips, *Georgia and State Rights,* 44–47.

24. *AC,* Feb. 13, 1791; July 21, 1792; Feb. 22, 1794; Wood, "From Town to City," 8–11.

25. Although the society was organized by May 7, 1791, sixteen mechanics petitioned the state legislature to incorporate the MSA three and a half years later. Exec. Dept. Mins., Dec. 24, 1794. These petitioners were William Longstreet (machinist/inventor), John Catlett (silversmith), Thomas Bray (jeweler), Robert Cresswell (carpenter), Edward Primrose (occupation unknown), Conrad Liverman (carpenter), Isaac Wingate (occupation unknown), Hugh Magee (miller), William Dearmond (carpenter), Baxter Pool (carpenter), John Cook (tailor), Joseph Stiles (silversmith), Angus Martin (occupation unknown), John Stiles (saddler), Hiel

Chatfield (occupation unknown), and Edward Primrose (occupation unknown). Only one additional name appeared in the newspaper notices listing MSA officers between 1791 and 1804, Francis Vallotton (shoemaker).

26. On MSA meetings see *AC* May 7, July 23, 1791; Jan. 28, Apr. 24, May 5, July 14, 1792; Jan. 27, Apr. 20, May 3, July 27, Aug. 10, 1793; Jan. 25, Mar. 14, May 1, 1794; Apr. 25, Nov. 7, 1795; Apr. 16, Oct. 29, 1796; Apr. 22, May 6, July 22, Oct. 27, 1797; Jan. 25, Mar. 10, Apr. 17, May 1, May 17, Aug. 28, 1798; Jan. 26, Apr. 13, July 27, Oct. 26, 1799; Feb. 1, July 26, 1800; Jan. 31, 1801; May 7, 1803; July 28, 1804 (the last announcement about MSA activities until the institution reorganized itself under new leadership in 1823). Unfortunately, it is impossible to determine MSA membership. While incomplete records of MSA officeholders have been preserved through newspaper records of election results, membership lists have not.

27. Alfred F. Young, "'By Hammer and Hand All Arts Do Stand': An Interpretation of Mechanics in the Era of the American Revolution" (unpublished paper, Organization of American Historians, San Francisco, Apr. 1980), quoted in Steffan, *Mechanics of Baltimore,* 283.

28. The charter is listed in H. Marbury and W. H. Crawford, *Digest of the Laws,* 145–46.

29. *AC,* May 4, 1793; May 5, 1792.

30. Thomas J. Schlereth, "Artisans and Craftsmen," 35–39. The state legislature of Georgia recognized the significance of artisan skills as property by giving all mechanics the franchise, regardless of real holdings, in Article IX of the state constitution of 1777, a radically democratic position to adopt. Albert B. Saye, *Constitutional History of Georgia,* 106 (rev. ed.).

31. MSA charter in Marbury and Crawford, *Digest of the Laws,* 145–46.

32. *AC,* May 7, 1791, and May 5, 1792. On the tradition of artisan promotion of political equality, see Wilentz, *Chants Democratic,* 93.

33. MSA leaders who served during the American Revolution included: Capt. Baxter Pool, *General Index to Compiled Military Service Records of Revolutionary War Soldiers,* part of War Department Collection of Revolutionary War Records, record group 93, M-860, roll 0041, National Archives and *Georgia Military Affairs,* vol. 1, 164, 168, 174–75; John Cook, see Alfred D. Candler [ed.], *The Revolutionary Records of the State of Georgia,* vol. 3, 169; and Hugh Magee, who was listed on the militia muster rolls between 1773 and 1793, *Georgia Military Affairs,* vol. 1, 23. William Dearmond served as captain of the Richmond Light Horse in the 1790s, *Georgia Military Affairs,* vol. 2, 424. John Catlett, John Cook, and William Longstreet were each listed on the militia muster rolls between 1791 and 1813, *Georgia Military Affairs,* vol. 1, 300; vol. 3, 46, 142.

On the relationship between political ambitions and militia leadership, see Lamplugh, *Politics on the Periphery,* 22. On the connections between popular societies and militia in the United States, see Eugene Perry Link, *Democratic Republican Societies,* 52, 111–12, 179–84.

34. *AC,* May 5, 179, and May 4, 1793.

35. *AC,* May 7, 1791, May 5, 1792, and May 4, 1793.

36. *AC,* May 7, 1791, May 5, 1792, and May 4, 1793.

37. *AC,* Dec. 15, 1802, and May 7, 1803.

38. For a description of Washington's visit, see Archibald Henderson, *Washington's Southern Tour,* xxiv–xxv, 238, 242, 245–49, and Jones, *Memorial History of Augusta,* 141–42.

39. *AC,* May 28, 1791. On Washington's promotion of mechanics see David Freeman Hawke, *Nuts and Bolts of the Past,* 41.

40. *AC,* Aug. 10, 1793; Lamplugh, *Politics on the Periphery,* 108, 136.

41. *Georgia Military Affairs,* vol. 2, part 2, 363–82, 424–25, 428.

42. Ibid., 366–67; in fact, Jackson and Watkins came to blows twice over their party differences.

43. Ibid., 380.

44. Ibid.

45. Ibid., 382.

46. Ibid., 377–80.

47. *AC,* May 5, 1792, Apr. 11, 1807, Apr. 9 and 16, 1808, Mar. 25, 1809; J. D. Wade, *Longstreet,* 3–11; Jones, *Memorial History of Augusta,* 135–36, 163.

48. *AC,* Aug. 2, 1805, Dec. 6, 1806, Oct. 31, 1807, Apr. 16, 1808; Jones, *Memorial History of Augusta,* 166–67.

49. *AC,* Mar. 20, 1798, and Apr. 19, 1806; Jones, *Memorial History of Augusta,* 135.

50. *AC,* Mar. 20, 1798, and Mar. 28, 1801.

51. *Southern Sentinel and Gazette of the State,* Feb. 13, 1794, from MESDA Research Files.

52. *AC,* Apr. 12, 1788; *Georgia Gazette,* Apr. 7, 1798; and Executive Department minutes, July 2, 1795, GDAH.

53. Telamon Cuyler Collection, Richmond County, box 36, June 3, 1797, Hargrett Library, University of Georgia.

54. Jones, *Memorial History of Augusta,* 166.

55. *Georgia Gazette* (Savannah), Sept. 7, 1786.

56. Ibid., Sept. 7, 21, 1786; Oct. 19, 1786; Lamplugh, *Politics on the Periphery,* 53–54.

57. Calculation based on data from Chatham County Tax Digest, 1798, microfilm, GDAH.

58. *Georgia Gazette,* Oct. 2, 1789.

59. Ibid., Feb. 19, 1789.

60. Ibid., Jan. 31, 1793.

61. Laura Mason, "Ca Ira," 22–38.

62. Mason, "Ca Ira," and *AC,* 20 July, 1793.

63. *Georgia Gazette,* Aug. 3, 1793.

64. *AC,* Aug. 3, 1793.

65. *AC,* Aug. 3, 1793.

66. *Georgia Gazette,* July 5, 1793.

67. Act of the Georgia General Assembly, Dec. 16, 1793, in Marbury and Crawford, *Digest of the Laws,* 145–46.

68. City of Savannah, City Council Minutes, 1791–1796, GDAH; MESDA Research Files, Chatham County, Georgia, 9; Theus, *Savannah Furniture,* 58–63.

69. Coleman, *History of Georgia,* 96–97.

70. *Georgia Gazette,* Mar. 19, 1795.

71. Circular published in *Georgia Gazette,* July 25, 1795.

72. *Georgia Gazette,* Sept. 10, 1795.

73. Ibid., Oct. 1, 1795.

74. Ibid., Nov. 5, 1795.

75. *Columbian Museum,* Sept. 23, 1796.

76. Ibid., Dec. 6, 1796; Strong, "Glimpses of Savannah," 28.

77. *Columbian Museum,* Mar. 3, 1797.

78. Ibid., Mar. 3, 1797.

79. *Georgia Gazette,* Mar. 22, 1799.

80. *Columbian Museum,* Oct. 24, 1797.

81. Strong, "Glimpses of Savannah," 28; Chatham County Tax List, 1798, GDAH.

82. *Columbian Museum,* Jan. 16, 1798.

83. *AC,* Jan. 3, 1801.

84. *Georgia Republican* (Savannah), Aug. 31, 1802.

85. Ibid., Dec. 15, 1802.

86. Dunlop, "A Scotsman Visits Georgia," 261, 263.

87. *Columbian Museum,* Jan. 17, 1800.

88. *Georgia Gazette,* June 16, 1800; June 25, 1801.

89. Lamplugh, *Politics on the Periphery,* 98–100.

90. William J. Cooper Jr., *Liberty and Slavery,* 81–95.

91. Phillips, *Georgia and State Rights,* pp. 38, 99; Francis Butler Simkins and Charles Pierce Roland, *A History of the South,* 92; Thomas Perkins Abernethy, *The South in the New Nation,* 302–3, 305, 310, 328, 408; Coleman, *History of Georgia,* 102–4.

92. Michele Gillespie, "Planters in the Making: Artisanal Opportunity in Georgia, 1790–1820," in *The American Artisan,* ed. Robert Asher, Paul Gilje, and Howard Rock, 33–47.

93. J. D. Wade, *Longstreet,* 4.

94. *The Story of Georgia: Biographical Volume* (New York, n.p., 1938), 683; Jones, *Memorial History of Augusta,* 146–47; J. D. Wade, *Longstreet,* 10–13.

95. Bailie Family Papers, Special Collections, Augusta College, Augusta, Georgia; J. D. Wade, *Longstreet,* 13; Jones, *Memorial History of Augusta,* 166–67, 292; *AC,* July 22, 1797.

96. J. D. Wade, *Longstreet,* 12.

97. The role of Longstreet's wife in his success should be more appreciated. The capital that Longstreet applied to his ventures probably originated from his wife's inheritance. His wife Hannah ran first a private and then a public boarding-house that bailed the family out of financial difficulties when the plantation failed. We need to know more about women's contributions to the household economy of southern artisans. J. D. Wade, *Longstreet,* 12–14, 20.

98. Allen D. Candler, *Colonial Records of Georgia,* vol. 10, 14, 75, 215, 628; Cutten, *Silversmiths of Georgia,* 136; *AC,* Apr. 23, 1791, Jan. 28, 1792, May 12, 1792, and June 13, 1792; Richmond County Ordinary Tax Digest, 1807, GDAH; Richmond County Probate Records, Richmond County Courthouse, 1811.

99. *AC,* Apr. 12, 1811, Dec. 8, 1810, and Feb. 6, 1808; Richmond County Tax Digest, 1809.

100. This upward mobility was in keeping with the history of the upcountry. Since the colonial era poor men who settled in the area often found themselves financially well off within a decade or so of their arrival. Harold E. Davis, *The Fledgling Province,* 42.

101. Richmond County Probate Records, 1816, Richmond County Courthouse, Augusta, Georgia.

102. Bray, *AC,* July, 4, 1801; Cook, Richmond Co. Ord. Tax Digest, 1800, *IHRBG,* 127; Dearmond, Richmond Co. Ord. Tax Digest, 1800; Liverman, Richmond Co. Ord. Tax Digest, 1800; Magee, *IHRBG,* 402, Richmond Co. Ord. Tax Digest, 1795, 1809, Richmond Co. Probate Records, Sept. 8, 1812; Martin, *IHRBG,* 409, Richmond Co. Ord. Tax Digest, 1800; Pool, *IHRBG,* 526, *AC,* Feb. 2, 1800, Aug. 12, 1809; Primrose (who may have been a brewer given the items such as casks, crockeryware, vinegar, and scales sold at his estate sale, *AC,* Oct. 29, 1808), *IHRBG,* 534; Vallotton, Richmond Co. Ord. Tax Digest, 1800, 1807.

103. Chatham County Estate Records, 1805–1823, GDAH.

104. Peter Miller in 1797, Theus, *Savannah Furniture,* 63–64; Thomas Palmer in 1800, *Columbian Museum,* Jan. 3, 1800.

105. *Columbian Museum,* Apr. 4, 1800.

106. Chatham County Tax List, 1798 and 1806, GDAH.

107. Richmond Co. Ord. Tax Digest, 1800.

108. Act of the Georgia General Assembly, Dec. 1, 1802, A. S. Clayton, *Compilations of the Laws of Georgia,* 94.

109. Chatham County Tax List, 1806, GDAH.

110. Douglas R. Egerton, "Gabriel's Conspiracy," 200.

111. Frey, *Water from the Rock,* 212, 222–42; Morgan, "Black Society in the Low-country," 138–40.

112. A number of Savannah city ordinances were passed to prevent such exchanges. For example, see the ordinance that forbade free blacks in the city to sell goods or liquor, *Georgia Gazette,* Feb. 12, 1795. No such ordinances were passed in Augusta during this period. Yet in the hinterland surrounding Augusta, field hands increasingly hired out their time, another new form of autonomy. See Frey, *Water from the Rock,* 223–24.

113. James Jackson letter, Dec. 24, 1776, Telamon Cuyler Collection, box 82, Georgia slavery file, slave rebellion folder, Hargrett Library, University of Georgia; Trial of a Negroe Slave Named Lewis, Telamon Cuyler Collection, box 71, Georgia slavery file, slavery trials folder, Hargrett Library, University of Georgia; Frey, *Water from the Rock,* 226–27; Morgan, "Black Society in the Lowcountry," 139, fn. 99.

114. Alfred N. Hunt, *Haiti's Influence,* 107–8.

115. The Savannah City Council, fearing the potential for racial conflict, refused to allow a vessel with 100 blacks from Kingston aboard to dock in the harbor in 1795. Four years later, it passed an ordinance requiring the registration of all free blacks and slaves seeking work in the city. The state legislature, equally worried about the influence of black Haitian émigrés on Georgian slaves, banned free blacks from the state of Georgia in 1793, temporarily banned the importation of all slaves in 1798, and prohibited the importation of blacks from the West Indies in 1803. *AC,* Oct. 5, 1799; Hunt, *Haiti's Influence,* 108; Marbury and Crawford, *Digest of the Laws,* 440–43; Oliver Prince, comp., *A Digest of the Laws of the State of Georgia,* 442.

116. Although the port cities of Charleston and Savannah bore the brunt of the exodus of St. Domingue planters, slaves, and free blacks, refugees had established a "French colony" in the eastern section of Augusta by 1800. Augusta Unit, Federal Writers' Project in Georgia. Works Progress Administration, comp. *Georgia* (American Guide Series) (Augusta, Ga.: WPA, 1938), p. 73; J. D. Wade, *Longstreet,* 15.

117. For example, the *Georgia Gazette,* Feb. 6, 1794, reported that three Savannah blacks had been hanged after being convicted of killing a white man on February 4, 1794.

118. *Georgia Gazette,* June 19, 1794.

119. Trial of a Negro Fellow Named George, belonging to Robert Forsyth, July 20, 1793, Telamon Cuyler Collection, box 71, slavery trials folder, Hargrett Library, University of Georgia.

120. George Fredrickson introduced this notion of a herrenvolk democracy in the antebellum South in *The Black Image in the White Mind*, 59–61, 66–68.

3. The Spread of Production

1. Elizabeth Fox-Genovese, *Within the Plantation Household*, 57.

2. Harold Woodman, *King Cotton and His Retainers*, 3–72; Allan R. Pred, *Urban Growth and the Circulation of Information*, 127–29, and *Urban Growth and City-Systems*, 116.

3. An extensive literature exists on these issues. To introduce them, see Eugene D. Genovese, *Political Economy of Slavery*, part 3; Bayrd Still, *Urban America*, 543–61; David R. Goldfield, *Urban Growth in the Age of Sectionalism*, intro.

4. This statement was less true of border states, however. See especially Barbara Jeanne Fields, *Slavery and Freedom on the Middle Ground*.

5. Pred, *Urban Growth and City-Systems*, 166–67, 169.

6. Jacob M. Price, "Economic Function," 123–86; Earle and Hoffman, "Staple Crops and Urban Development," 7–78; Ernst and Merrens, "Camden's turrets," 549–74.

7. Stuart Bruchey, comp. and ed., *Cotton and the Growth of the American Economy*, 7–42; James C. Bonner, *History of Georgia Agriculture;* Willard Range, *Century of Georgia Agriculture*, ch. 1; Kenneth Coleman, ed., *History of Georgia*, 162–65.

8. Milton Sydney Heath, *Constructive Liberalism*, ch. 7.

9. Ulrich B. Phillips, *Georgia and State Rights*, ch. 2.

10. Coleman, ed., *History of Georgia*, ch. 12.

11. Phillips, *Georgia and State Rights*, ch. 2; Ralph B. Flanders, *Plantation Slavery in Georgia*, 22–64; Heath, *Constructive Liberalism*, 69–158; Woodman, *King Cotton and His Retainers*.

12. Joan Niles Sears, *Town Planning in Georgia*, chs. 4, 5; William Lamar Cawthon Jr. "Clinton," 151–52.

13. Lamplugh, *Politics on the Periphery*, chs. 1, 2.

14. Albert B. Saye, *Constitutional History of Georgia*, 165–74.

15. Edmund S. Morgan, *American Slavery, American Freedom*, 380–87.

16. Sears, *Town Planning in Georgia*, 12–13; Peter Wallenstein, *From Slave South to New South*, 20.

17. Sears, *Town Planning in Georgia*, 12–13, 29.

18. Ibid., 12–13. Legislative commitment to town planning was commonplace throughout frontier settlements. See Richard C. Wade, *Urban Frontier*, ch. 3.

19. Manuscript Census, Georgia, Hancock County, Burke County, Jefferson County, Twiggs County, 1810, 1820, 1830, GDAH.

20. Cawthon, "Clinton," 25–29, 34. Augusta, of course, was an exception to this

rule, because its primary function as distribution center and supplier for the South Carolina and Georgia upcountry encouraged expansion of the urban economy and population growth.

21. Sears, *Town Planning in Georgia,* ch. 6.

22. For background on these new towns see Works Project Administration, *Georgia;* George White, *Statistics,* and *Historical Collections.* On the impact of railroads on town development, see Phillips, *History of Transportation,* and Goldfield, *Urban Growth in the Age of Sectionalism,* xx–xxi; see also John C. Butler, *Historical Record of Macon,* chs. 4 and 5, which chronicles Macon town fathers' willingness to alter the town economy in response to the railroad's impact; and for another look at urban Georgia's attitude toward railroads, see Wallenstein, *From Slave South to New South,* 28–35, 51–54.

23. For an analysis of the importance of the fall-line for successful town-building see John Richard De Treville, "Fall-Line Cities," intro. and ch. 1.

24. Ulrich B. Phillips, *History of Transportation,* ch. 4; Coleman, ed., *History of Georgia,* 168–73.

25. Joseph Patrick Reidy, "Masters and Slaves, Planters and Freedmen," ch. 1.

26. Reidy, "Masters and Slaves, Planters and Freedmen," 16. Also see Butler, *Historical Record of Macon,* for a description of Macon's economic growth.

27. A. T. Havens, "Journal on a Trip to Georgia and Florida, 1842–1844," Hargrett Library, University of Georgia, Apr. 20, 1842.

28. Robert Scott Davis Jr., "Robert Findlay," 17–43.

29. John H. Martin, *Columbus, Georgia,* provides a detailed social, political, and economic history of Columbus's antebellum development.

30. For a descriptive history of Milledgeville, see James C. Bonner, *Milledgeville;* quote from James Silk Buckingham, *The Slave States of America,* vol. 2, 535–36.

31. Ernest C. Hynds, *Antebellum Athens;* Augustus Longstreet Hull, *Sketches of Athens.*

32. James Michael Russell, *City-Building,* 14–37; Franklin M. Garrett, *Atlanta and Environs,* vol. 1, ch. 6. On the interdependent relationship between market center, staple-producing countryside, and urban development, see Earle and Hoffman, "Staple Crops and Urban Development," 64–68.

33. The manuscript census for De Kalb County, 1860, Schedule I, lists 847 artisans and mechanics. They represent about 44 percent of the adult white male population. See also Russell, *City-Building,* 70–71.

34. Claudia Goldin, *Urban Slavery,* 9–10, 123–25.

35. Ibid., 124.

36. Kent Anderson Leslie, *Woman of Color;* Whittington B. Johnson, *Black Savannah;* Adele Logan Alexander, *Ambiguous Lives.*

37. Statistics derived from *Census for 1820; Fifth Census; or Enumeration of the Inhabitants of the U.S.; Enumeration of the Inhabitants and Statistics of the U.S., Sixth Census; The Seventh Census of the U.S., 1850; Population of the U.S. in 1860, Compiled from the Original Returns of the Eighth Census.*

38. Cawthon, "Clinton," 149–50.

39. Records of the 1820 Census of Manufactures, roll 19, schedules for North Carolina, South Carolina, and Georgia, Clarke County, GDAH.

40. Manufacturing Census, Hall County.

41. This statement is taken from published returns in *Digest of Accounts of Manufacturing.*

42. *Digest of Accounts of Manufacturing.*

43. Records of the 1820 Census of Manufactures, Washington County, GDAH.

44. Records of the 1820 Census of Manufactures, Bryan and Liberty Counties, GDAH.

45. Based on a comparison of the manuscript returns for Chatham County in the records of the 1820 Census of Manufactures and the *Digest of Accounts of Manufacturing.*

46. Records of the 1820 Census of Manufactures, Richmond County, GDAH.

47. Quote from records of the 1820 Census of Manufactures, Laurens County, GDAH.

48. Records of the 1820 Census of Manufactures. Baldwin County supported 5 saddlers, 16 shoemakers, 12 blacksmiths, 12 carriage- and wagonmakers, 16 carpenters, and 12 tanners, for a total of 73 artisans.

49. Records of the 1820 Census of Manufactures, Baldwin County, GDAH, and *Census for 1820.*

50. Records of the 1820 Census, Warren, Franklin, Baldwin, and Jasper Counties, GDAH.

51. Records of the 1820 Census, Richmond, Pulaski, and Jackson Counties, GDAH.

52. U.S. Bureau of the Census, "1840 Mines, Manufacturing, and Agricultural Schedule," microfilm, GDAH.

53. U.S. Bureau of the Census, "1840 Mines, Manufacturing, and Agricultural Schedule," microfilm, GDAH.

54. David Freeman Weiman, "Petty Commodity Production," 240–41.

55. For ease of computation, "adult" is herein defined as sixteen and over. The records of the 1820 Census of Manufactures listed 3,427, or 3 percent of all white males in Georgia sixteen and over, engaged in manufacturing.

56. J. D. B. De Bow, *Statistical View of the U.S., Being a Compendium of the Seventh Census,* 215–18.

57. On the Panic of 1837 and its consequences, see Peter Temin, *The Jacksonian Economy,* chs. 4 and 5. On local disasters that included a drought, a flood, and a yellow fever epidemic, see Florence Fleming Corley, *Confederate City,* 7.

58. *President's Report to the Stockholders of the Georgia Railroad and Banking Company, May 17, 1845,* 6–9.

59. *Southern Business Directory and General Commercial Advertiser,* 282–96.

60. *Manufactures of the U.S. in 1860, Compiled from the Original Returns of the Eighth Census,* Richmond County.

61. On the textile industry in Richmond County, see Richard W. Griffin, "The Augusta Manufacturing Company," 60–73, and W. K. Wood, "A Note on Pro-Urbanism," 23–31; Clark, *History of Manufactures,* 553–58.

62. Savannah *News,* cited in *De Bow's Review* 11 (1851): 322.

63. Frederick Law Olmsted, *A Journey in the Seaboard States,* 542–44; William Gregg, "Practical Results of Southern Manufactures," 777–91.

64. For a discussion of these changes, see Phillips, *History of Transportation.*

65. *Report of R. D. Arnold, Mayor of the City of Savannah, for the Year Ending September 30th, 1860, etc.,* 26.

66. U.S. Bureau of the Census, 1840 Mines, Manufacturing, and Agricultural Census, Chatham County, GDAH.

67. Joseph Bancroft, *Census of the City.*

68. *Statistical View of the U.S., Being a Compendium of the Seventh Census,* p. 211.

69. James H. Stone, "Economic Conditions in Macon," 209–52; for a detailed description of the relationship between Macon and the countryside, see Reidy, "Masters and Slaves, Planters and Freedmen," ch. 3.

70. *Georgia Telegraph* (Macon), Jan. 29, 1839.

71. *Georgia Journal and Messenger* (Macon), Dec. 7, 1859.

72. Davis, "Robert Findlay," 17–43, has meticulously researched Findlay's early career.

73. *Georgia Telegraph* (Macon), Sept. 21, 1839.

74. Davis, "Robert Findlay," 21.

75. De Treville, "Fall-Line Cities," 125.

76. *Messenger* (Macon), Jan. 2, 1840.

77. *Georgia Telegraph,* May 11, 1841, Mar. 13, 1855; *Georgia Journal and Messenger,* Sept. 27, 1848, and May 27, 1857.

78. Davis, "Robert Findlay," 23–24.

79. *The State Press* (Macon), Nov. 5, 1857; *Georgia Citizen* (Macon), Apr. 2, 1853; White, *Historical Collections,* 271–72.

80. R. G. Dun and Company, Georgia, volume 6, 155, Baker Library, Harvard University Graduate School of Business Administration.

81. *Weekly Georgia Telegraph* (Macon), Dec. 6, 1859.

82. George Tucker, *Progress of the United States in Population and Wealth in Fifty Years,* 64.

83. Richard W. Griffin, "Origins of the Industrial Revolution," 355–75; Clement Eaton, *Growth of Southern Civilization,* ch. 10.

84. Gavin Wright, *The Political Economy of the Cotton South,* 43–88.

4. *"Thriving and Money-Making Men"*

1. Sean Wilentz, *Chants Democratic,* 107–42.

2. Peter Wallenstein, *From Slave South to New South,* 12–18.

3. Eugene D. Genovese discusses these "men of skill" in all their diversity in *Roll, Jordan, Roll,* 388–98.

4. Harriet Gift Castlen, *That Was a Time,* 22–23.

5. This argument began with Carl Bridenbaugh's *The Colonial Craftsman,* but it continues to be used. "Many planters considered mechanical labor fit only for blacks." Quote from Rorabaugh, *The Craft Apprentice,* 178, also see discussion, 174–79.

6. Eugene Genovese, *Political Economy of Slavery,* 162; Leslie Owens, *This Species of Property,* 178.

7. See for example the Harden-Jackson-Carrithers Collection, Hargrett Library, University of Georgia, which contains receipts for carpentry work done in 1856.

8. Robert William Fogel, *Without Consent or Contract,* ch. 2; Michael P. Johnson, "Work, Culture, and the Slave Community," 325–55.

9. Castlen, *That Was a Time,* 22–23.

10. David Crenshaw Barrow Papers, Hargrett Library, University of Georgia, box 9, folders 4–8, names and services quoted occurred on January 6, March 22, May 4, 15, 27, 1851, March 24–25, September 21, December 16–18, 1852, December 12, 15, 17, 1856.

11. Ibid., box 9, folder 5, May 15 and 27, 1851.

12. For some examples, see Howell Cobb Papers, Hargrett Library, University of Georgia, box 95, folder 20, J. T. Brown to John B. Lamar, undated receipt for $77.00 worth of carpentry work on slave cabins; box 94, folder 1, undated receipt for $450.00 worth of well-digging; box 37, folder 9, June 24, 1854, John A. Breedlove to Howell Cobb, long overdue receipt for blacksmith's work; box 3, folder 7, June 10, 1839, William Hansell to Howell Cobb, requests payment for $662 worth of masonry work.

13. Ibid., box 20, folder 4, Sept. 24, 1849; box 9, folder 13, Feb. 17, 1845, John B. Lamar to Howell Cobb.

14. Joseph Henry Lumpkin Collection, Carr Division, bills and receipts, Hargrett Library, University of Georgia. Robert Espy collected $100 "in part for his

blacksmith's account" on July 8, 1837. William Morton collected $58.11 due him for blacksmith work completed in 1837 on July 30, 1839. Samuel Clark Plantation Records, Hargrett Library, University of Georgia.

15. Blacksmith account book, 1821–1823, 1863, Baldwin County, GDAH.

16. Blacksmith account book [John Castleberry], 1854–1856, Fort Valley, Georgia, GDAH.

17. Blacksmith account book, 1821, Sparta, Georgia, Hancock County, GDAH.

18. Baber-Blackshear Collection, Hargrett Library, University of Georgia, Ambrose Baber to Mary Baber, Aug. 8, 1827.

19. Jane Webb Smith, *Georgia's Legacy*, 20–22, 53; Mary Levin Koch, "A History of the Arts in Augusta, Macon, and Columbus, Georgia, 1800–1860;" Henry D. Green, *Furniture of the Piedmont Before 1830*.

20. Smith, *Georgia's Legacy*, 53.

21. Hal S. Barron, *Those Who Stayed Behind*, 51–77.

22. Frederick Adolphus Brahe Papers, Hargrett Library, University of Georgia; Cutten, *Silversmiths of Georgia*, 21.

23. *Augusta City Directory, 1841* (Augusta: n.p., 1842); Cutten, *Silversmiths of Georgia*, 20–40.

24. Cutten, *Silversmiths of Georgia*, 68.

25. Hatton-Lovejoy Memoirs, Hargrett Library, University of Georgia, 16, 25. Although this memoir is not dated, context indicates the 1850s.

26. Atlanta Historical Society, *Neat Pieces*, 175; Smith, *Georgia's Legacy*, 22.

27. U.S. Bureau of the Census, "1840 Mines, Manufacturing, and Agriculture Schedule," Bibb County, microfilm, GDAH; Stone, "Economic Conditions in Macon," 220.

28. *Macon Messenger*, Aug. 2, 1838; *Macon Journal*, Nov. 3, 1847.

29. DuBose Family Papers, Hargrett Library, University of Georgia, box 6, receipts of Mrs. P. W. Booth, 1835–1855.

30. David R. Goldfield, *Urban Growth in the Age of Sectionalism*, intro.; Wallenstein, *From Slave South to New South*, 33–39.

31. *AC*, May 27, 1851.

32. Richard H. Haunton, "Savannah in the 1850s," 51.

33. Stephen Ray Henson, "Industrial Workers," 2, 24–27; description of engine house and machine in Atlanta of the Georgia R.R., *AC*, Nov. 5, 1949.

34. Quote in Davis, "Robert Findlay," 19, out of *American Railroad Journal and Advance of Internal Improvements* 5 (1836), 179–80.

35. Henson, "Industrial Workers," 64.

36. Eaton, *Growth of Southern Civilization*, 68.

37. *Augusta City Directory, 1841;* U.S. Bureau of the Census, Fourth Census, 1840, Richmond County, Schedule I. City directories pose certain problems for histori-

ans, not the least of which is the likelihood that many artisans were excluded from their pages. Thus, these numbers can only serve as a rough guide.

38. *Augusta City Directory, 1841;* U.S. Bureau of the Census, Fourth Census, 1840, Richmond County, Schedule I.

39. Manuscript returns, U.S. Census Bureau, Seventh and Eighth Census, 1850 and 1860, Clarke County.

40. Lacey K. Ford, *Origins of Southern Radicalism,* 2, 134, 79–80, 372–73. Also see Cooper, *Liberty and Slavery,* and Morgan, *American Slavery, American Freedom.*

41. The R. G. Dun and Company Reports for Clarke and Bibb Counties assessed the business prospects of many artisans. Unless the subject owned fairly substantial property, in the form of real estate, capital, and/or slaves, assessors were unwilling to recommend the individual as a loan risk. Georgia, vol. 3, R. G. Dun and Co., Baker Library, Harvard University Graduate School of Business Administration.

42. Dale L. Couch, "John Riley Hopkins," 43–55.

43. Howell Cobb Papers, box 95, folder 20, undated letter, Oliver Hillhouse Prince to John B. Lamar.

44. John C. Carter cashbook and ledger, Hargrett Library, University of Georgia. Carter described this episode on the last page (34) of his accounting book.

45. David C. Barrow Papers, Hargrett Library, University of Georgia, box 8, folder 3, June 4, 1858.

46. DuBose Family Papers, Hargrett Library, University of Georgia, Warren DuBose to Major Reuben Thornton, Gainesville, Georgia, Apr. 24, 1837.

47. Governor Joseph E. Brown correspondence, Hargrett Library, University of Georgia, Copy of letter from Governor Brown to Daniel Grambling, Milledgeville, Apr. 5, 1858.

48. Governor Joseph E. Brown to Daniel Grambling, Milledgeville, Apr. 9, 1858.

49. Godfrey Barnsley Papers, Hargrett Library, University of Georgia, typescript from letterbooks, Godfrey Barnsley to John Reid, Aug. 5, 1842.

50. Godfrey Barnsley Papers, Hargrett Library, Godfrey Barnsley to John Conally, Dec. 8, 1849.

51. Godfrey Barnsley Papers, Hargrett Library, Godfrey Barnsley to Ed Parsons, Dec. 13, 1849.

52. Godfrey Barnsley Papers, Hargrett Library, Godfrey Barnsley to Ed Parsons, Dec. 13, 1849, and Godfrey Barnsley to William Russell, Dec. 13, 1849.

53. Data on Augusta artisans tabulated from the *Augusta City Directory, 1841,* and manuscript returns, U.S. Bureau of the Census, Fifth Census, 1840, Schedule II; on Athens from the manuscript returns, U.S. Bureau of the Census, Sixth Census, 1850, Schedules I and II.

54. Inventory of James Thomas Estate, 1836, Wilkes County, microfilm, GDAH.

55. Inventory of James Thomas, Washington County, Mar. 1836; description of James Thomas property in the private collection of Thomas Family Papers owned by Marguerite Hodgson, Athens, Georgia.

56. Jackson County, unfiled court records, 1796–1800, microfilm, GDAH.

57. Bonner, *Milledgeville,* 27.

58. For background on Marlor, see Bonner, *Milledgeville;* Ulrich B. Phillips, "Historical Notes of Milledgeville, Georgia," *Gulf States Magazine,* Nov. 1903; Daniel Larson, "A Historic Survey of Outstanding Examples of Federal and Greek Revival Architecture in Milledgeville, Georgia"; Kenneth Coleman and Charles Stephen Gurr, eds. *Dictionary of Georgia Biography,* vol. 1, 685–86.

59. Randall M. Miller, "Daniel Pratt's Industrial Urbanism," 5–35.

60. Bonner, *Milledgeville,* 32–35, offers a good description of the effects of the maturing plantation society on town and countryside.

61. William Nathaniel Banks, "The Architectural Legacy of Daniel Pratt," 53–62; Mrs. S. F. H. Tarrant, *Hon. Daniel Pratt: A Biography* (Richmond, Va: Whittet & Shipperson, 1904), 40–64; Randall M. Miller, "Daniel Pratt's Industrial Urbanism," 5–19.

62. John C. Butler, *Historical Record of Macon,* vol. 1, 91, 96.

63. Ibid., 99, 179–81.

64. Ibid., 179–81; Coleman and Gurr, *Dictionary of Georgia Biography,* vol. 1, 14–15. Elam's boosterism included financial support for a steam-powered textile mill in Macon, along with other local manufacturers, including iron-founder Robert Findlay. *Telegraph* (Macon), Apr. 14, 16, and 28, 1846.

65. Ariadne Lea Kelley, "The Plantation Homes of John Wind."

66. Buckingham, *The Slave States of America,* vol. 2, 540.

67. Manuscript returns, U.S. Bureau of the Census, Seventh Census, 1850, Clarke County.

68. An unskilled white laborer earned $0.74 in the South Atlantic states in 1850. A skilled journeyman earned $1.59. See Robert A. Margo and Georgia C. Villaflor, "Growth of Wages," 893, 894.

69. Thomas Sanson, account books, 1849–1852, Athens, Georgia, Clarke County, Hargrett Library, University of Georgia.

70. William Jones, account books, 1836–1840, Hargrett Library, University of Georgia. Although he sold gins and gin parts to clients as far away as New Orleans, most of his customers came from nearby counties (for example, Jefferson, Morgan, Baldwin, Burke, and Lincoln Counties).

71. Ralph B. Flanders, *Plantation Slavery in Georgia,* 204. Jones owned three slaves, a boy, a man, and a woman, in 1830. They are listed in the Richmond County Slave Schedules, however, because Jones had yet to establish his gin manu-

factory in nearby Columbia County. Manuscript returns, U.S. Bureau of the Census, Fifth Census, 1830.

72. U.S. Census Office, Eighth Census, Population Schedules, 1860, Clarke County, Georgia, 1016.

73. J. M. Hodgson, "Looking Back" (number 2), pp. 1–2, Hodgson Papers.

74. Ibid.

75. J. M. Hodgson, "Looking Back" (number 2), 1–2; letter from J. M. Hodgson to John, 1–2; Anna Bishop Campbell, "The Bishop Family," Sept. 2, 1946, unpublished typescript in the Hodgson Papers; *Athens Daily Times,* May 8, 1935.

76. Tax Digests, Clarke County, 1841–1845, microfilm, GDAH. The three brothers paid only poll taxes during this period. For many Georgians, however, even the poll tax was an onerous burden in the 1840s. Indeed it was equal to the tax due on a slave whose value probably averaged $900 during this period. See Wallenstein, *From Slave South to New South,* 45.

77. Tax Digests, Clarke County, 1846–1855; 1856–1866, microfilm, GDAH. In 1858 the Hodgsons' taxable income stood at approximately $39,000. They owned nine slaves valued at $5,000, $3,000 worth of rural property, $7,500 worth of town property, $7,000 worth of capital, and $16,000 worth of capital investments (i.e., their business).

78. Manuscript returns, U.S. Census Office, Seventh Census, 1850, Slave Schedules, Clarke County, Georgia.

79. The average price of a strong field hand had risen from a low of $600 in 1844 to $1,000 in 1851. By 1860 the price had reached a high of $1,800. See U. B. Phillips, "Economic Cost of Slaveholding," 266.

80. Georgia, vol. 6, 92, R. G. Dun and Company, Baker Library, Harvard University Graduate School of Business Administration.

81. *Athens Daily Times,* May 8, 1935; Frank J. Huffman Jr., "Town and Country in the South," 369.

82. Blacksmith account book, 1821, Sparta, Georgia, Hancock County, GDAH.

83. Tailor account books, 1847–1848, Macon, Georgia, Bibb County, GDAH; Margo and Villaflor, "Growth of Wages," 893, 894.

84. Thomas Sanson, account books, Hargrett Library, University of Georgia, Mar. 2 through May 25, 1850.

85. For background information on Godfrey Barnsley, see Nelson Hoffman Jr., "Godfrey Barnsley, 1805–1873."

86. Godfrey Barnsley Papers, Hargrett Library, John Connally to Godfrey Barnsley, Feb. 18, 1853.

87. Godfrey Barnsley Papers, Hargrett Library, Godfrey Barnsley to John Connally, May 16, 1855.

88. Hodgson Family Papers, Joseph Watts to E. R. Hodgson, Jan. 5, 1846.

89. Manuscript returns, U.S. Bureau of the Census, Seventh Census, 1850, Union County, Georgia. His real estate was valued at a modest $400.

90. Manuscript returns, U.S. Bureau of the Census, Eighth Census, 1860, Muscogee County, Georgia.

91. Wood and Wood, eds., *Journal.*

92. Bruce Laurie, *Artisans into Workers,* 47–73.

93. William Price Talmage diary, Hargrett Library, University of Georgia, Athens, Georgia, 1. Xerox Copy. Original in the possession of Robert Henry Kimbrell, Athens, Georgia. William Talmage's cousin Aaron was the great-grandfather of Georgia governor Eugene Talmadge. William Talmage dropped the "d" from his name after a dispute with his brother John over the ownership of a cow.

94. Talmage diary, 1.

95. Ibid.; *New Jersey: A Guide to Its Past and Present,* comp. and written by the Federal Writers' Project of the Works Progress Administration for the State of New Jersey (New York: Hastings House, 1939), 497, 478. Talmages appear to have resided in this area since the eighteenth century. Theodore Thayer, *Colonial and Revolutionary Morris County* (Morristown, N.J.: Compton Press, 1975), 293, 302.

96. W.P.A., *New Jersey: A Guide,* 80–81, 320; Clark, *History of Manufactures,* 475–76.

97. Milton Nadworny, "New Jersey Working Men and the Jacksonians," *Proceedings of the New Jersey Historical Society* 67 (1949): 185–98; Susan E. Hirsch, *Roots of the American Working Class.*

98. Talmage offers no explanation for his sudden departure. Nor does he explain what he was doing in Newark during this period. Talmage diary, 1. Talmage is also exceedingly elusive about politics in his journal. He noted presidents' deaths, kept a detailed record of the battles of the Mexican War, and attended both the state conventions of the Whigs and of the Democrats in 1848. While on tour through Alabama in 1841 he mentioned visiting the Hagerty family, who were staunch Democrats in their community. This is the extent of Talmage's account of his politics before the Civil War. Talmage diary, 8, 15–20. W. G. Robertson, *Recollections of the Early Settlers of Montgomery County and Their Families* (Montgomery, Ala: Excelsior Printing Co., 1892), 25.

99. Talmage diary, 1–2.

100. Ibid.

101. Frank J. Huffman Jr., "Town and Country in the South," 366–81; Kenneth Coleman, *Confederate Athens,* 2–7; Kenneth Coleman ed., *History of Georgia,* 176.

102. Henry Newton (1822–1913), "Some Early Reminiscences of Early Life and Times," unpublished manuscript, Hargrett Library, University of Georgia, Athens, Georgia.

103. Ibid.; Hull, *Sketches of Athens,* 474; John Talmage obituary, *Southern Whig* [Athens], Aug. 2, 1849, 3.

104. Clarke County, Tax List, 1838, GDAH. John Talmage's obituary states that he "accumulated a handsome fortune of about $20,000" but went insane. *Southern Whig,* Aug. 2, 1849, 3. William Talmage made no mention of his brother's mental health, nor of his brother's death in 1849, though he did note that his brother's "moveable property was sold Oct. 19th [1841]," presumably following the onset of his illness. Talmage diary, 12.

105. Talmage diary, 2–4. William could not remember whether he visited Aaron once or twice during this time. According to Talmage family history, Aaron's father traveled on foot from Newark, New Jersey, to Monroe County, Georgia, in 1798. He purchased land for a farm, returned to Newark a year later, married, and brought his new wife back to Georgia aboard a donkey. Aaron Talmage, William's cousin, was the great-grandfather of the infamous Georgia governor Eugene Talmadge. *The Story of Georgia,* Biographical Volume (New York: The American Historical Society, 1938), 14; Harold Martin, *Atlanta and Environs: A Chronicle of Its People and Events,* vol. 3, 44.

106. Talmage diary, 2–4.

107. W.P.A., *New Jersey: A Guide,* 240.

108. Talmage diary, 4. Talmage offered no explanation for why he returned to New Jersey. He simply stated his movements and actions in chronological order.

109. Graves Family Papers, 1840–1931, Special Collections Department, Robert W. Woodruff Library, Emory University, Atlanta, Georgia; William Bailey Williford, *The Glory of Covington,* 50–51; *History of Newton County,* 706–7.

110. Manuscript Census Returns, U.S. Bureau of the Census Office, *Seventh Population Census, 1850,* Newton County, Georgia.

111. Talmage diary, 4–6.

112. Georgia miscellany. Blacksmith shop account book, 1830–1836. Special Collections Department, Robert W. Woodruff Library, Emory University, Atlanta, Georgia.

113. Talmage diary, 5, 10, 12.

114. Ibid., 6–7.

115. Likewise, Steven Hahn observes that yeoman farmers in the more mountainous regions of northwestern Georgia relied on artisans who followed prescribed routes, or rounds, in search of custom work, in *The Roots of Southern Populism,* 71.

116. *Alabama: A Guide to the Deep South,* compiled by Workers of the Writers' Program of the Works Project Administration in the State of Alabama (New York: Richard R. Smith, 1941), 69.

117. Ibid., 339.

118. George E. Brewer, "Early Alabama," *Alabama Historical Quarterly* 4, nos. 1–2 (Spring–Summer 1942): 17–19; Manuscript Census Returns, Slave Schedules, U.S. Bureau of the Census Office, *Sixth Population Census, 1840,* Coosa County, Alabama.

119. *Alabama: A Guide,* 229, 338.

120. Virginia O. Foscue, *Place Names in Alabama* (Tuscaloosa: University of Alabama Press, 1989), 98; W. G. Robertson, *Recollections,* 38–59.

121. Talmage diary, 5–6.

122. Marilyn Davis Hahn, comp. *Old Cahaba Land Office and Military Warrants: 1817–1853* (Mobile, Ala.: Old South Printing and Publishing Co., 1981), 35. Marks is listed as a landowner in Montgomery County by 1825.

123. Thomas P. Abernethy, *The Formative Period in Alabama, 1815–1828,* (Montgomery, Ala.: Brown Printing Co., 1922), 26–27; *Alabama: A Guide,* 221–23.

124. Robertson, *Recollections,* 72; Abernethy, *Formative Period,* 22.

125. Manuscript Census Returns, Slave Schedules, U.S. Bureau of the Census Office, *Fifth Census of the U.S., 1830,* Montgomery County, Alabama; Nicholas Marks, Probate Records, Will, Sept. 3, 1847, Montgomery County, Alabama State Archives (hereafter ASA), Montgomery, Alabama; marriage of Nicholas Marks to Rebecca Wright, Mar. 8, 1820, Montgomery County, Alabama Marriages, book C, ASA, Montgomery, Alabama; Robertson, *Recollections,* 72, 79–80; Hahn, *Old Cahaba,* 35.

126. None of these names appeared in the Manuscript Census Returns, Slave Schedules, U.S. Bureau of the Census Office, *Sixth Census of the U.S., 1840,* Montgomery Co., Alabama.

127. Matthew William Clinton, *Tuscaloosa, Alabama: Its Early Days, 1816–1865* (Tuscaloosa: n.p., 1968), 34.

128. Grace E. Jemison, *Historic Tales of Talladega* (Montgomery, Ala.: Paragon Press, 1959), 84, 208–11; Foscue, *Place Names,* 32; Thomas McAdory Owen, *History of Alabama and Dictionary of Alabama Biography,* vol. 3 (Chicago: S. J. Clarke Publishing Co., 1921), 902.

129. Talmage diary, 10–12.

130. R. C. Fain, store and blacksmith account books, 1836–1868, Paulding County, GDAH.

131. On the importance of kinship networks in southern culture see Bertram Wyatt-Brown, *Southern Honor,* 117, and Hahn, *The Roots of Southern Populism,* 53; James Oakes, *The Ruling Race.*

132. Talmage diary, 12–13.

133. Manuscript Census Returns, U.S. Bureau of the Census Office, *Sixth Population Census, 1840* and *Seventh Population Census, 1850,* Clarke County, Georgia.

134. Huffman, "Town and Country in the South," 366–81; Coleman, *Confederate Athens,* 2–7; Kenneth Coleman, ed., *History of Georgia,* 176.

135. Coleman, *Confederate Athens,* 2–7.

136. Clarke County, Tax Digest, 1846, GDAH.

137. Clarke County, Tax Digests, 1842, 1852, GDAH.

138. Hynds, *Antebellum Athens,* 54–55.

139. Talmage diary, 26. "Feb 8 Athens 1851 I took an interest in the Athens Steam Company to the amount of $1500."

140. Hynds, *Antebellum Athens,* 55.

141. While Talmage's fellow investors in the paper mill were labeled "manufacturers" in the R. G. Dun Reports, Talmage was listed as a "blacksmith." Moreover, he was known throughout the town as a blacksmith. See Georgia, vol. 6, 94, R. G. Dun and Co., Harvard University Graduate School of Business Administration, Baker Library, Cambridge, Massachusetts; Hull, *Sketches of Athens,* 296.

142. Manuscript Census Returns, U.S. Bureau of the Census Office, *Sixth Population Census, 1840,* Clarke County, Georgia.

143. Data tabulated for Athens based on the manuscript returns, U.S. Bureau of the Census, Sixth Census, 1850, Schedules I and II.

144. Talmage diary, 7.

145. Ibid. Colonel John A. Cobb had been badly hit by the Panic of 1837 and was forced to sell his large plantation property to pay his creditors. He initially offered 150 slaves from his Cherry Hill Plantation in Jefferson County for private sale in November 1840. Sixty-one of his slaves were then advertised for purchase at the February Clarke County Sheriff's sale. It is this latter sale that Talmage records. See *The Southern Banner* [Athens], Nov. 6, 1840, and Jan. 22, 1841; Hull, *Sketches of Athens,* 124.

146. Fox-Genovese, *Within the Plantation Household,* ch. 2, quote from page 99.

147. Talmage diary, 13–14.

148. Fogel, *Without Consent or Contract;* Goldin, *Urban Slavery,* 122.

149. *Compendium of the Sixth Census,* 40–46.

150. Edward L. Ayers, *Vengeance and Justice,* 103.

151. For examples of these state and local laws, see Prince, *Digest,* 788, and the *AC,* Dec. 16, 1837. Edward F. Sweat, "The Free Negro in Ante-Bellum Georgia," offers a full account of the changing laws against blacks, slave and free, in antebellum Georgia.

152. A. T. Havens, "Journal on a Trip."

153. *AC,* Dec. 17, 1836.

154. W.P.A. Georgia Writer's Project, box 2, folder 1, typescript, Hargrett Library, University of Georgia.

155. Wade, *Slavery in the Cities,* 143–79; Ira Berlin, *Slaves without Masters,* 284–315.

156. Howell Cobb Papers, box 24, folder 10, John B. Lamar to Maryann Cobb, Dec. 3, 1850.

157. Ibid., box 24, folder 12, John B. Lamar to Johnny A., Nov. 17, 1851.

158. Ibid., box 24, folder 12, Maryann Cobb to Howell Cobb, Dec. 9, 13, and 17, 1850.

159. Ibid., Godfrey Barnsley to Edward, May 16, 1860.

160. Milledgeville *Federal Union,* Mar. 18, 1836.

161. Cited in description of an accident at the courthouse in the William Warren Thomas Papers, Hargrett Library, University of Georgia.

162. Davis, "Robert Findlay," 41.

163. John Phillips diary, Hargrett Library, University of Georgia, see especially entries dated Apr. 30, May 2, May 7, May 12, May 17, and May 19, 1853.

164. Hodgson Family Papers, Joseph Watts to E. R. Hodgson, Jan. 5, 1846.

165. Manuscript returns, U.S. Bureau of the Census, Seventh Census, 1850, Clarke County.

166. Anonymous Savannah carpenter's book, 1853–1854, Georgia Historical Society, Savannah, Georgia. Wage rates for the South Atlantic in 1854 quoted from Margo and Villaflor, "Growth of Wages," 893–94.

167. John C. Caldwell to Mr. Hodgson, Augusta, Aug. 3, 1849, Hodgson Papers; Margo and Villaflor, "Growth of Wages," 893.

168. W. H. Cooper to E. R. Hodgson and Brothers, Augusta, Jan. 10, 1849, Hodgson Papers. This figure assumes the hired slave works six days a week throughout the year. Margo and Villaflor, "Growth of Wages," 893–94.

169. T. Harrison to Hodgsons, Mar. 27, 1847, letter informs Hodgsons that a skilled slave may be available for hire. W. H. Cooper to Hodgsons, Jan. 10, 1849, has a skilled slave carriagemaker for hire. Margo and Villaflor, "Growth of Wages," 893–94.

170. Conger's real estate was valued at $4,000 in 1850. Manuscript returns, U.S. Bureau of the Census, Seventh Census, 1850 and Eighth Census, 1860; Conger's history in the Conger family papers in the possession of Marguerite Hodgson, Athens, Georgia.

171. Indenture, dated Jan. 1, 1840, between Abijah Conger and Mrs. Thomas regarding Mrs. Thomas's slaves Ned and Sanders, in the possession of Marguerite Hodgson, Athens, Georgia.

5. Politics in a Slaveholders' Republic

1. My understanding of party principles and ideology is informed by John Ashworth, *Agrarians and Aristocrats: Party Political Ideology in the United States, 1837–1846.*

2. On the significance of artisanal republicanism as a radical political critique, see Eric Foner, *Tom Paine and Revolutionary America;* Gary B. Nash, *The Urban Crucible;* Rock, *Artisans of the New Republic;* and especially Wilentz, *Chants Democratic.*

Explorations of artisanal republicanism in the South include Steffan, *Mechanics of Baltimore,* and Douglas R. Egerton, "Gabriel's Conspiracy," 191–214, both of which examine urban worlds in the upper South.

3. Bonner, *History of Georgia Agriculture;* Dodd and Dodd, *Historical Statistics;* Klein, *Unification of a Slave State;* Kulikoff, "Uprooted Peoples," 143–71.

For firsthand accounts of these opportunities see Strong, "Glimpses of Savannah," 28–36, and Wood and Wood, eds., *Journal.*

On the nature of urban developments that accompanied the growth of staple-crop economies, see Ernst and Merrens, "Camden's turrets," 549–74; Earle and Hoffman, "Staple Crops and Urban Development," 7–78: and Price, "Economic Function," 123–86.

4. Phillips, *Georgia and State Rights,* 38, 99; Simkins and Roland, *A History of the South,* 92; Thomas Perkins Abernethy, *The South in the New Nation,* 302–3, 305, 310, 328, 408; Coleman, ed. *History of Georgia,* 102–4.

5. By 1820, 60 percent of upcountry farmers grew cotton. Production had increased from one thousand bales in 1790 to ninety thousand. Coleman, ed., *History of Georgia,* 112. Settlement of an expanding upcountry was encouraged by the Georgia cessions of 1802, 1804, 1817, 1818, 1819, and 1821 when the state appropriated Cherokee lands in northeast Georgia and Creek lands westward to the Flint River. This land was distributed to white heads of household by a relatively democratic land lottery system. Phillips, *Georgia and State Rights,* 48–56, and Coleman, ed., *History of Georgia,* 107–8.

6. Indeed, they probably based their opinion on the growing number of advertisements in local newspapers warning residents not to hire certain disreputable journeymen. For examples in the *AC,* see David Crane's account of the "villainous" turner and bricklayer who stole from him, May 23, 1822; tailor Joel Stevenson's description of his negligent journeyman, Jan. 15, 1825; shoemaker John Haynes's description of the journeyman shoemaker who ran away with his tools and in his debt, Nov. 8, 1826; coachmaker Thomas G. Hall's account of a wayward journeyman carpenter, Apr. 3, 1830, tailor Etienne Lartigue's bad experience with a journeyman tailor who gambled, Apr. 21, 1832, and the itinerant journeyman tailor named George T. Bush, who swindled his way through Eatonton and on to Milledgeville, Aug. 20, 1836.

7. For example, on the effect of the Masons' lottery on the "profligate workingmen" see the *AC,* Aug. 17, 1825. On the need for a savings bank to halt "the intemperance which we daily witness among the lower classes," see the *AC,* Oct. 24, 1827.

8. *AC,* May 5, 1832, "Essays on Useful Knowledge, No. 2."

9. The movement in Georgia began with Baptist minister Adiel Sherwood's Manual Labor School near Eatonton. See the *Federal Union* (Milledgeville), Dec. 29, 1831; *AC,* Feb. 21, 1835.

10. Quoted in E. Merton Coulter, "The Ante-bellum Academy Movement in Georgia," *Georgia Historical Quarterly,* 5 (1921): 23.

11. Coulter, "The Ante-bellum Academy Movement," 23.

12. William Thomson, *A Tradesman's Travels in the U.S. and Canada,* 3–5, 14–16, 117.

13. No information could be located on the Macon Mechanic Society except that the General Assembly passed an act incorporating it in 1833. *Acts of the General Assembly . . . 1833,* 129–30. Here I am assuming that the Macon Mechanic Society and its membership mirrored that of the other newly created mechanics' societies.

14. *AC,* Sept. 20, 1823; *Acts of the General Assembly . . . 1823,* 143. At the same time, the General Assembly repealed the 1794 act that incorporated the original MSA.

15. Occupations taken from *Augusta City Directory, 1841,* the earliest extant directory available, newspaper advertisements, *AC,* May 30, 1818, Apr. 21, 1819, Sept. 16, 1814, Dec. 17, 1817, Feb. 13, 1819, and MESDA Research Files. *AC,* Apr. 1, 1820, Aug. 22, 1818, and Oct. 11, 1819; Richmond County Ordinary Tax Digest, 1820 and 1827, and the U.S. Manuscript Census Returns, Richmond County, 1820 and 1830. Jones, *Memorial History of Augusta,* 338–39, 341, 344–45, 398.

16. See announcements about the MSA in the *AC,* Sept. 23, 1823; Jan. 24 and May 5, 1824.

17. The AMMAA was incorporated by the state in 1837. *Acts of the General Assembly . . . 1837,* 126. The AMMAA reported its first meetings in the *Southern Banner,* May 12, June 25, Oct. 15, and Nov. 12, 1836.

In addition to their printing, bakery, shoe-making, and cabinetmaking shops, several of these men held a partnership in an auctioneering house, one owned the popular Temperance Coffee House, and one was elected town commissioner. Hynds, *Antebellum Athens,* 30, 130, 175, 178, 183.

18. Quote, purpose, and membership criteria from the organization's constitution printed in the *Southern Banner,* June 2, 1838.

19. Hodgson Papers, in the possession of Marguerite Hodgson, Athens, Georgia.

20. The resolutions of the Newton County Mechanics' Society were printed in the *AC,* July 28, 1840. Information could not be located on all thirty-three of the members. Sixteen of the members were slaveholders, averaging 4.5 slaves each. Most owned their own shops. Their occupations included master carpentry, carriage-making, wagoning, manufacturing, blacksmithing, tailoring, cabinetmaking, and silversmithing. Unlike the mechanics of Savannah and Augusta in the early republic, the majority of these men were born in Georgia or South Carolina. They were a stable group. Twenty-five of the original thirty-three members remained in Newton County a decade later. U.S. Bureau of the Census, Fifth Census, 1840, Schedule I and the Sixth Census, 1850, Schedule I and II.

21. Resolution, *AC,* July 28, 1840.

22. Resolution, *AC,* July 28, 1840.

23. See, for example, the editorial on mechanics in the *Federal Union* (Milledge-ville), Mar. 18, 1845, and "A Mechanic to Brother Mechanics" in the *Southern Banner,* Apr. 15, 1845.

24. See, for example, editorials in the *AC,* Oct. 6, 1837; May 12, 1832; June 6, 1835; the *Savannah Georgian,* Aug. 13, Nov. 5, 1833, and the *Southern Whig,* June 7, 1846.

25. *Acts of the General Assembly of the State of Georgia passed at Milledgeville at an Annual Assembly in November and December, 1820* (Milledgeville, 1821), 13, 55; *Acts of the General Assembly . . . 1821,* 7; *Acts of the General Assembly . . . 1825,* 178; *Acts of the General Assembly . . . 1827,* 141–42; *Acts of the General Assembly . . . 1834,* 187–89; *Acts of the General Assembly . . . 1835,* 146–47; *Acts of the General Assembly . . . 1836,* 161; *Acts of the General Assembly . . . 1837,* 169; *Acts of the General Assembly . . . 1840,* 123–24.

26. *Southern Banner,* Jan. 13, 1838.

27. Paul Murray, *The Whig Party in Georgia, 1825–1853,* 140–76, 199.

28. Coleman, ed. *History of Georgia,* 162, 168.

29. Governor Forsyth's address to the state, reprinted in the *AC,* Nov. 8, 1828.

30. Statement in the *AC,* Apr. 11, 1829; Murray, *The Whig Party in Georgia,* 12.

31. *Mercury* editor quoted in the *AC,* June 25, 1828. On similar opinions expressed by Augusta editors, see Aug. 2 and 6, 1828.

32. Richard W. Griffin, "Origins of the Industrial Revolution," 356; Adiel Sherwood, *A Gazetteer of Georgia,* 172–73.

33. Ashworth, *Agrarians and Aristocrats,* 54–77.

34. Thomas Brown, "The Southern Whigs and Economic Development," esp. 27–28. Of course the Whigs were not the only advocates of this balanced economy. See Robert S. Starobin, *Industrial Slavery in the Old South,* 163, 231–32.

35. Murray, *The Whig Party in Georgia,* 112–39.

36. Coleman, ed. *History of Georgia,* 168–73.

37. Coleman, *History of Georgia,* 140–76, 201–2.

38. For some examples see the *Savannah Georgian,* Aug. 13 and Nov. 5, 1833, and the *AC,* May 12, 1832, and June 6, 1835.

39. *AC,* July 17, 1840, and Mar. 16, 1851.

40. *AC,* May 22, 1853.

41. Ashworth, *Agrarians and Aristocrats,* 64–77.

42. *AC,* Oct. 6, 1837.

43. *AC,* Aug. 15, 1840.

44. *Southern Whig,* June 7, 1846.

45. Report of the Committee of Manufacturers of the Georgia legislature, 1847.

46. *Savannah Republican,* May 11, 1843. The editor challenged planters to

throw off the yoke of the North by encouraging a self-sufficient economy. See also the *Georgia Journal and Messenger* (Macon), Apr. 11 and 18, June 1, and Aug. 1, 1849; the *Chronicle* (Augusta), Oct. 4, 1841, Jan. 10, 1845, Dec. 11, 1846, and June 8, 1849.

47. Howell Cobb, *Compilation of the General and Public Statutes of the State of Georgia,* 215–16.

48. *Georgia Reports,* Supreme Court of Georgia, vol. 25, 571–73.

49. Ashworth, *Agrarians and Aristocrats,* 12–51.

50. Quote from the *Federal Union,* Mar. 18, 1845. On Monroe see the *Little Georgian,* reprinted in the *AC,* Jan. 29, 1845.

51. "A Mechanic to Brother Mechanics of Georgia, and Especially of Our Own Village," *Southern Banner,* Apr. 15, 1845.

52. Talmage diary, Hargrett Library, University of Georgia. Aug. 14 and Sept. 13, 1848, entries. Talmage did not reveal his party preference in his journal.

53. *AC,* July 3 and 7, 1830.

54. The resolutions of the Newton County Mechanics' Meeting printed in the *AC,* July 28, 1840.

55. Ashworth, *Agrarians and Aristocrats,* 87–110.

56. Ashworth, *Agrarians and Aristocrats,* 87–110.

57. This information is based on the manuscript returns, U.S. Bureau of the Census, Fifth Census, 1840, Schedule I. The returns for the Sixth Census, 1850, Schedules I and II, show that twenty-five of the original thirty-three men lived in the county a decade later. Fifteen of them owned slaves at an average of 5.8 each.

58. *Newton County History,* pp. 31, 111, 287. Census information located only twenty of the thirty-three men in 1850.

59. On the emergence and impact of free labor ideology, see Eric F. Foner, *Free Soil, Free Labor, Free Men.*

60. *AC,* Aug. 4, 1842.

61. *AC,* Aug. 4, 1842.

62. *AC,* Aug. 8 and 9, Jan. 14, and Apr. 6, 1843.

63. Hynds, *Antebellum Athens,* 30, 130, 163, 175, 178, 183.

64. *Southern Banner,* May 12, 1836.

65. *Southern Banner,* May 12, 1836. Articles 10, 11, and 12 of the AMMAA constitution.

66. *Southern Banner,* Mar. 14, July 4, 1844.

67. *Southern Banner,* May 12, 1836, Article 2.

68. Howell Cobb Papers, box 13, folder 13, AMMAA to Howell Cobb, Nov. 12, 1846; box 19, folder 12, Charles L. Oliver to Howell Cobb, Apr. 2, 1849.

69. Howell Cobb Papers, box 24, folder 9, William H. Hull to Howell Cobb, Nov. 29, 1850.

70. Hynds, *Antebellum Athens,* 175–78.

71. No other notices in area newspapers listed Newton County mechanic meeting announcements after the original one. *AC,* July 28, 1840.

72. For a description of one prisoner's experience as an inmate artisan see Lewis Paine, *Six Years in a Georgia Prison;* also see Bonner, *Milledgeville,* 127–29, 136–39; and Edward L. Ayers, *Vengeance and Justice,* 65.

73. Bonner, *Milledgeville,* 128.

74. *Milledgeville Statesman and Patriot,* Nov. 25, 1829.

75. *Report of the Principal Keeper of the Georgia Penitentiary, 1872–1873,* 16–17; Ayers, *Vengeance and Justice,* 47–48.

76. *Georgia Banner,* reprinted in the *Federal Union,* Apr. 15, 1845, quoted in Ayers, *Vengeance and Justice,* 296.

77. *AC,* Sept. 30, 1845.

78. Ayers, *Vengeance and Justice,* introduction and appendices.

79. Richard Morris, "Labor Militancy in the Old South," 36; *AC,* Nov. 21, 1829; *Southern Banner,* Nov. 19, 1836; Richard H. Haunton, "Savannah in the 1850s," 53.

80. On Augusta mechanics' societies, see *AC,* July 3, 1840, July 4, 1842; Feb. 21, 1843; June 29, 1851; May 28, 1850. On Macon mechanics' societies see the *Georgian,* Dec. 31, 1833; *Albany Patriot,* Aug. 17, 1849. Records of the Troup County Agricultural and Mechanic Society, minute books, 1850–1853, in GDAH. Etowah Agricultural and Mechanic Fair, reported in the *AC,* Oct. 16, 1852.

81. Franklin M. Garrett, *Atlanta and Environs,* vol. 1, 318.

82. *AC,* Aug. 23, 1848; Sept. 15, 1849. The success of the state fair prompted envious Augusta boosters to propose organizing a Farmers and Mechanics Institute modeled after the Stone Mountain Fair but intended for the farmers and mechanics in the South Carolina and Georgia upcountry around Augusta. Ibid., Aug. 26, 1848; Aug. 29, 1849.

83. *Southern Banner,* Oct. 23, 1851.

84. Findlay may have imported Scotsmen to meet his labor needs. See Davis, "Robert Findlay," 41, 43.

85. For a discussion of the institute see the *Macon Citizen,* Feb. 24, 1852.

86. *Georgia Journal and Messenger,* Apr. 30, May 28, Oct. 15, 1851; *AC,* Sept. 8, 1852.

87. *Macon Georgia Citizen,* Oct. 29, 1853.

88. *AC,* July 9, 1828.

89. Harold Papers, box 1, letter to David Valentine, Oct. 14, 1836, Emory Archives, Emory University.

90. *Southern Banner,* Jan. 13, 1838.

91. Ronald Takaki, *A Proslavery Crusade,* 47, 337.

92. Percentages calculated from the *Compendium of the Sixth Census,* 40–46; *Sev-*

enth Census of the U.S., 366; *Eighth Census of the U.S.* On the decline of urban slavery in the 1850s as a result of agricultural demand, see Goldin, *Urban Slavery.*

93. See Siegel, "Artisans and Immigrants," 221–30.

94. See Betty Wood, *Slavery in Colonial Georgia;* Richard C. Wade, *Slavery in the Cities,* 81–110; Ralph B. Flanders, *Plantation Slavery in Georgia,* 233–39.

95. *Acts of the State of Georgia, 1845,* 49.

96. *Georgia Journal and Messenger,* May 9, 1849, Apr. 24, 1850; *Georgia Citizen,* Apr. 5 and May 17, 1851; *Macon Southern Museum,* Sept. 22, 1849.

97. *Atlanta Intelligencer,* July 10, 1851.

98. *Atlanta Intelligencer,* July 10, 1851.

99. Reprinted in the *Albany Patriot,* Aug. 17, 1949.

100. *Columbus Times,* May 2, 1851.

101. U.S. Manufacturing Census of 1860, Seventh Census, Georgia.

102. Seventh Census of the United States, 1850, Schedule I: An Enumeration of the Free Population, microfilm, GDAH.

103. Coleman, ed., *History of Georgia,* 171–73.

104. White, *Statistics,* 156; Bureau of the Census, Rolls 1 and 2, Schedule of Mines, Agriculture, Commerce, and Manufacturing, Georgia, 1840, microfilm, GDAH. The 1860 U.S. Manufacturing Census lists only a cooperage, a bookbindery, a carriage-making establishment, a furniture-making establishment, four print shops, four bakeries, and five machine shops among its factories. This figure clearly excludes the small workshops that proliferated in the city but suggests how limited factory production actually was. *Manufactures of the U.S. in 1860, Compiled from the Original Returns of the Eighth Census,* 63–64.

105. Jane Webb Smith, *Georgia's Legacy,* 63–66, 71.

106. George Barton Cutten, *Silversmiths of Georgia,* 21, 40, 68; Smith, *Georgia's Legacy,* 20–22, 53; Barron, *Those Who Stayed Behind,* 51–77; Atlanta Historical Society, *Neat Pieces,* 175; Haunton, "Savannah in the 1850s," 51.

107. *Columbian Museum and Savannah Daily Gazette,* Feb. 13, 1817; June 13, 1820; *Georgian,* July 7, 1835; July 27, 1837; Dec. 3, 1838; Aug. 27, 1839; Chatham County, Wills, 1860, microfilm, GDAH.

108. U.S. Population Census, Chatham County, Georgia, 1850 and 1860, microfilm, GDAH. Of these twenty-four cabinetmakers in 1850, eight were German natives, six Irish natives, two English natives, one Swiss native, two New Jersey natives, one New York native, one South Carolina native, one Florida native, and one Georgia native. Two sets of these men were brothers, and another set was a father and son team.

109. The William Harris Garland Papers, 1819–1873, Southern Historical Collection, University of North Carolina, Chapel Hill, North Carolina (hereafter cited as the Garland Papers).

110. Ernst and Merrens, "Camden's turrets," 572–74; Earle and Hoffman, "Staple Crops and Urban Development," 64–67.

111. Victor S. Clark, *History of Manufactures in the United States, Volume 1, 1607–1860* (New York: Carnegie Institution of Washington, 1929), 403, 417, 419, 507–9.

112. Gavin Wright, *The Political Economy of the Cotton South,* 119, 123, 126–27.

113. Whittington B. Johnson, *Black Savannah,* 145–50.

114. George Kollock, plantation books, vol. 6, Nov. 1846, Georgia Historical Society, Savannah.

115. For example, see advertisement for "100 able-bodied Negro men" in the Savannah *Daily Georgian,* Jan. 5, 1848; Buckingham, *The Slave States of America,* vol. 1, 137.

116. Bancroft, *Census,* 34–36; John A. Eisterhold, "Savannah: Lumber Center of the South Atlantic," *GHQ* 57 (Winter 1973): 527–29; Ball, *Fifty Years in Chains,* 417.

117. Anonymous carpenter's account book, Savannah, 1853–1854, Georgia Historical Society, Savannah, Georgia.

118. Register of Free Persons of Color, 1848, Savannah, Clerk of the Ordinary, Chatham County, microfilm, GDAH.

119. U.S. Office of the Census, 1860, Chatham-Chattahoochee Counties, Georgia, microfilm, GDAH.

120. David Roediger raises this point in more abstract fashion in *Wages of Whiteness,* 24.

121. The author is grateful to Timothy J. Lockley for bringing this case to her attention. Lockley addresses its larger implications in his paper " 'Partners in Crime': The Criminal Relationship Between Afro-Americans and Non-Slaveholding Whites in Lowcountry Georgia, 1835–1840."

122. Chatham County, Superior Court minutes, book 14, 1836–1839, GDAH; Lockley, "Partners in Crime," 7; Betty Wood, *Women's Work, Men's Work,* 94–95, 147.

123. Preamble and regulations of the Savannah River Anti-Slave Traffick Association, Georgia Historical Society, Savannah.

124. Mother Garland, Beaufort, to William H. Garland, Savannah, Oct. 31, 1838; Mrs. Osborn, Beaufort, to William H. Garland, Apr. 17, 1840; M. B. Bell, Beaufort, to William H. Garland, July 29, 1851; Oct. 26, 1851; Garland Papers.

125. This lack of respect for white mechanics was expressed in local newspapers as early as the 1820s. On "profligate workingmen," see the *Georgia Republican,* Aug. 17, 1825. On the need to halt "the intemperance which we daily witness among the lower classes," see the *AC,* Oct. 24, 1827. Henry Merrell, a New York native who managed the Roswell Manufacturing Company in the 1840s, described his disgust at having to hire engineers who were not only unreliable but who

"treated steam as a mystery." Quoted in *Autobiography of Henry Merrell,* ed. James L. Skinner III, 133, 170.

126. Siegel, "Artisans and Immigrants," 225.

127. Figures from Herbert Weaver, "Foreigners in Ante-bellum Savannah," 1–4.

128. Corley, *Confederate City,* 48–52.

129. These Macon figures are from Joseph Patrick Reidy, "Masters and Slaves, Planters and Freedmen," 480.

130. Figures from manuscript returns, U.S. Bureau of the Census, Sixth and Seventh Census, 1850 and 1860, Clarke County, Schedule I.

131. Russell, *City-Building,* 69–70.

132. The foreign-born population in Georgia represented 1 percent of the free population in 1850 and 2 percent in 1860, *Compendium of the Seventh Census* and *Population of the U.S. in 1860,* 76.

133. Data on Augusta artisans tabulated from the *Augusta City Directory, 1841,* and manuscript returns, U.S. Bureau of the Census, Fifth Census, 1840, Schedule II; on Athens from the manuscript returns, U.S. Bureau of the Census, Sixth Census, 1850, Schedules I and II.

On the threat to southern society posed by immigrants in the 1850s, see Berlin and Gutman, "Natives and Immigrants," 1175–1200; Randall M. Miller, "The Enemy Within," 30–53; Fred Siegel, "Artisans and Immigrants," 221–30.

134. Wade, *Slavery in the Cities,* 41; Edward M. Shoemaker, "Strangers and Citizens," 266–70.

135. Wilson, *Digest,* 418–20.

136. Wilson, *Digest,* 7–8, 417–18; William Andrew Byrne, "The Burden and Heat of the Day," 190.

137. Figures from Peter Wallenstein, *From Slave South to New South,* 14.

138. Ayers, *Vengeance and Justice,* 105, shows that these changes precipitated urban violence as a means of venting the effects of so much dislocation and social tension.

139. James Oakes, *The Ruling Race,* 67.

Bibliography

Manuscript Collections

Baker Library, Harvard University Graduate School of Business Administration, Cambridge: Dun and Bradstreet Reports. Georgia.

Georgia Department of Archives and History, Atlanta: Augusta Store Account Book, 1795–1796; Barrington King, General Ledger, 1834–1864; Blacksmith Account Book, Sparta, 1821; Blacksmith Account Book, Baldwin County, 1821–1823, 1863; Blacksmith Account Book, Sparta, 1826–1829; Blacksmith Account Book, Crawford County, 1854–1856; John Castleberry Blacksmith Account Book, Fort Valley, 1854–1856; R. C. Fain Store and Blacksmith Account Books, 1836–1868; Little and Harrison Blacksmith Account Book, Franklin County, 1856; W. B. Myers Sawmill Account Book, Morgan County, 1840.

Georgia Historical Society, Savannah: Anonymous, Carpenter's Day Book, Savannah, 1853–1854; Invoice Book, Macon Clothier and Tailor, 1848; John Handy Account Book, Savannah; William H. May and Company Papers, Savannah Saddlers, 1850–1853, 1858–1860; George Walton, "A Note on the Pine Land of Georgia," Augusta, May 1, 1793.

Hargrett Library, University of Georgia, Athens: Baber-Blackshear Collection; Godfrey Barnsley Papers; David Crenshaw Barrow Papers; Basinger Collection; Frederick Adolphus Brahe Papers; Joseph E. Brown Papers; Carlton-Newton-Mell Collection; Champion Family Letters; Samuel Clark Plantation Records, Burke County; John C. Carter Cashbook and Ledger, 1831–1836; John C. Carter Daybook, 1829–1836; Howell Cobb Papers; Du Bose Family Papers; A. T. Havens Journal on a Trip to Georgia and Florida, 1842–1844; Harden-Jackson-Carithers Collection; Hatton-Lovejoy Memoirs; Jewell Family Collection (Thomas Sanson Ledger); William Jones Account Book, 1836–1840; John W. Jordan Ledger, Crawfordville, 1819–1830. Joseph Henry Lumpkin Collection, Carr Division; Henry Newton Manuscript. Some Early Reminiscences; Newton

Memoirs; John Phillips Diary; Keith Reid Collection; Right Rogers Account Book, Athens Shoemaker, 1835–1837; Telamon Cuyler Collection; William Price Talmage Diary; William Warren Thomas Papers; John Toles Daybook, Tanner and Shoemaker, Clinton, 1832.

Southern Historical Collection, University of North Carolina, Chapel Hill: William Garland Papers.

Special Collections, Augusta College, Augusta: Bailie Family Papers.

Robert W. Woodruff Library, Emory University, Atlanta: Godfrey Barnsley Papers; Graves Family Papers, 1840–1931; Harold Papers.

Government Documents

Abstract of Returns, Fifth Census. Washington, D.C.: Duff Green, 1833.

Aggregate Amount of Persons Within the United States in the Year 1810. Washington, D.C.: Gales and Seaton, 1821.

Candler, Allen D. *Colonial Records of Georgia.* 19 vols. Atlanta: Franklin-Turner Company, 1904–1916.

Candler, Allen D., comp. *Revolutionary Records of the State of Georgia.* Atlanta: Franklin-Turner Company, 1916.

Census for 1820. Washington, D.C.: Gales and Seaton, 1821.

Clayton, A. S. *Compilations of the Laws of Georgia.* Augusta: Adams and Duyckinch, 1802.

Cobb, Howell. *Compilation of the General and Public Statutes of the State of Georgia.* New York: Edward O. Jenkins, 1859.

De Bow, J. D. B., comp. *Statistical View of the U.S., Being a Compendium of the Seventh Census.* Washington, D.C.: Beverly Tucker, 1854.

Digests of Accounts of Manufacturing in the U.S. Washington, D.C.: Gales and Seaton, 1823.

Enumeration of the Inhabitants and Statistics of the U.S., Sixth Census. Washington, D.C.: n.p., 1841.

Fifth Census; or Enumeration of the Inhabitants of the U.S. Washington, D.C.: Duff Green, 1832.

Georgia, State of. *Acts of the State of Georgia, 1845.* Columbus: 1845.

Georgia, State of. Executive Department Minutes.

Georgia Reports of Cases in Law and Equity Argued and Determined in the Supreme Court of the State of Georgia.

Lamar, Marie de, and Elisabeth Rothstein. *The Reconstructed Census of Georgia.* Baltimore: Genealogical Publishing Co., 1985.

Manufactures of the U.S. in 1860, Compiled from the Original Returns of the Eighth Census. Washington, D.C.: Government Printing Office, 1865.

Marbury, H., and W. H. Crawford. *Digest of the Laws of the State of Georgia*. Savannah: Seymour, Woolhopter, and Stebbins, 1802.

Population of the U.S. in 1860, Compiled from the Original Returns of the Eighth Census. Washington, D.C.: Government Printing Office, 1864.

Prince, Oliver Hillhouse, comp. *A Digest of the Laws of the State of Georgia*. Athens: Oliver Hillhouse Prince, 1837.

Report of the Principal Keeper of the Georgia Penitentiary, 1872–1873. Atlanta: n.p., 1873.

Return of the Whole Number of Persons Within the Several Districts of the United States. Philadelphia: Childs and Swaine, 1791.

Second Census of the United States. Washington, D.C.: Duane Printer, 1801.

The Seventh Census of the U.S., 1850. Washington, D.C.: n.p., 1853.

U.S. Bureau of the Census, 1840 Mines, Manufacturing, and Agriculture Schedule, Georgia. Manuscript Returns.

U.S. Bureau of the Census. Population Schedules and Slave Schedules. Georgia. Manuscript Returns.

U.S. Bureau of the Census. Records of the 1820 Census of Manufactures. Schedules for North Carolina, South Carolina, Georgia. Manuscript Returns.

Newspapers

The following newspapers were consulted: *Albany Patriot; Athenian; Athens Daily Times; Atlanta Daily Intelligencer; Atlanta Intelligencer; Augusta Chronicle; City Gazette and the Daily Advertiser* (Charleston); *Columbian Museum and Savannah Advertiser; Columbus Times; Daily Georgian* (Savannah); *Federal Union* (Milledgeville); *Georgia Citizen* (Macon); *Georgia Express* (Athens); *Georgia Gazette* (Savannah); *Georgia Journal and Messenger* (Macon); *Georgia Republican* (Savannah); *Georgia State Gazette* (Savannah); *Georgia Telegraph* (Macon); *Georgian* (Savannah); *Macon Citizen; Macon Messenger; Macon Journal; Macon Southern Museum; Milledgeville Statesman and Patriot; Savannah Republican; Southern Banner* (Athens); *Southern Recorder* (Milledgeville)

Other Printed Primary Sources

Andrews, Garnett. *Reminiscences of an Old Georgia Lawyer*. Reprint. Atlanta: n.p., 1984.

Augusta Directory and City Advertiser for 1841. Augusta: K. Woodward, 1841.

Bancroft, Joseph. *Census of the City*. 2d ed. Savannah: n.p., 1848.

Blair, Ruth. *Some Early Tax Digests of Georgia*. 1926. Reprint, Easley, S.C.: Southern Historical Press, 1971.

Brown, John. *Slave Life in Georgia: A Narrative of the Life, Sufferings, and Escape of John*

Brown, a Fugitive Slave. Edited by F. Nash Boney. Savannah: Bee Hive Press, 1992, previously published 1972.

Buckingham, James Silk. *The Slave States of America.* 2 vols. 1842. Reprint, New York: Negro University Press, 1968.

Butler, John C. *Historical Record of Macon and Central Georgia.* Vol. 1. Macon: J. W. Burke and Company, 1879.

Cooper, Thomas, M.D. *Two Tracts on the Proposed Alteration of the Tariff; and on Weights and Measures Submitted to the Consideration of the Members from S.C., in the Ensuing Congress of 1823–1824.* Charleston: Black and Kearn, 1824.

Coxe, Tench, ed. *A Statement of the Arts and Manufactures of the United States of America for the Year 1810.* Philadelphia: A. Corman Jr., 1814.

Craft, William, and Ellen Craft. *Running a Thousand Miles to Freedom.* New York: Arno Press, 1969.

Cumming, Mary G. *Georgia Railroad and Banking Company, 1833–1945.* Augusta: Walton Printing Company, 1945.

De Bow, J. D. B. *The Industrial Resources, Etc., of the Southern and Western States: Embracing a View of Their Commerce, Agriculture, Manufactures, Internal Improvements, Slave and Free Labor, Slavery Institutions, Etc. of the South.* 4 vols. New Orleans: Office of De Bow's Review, 1853.

Digest of Accounts of Manufacturing Establishments in the U.S. Washington, D.C.: Gales and Seaton, 1823.

Fitzpatrick, John C., ed. *The Diaries of George Washington, 1748–1799.* 4 vols. Boston: Little and Brown, 1925.

Gilmer, George R. *Sketches of Some of the First Settlers of Upper Georgia, of the Cherokees, and the Author.* Americus: Americus Book Company, 1926.

Hardee, Charles Seton Henry, *Reminiscences and Recollections of Old Savannah.* Edited by Martha Gallaudet Waring. N.p., 1934.

Hull, Augustus Longstreet. *Sketches of Athens, Georgia, from 1830–1865.* Athens: Woman's Work Print, 1906.

Hundley, Daniel R. *Social Relations in Our Southern States.* Edited, with an introduction by William J. Cooper Jr. Baton Rouge: Louisiana State University Press, 1979.

Longstreet, A. B. *Georgia Scenes.* 1835. Reprint, New York: Sagamore Press, 1957.

Lyell, Charles. *Second Visit of the U.S.* New York: Harper and Brothers, 1849.

Martin, John H. *Columbus, Georgia, from Its Selection as a "Trading Town" in 1827 to Its Partial Destruction by Wilson's Raid in 1865,* 2 vols. Columbus: T. Gilbert, 1874–1875.

Mellish, John. *Travels in the United States of America,* 2 vols. Philadelphia: n.p., 1812.

Museum of Early Southern Decorative Arts. Index of Early Southern Artists and Artisans.

Olmsted, Fredrick Law. *A Journey in the Seaboard States.* New York: Dix and Edwards, 1856.

Paine, Lewis. *Six Years in a Georgia Prison: A Narrative of Lewis W. Paine, who suffered imprisonment six years in Georgia, for the crime of aiding the escape of a fellow-man from that state, after he had fled from slavery.* Boston: B. Marsh, 1852.

Phillips, Ulrich Bonnell, ed. *The Correspondence of Robert Toombs, Alexander H. Stephens, and Howell Cobb.* 2 vols. 1911. Reprint, New York: Da Capo Press, 1970.

President's Report to the Stockholders of the Georgia Railroad and Banking Company, May 17, 1845. Augusta: n.p., 1845.

Rawick, George P., ed. *The American Slave: A Composite Autobiography,* vol. 12, *Georgia Narratives,* parts 1 and 2. Westport: Greenwood Press, 1972.

Report of R. D. Arnold, Mayor of the City of Savannah, for the Year ending September 30th, 1860, etc. Savannah: n.p., 1860.

Sherwood, Adiel. *A Gazetteer of Georgia.* Atlanta: J. Richards, 1860.

Skinner, James L., III, ed. *The Autobiography of Henry Merrell: Industrial Missionary to the South.* Athens: University of Georgia Press, 1991.

Southern Business Directory and General Commercial Advertiser. Charleston: Press of Walker and James, 1854.

Thomson, William. *A Tradesman's Travels in the U.S. and Canada in the Years 1840, 1841 and 1842.* Edinburgh: n.p., 1842.

Tucker, George. *Progress of the United States in Population and Wealth in Fifty Years.* 1855. Reprint, New York: Augustus M. Kelley, 1964.

White, George. *Historical Collections of Georgia.* New York: Pudney and Russel, 1854.

———. *Statistics of the State of Georgia.* Savannah: W. T. Williams, 1849.

Wood, Virginia Steele, and Ralph Van Wood, eds. *Collections of the Georgia Historical Society,* vol. 15: *The Reuben King Journal, 1800–1806.* Savannah: Georgia Historical Society, 1971.

Secondary Sources

Abernethy, Thomas P. *The South in the New Nation, 1789–1819.* Baton Rouge: Louisiana State University Press, 1961.

Adams, Donald R. "Prices and Wages in Maryland, 1780–1850." *Journal of Economic History* 46 (1986): 625–45.

———. "Wage Rates in the Early National Period: Philadelphia, 1785–1830." *Journal of Economic History* 28 (1968): 404–26.

Adams, Samuel, "The Yazoo Fraud." *Georgia Historical Quarterly* 7 (1923): 155–65.

Alexander, Adele Logan. *Ambiguous Liver: Free Women of Color in Georgia, 1789–1879.* Fayetteville: University of Arkansas Press, 1991.

Alexander, John K. "Urban America in the Revolutionary Era: Studies in the Neglected Period of American Urban History." *Journal of Urban History* 5 (1979): 241–53.

Appleby, Joyce. *Capitalism and a New Social Order: The Republican Vision of the 1790s.* New York: New York University Press, 1984.

Aptheker, Herbert. *The Labor Movement in the South During Slavery.* New York: International Publishers, 1955.

Asher, Robert, Paul Gilje, and Howard Rock, eds. *The American Artisan: Explorations in Social Identity.* Baltimore: Johns Hopkins University Press, 1995.

Ashworth, John. *Agrarians and Aristocrats: Party Political Ideology in the United States, 1837–1846.* Cambridge: Cambridge University Press, 1983.

————. "The Democratic-Republicans before the Civil War: Political Ideology and Economic Change." *Journal of American Studies* 20 (1986): 375–91.

Atlanta Historical Society. *Neat Pieces: The Plain-Style Furniture of Nineteenth-Century Georgia.* Atlanta: Atlanta Historical Society, 1983.

Averitt, John Nelson. "The Democratic Party in Georgia, 1824–1837." Ph.D. diss., University of North Carolina, 1957.

Ayers, Edward L. *Vengeance and Justice: Crime and Punishment in the Nineteenth-Century South.* New York: Oxford University Press, 1984.

Banks, William Nathaniel. "The Architectural Legacy of Daniel Pratt." In *The Papers of the Athens Historical Society,* vol. 2. Athens: Athens Historical Society, 1979, 53–62.

Barney, William L. *The Secessionist Impulse: Alabama and Mississippi in 1860.* Princeton: Princeton University Press, 1974.

Barron, Hal S. *Those Who Stayed Behind: Rural Society in Nineteenth-Century New England.* Cambridge: Cambridge University Press, 1984.

Bateman, Fred. *A Deplorable Scarcity: The Failure of Industrialization in the Slave Economy.* Chapel Hill: University of North Carolina Press, 1981.

Bateman, Fred, and Thomas Weiss. "Comparative Regional Development in Antebellum Manufacturing." *Journal of Economic History* 35 (1975): 182–215.

Beatty, Bess. "Lowells of the South: Northern Influences on the Nineteenth-Century North Carolina Textile Industry." *Journal of Southern History* 52 (1987): 37–62.

————. "Textile Labor in the North Carolina Piedmont: Mill Owner Images and Workers' Responses, 1830–1900." *Labor History* 25 (1984): 485–503.

Beck, John J. "Building the New South: A Revolution from Above in a Piedmont County." *Journal of Southern History* 53 (1987): 441–70.

Berlin, Ira. *Slaves without Masters: The Free Negro in the Antebellum South.* New York: Pantheon Books, 1974.

Berlin, Ira, and Herbert G. Gutman. "Natives and Immigrants, Free Men and

Slaves: Urban Workingmen in the Antebellum American South." *American Historical Review* 88 (1983): 1175–1200.

Bishir, Catherine W. "A Proper Good Nice and Workmanlike Manner: A Century of Traditional building Practice." In *Architects and Builders in North Carolina: A History of the Practice of Building,* ed. Catherine W. Bishir, Charlotte V. Brown, Carl R. Lounsbury, and Ernest H. Wood III. Chapel Hill: University of North Carolina Press, 1990.

Blewett, Mary H. *Men, Women, and Work: Class, Gender, and Protest in the New England Shoe Industry.* Urbana: University of Illinois Press, 1988.

Boles, John B. *Black Southerners, 1619–1869.* Lexington: University of Kentucky Press, 1983.

Boles, John B., and Evelyn Thomas Nolen, eds. *Interpreting Southern History: Historiographical Essays in Honor of Sanford W. Higginbotham.* Baton Rouge: Louisiana State University Press, 1987.

Bonner, James C. "The Georgia Penitentiary at Milledgeville, 1817–1874." *Georgia Historical Quarterly* 60 (1971): 303–28.

———. *A History of Georgia Agriculture, 1732–1860.* Athens: University of Georgia Press, 1964.

———. *Milledgeville: Georgia's Antebellum Capital.* Athens: University of Georgia Press, 1978.

———. "Profile of a Late Antebellum Community." *American Historical Review* 49 (1944): 663–80.

Bridenbaugh, Carl. *Cities in Revolt: Urban Life in America, 1743–1776.* New York: Alfred Knopf, 1955.

———. *The Colonial Craftsman.* New York: New York University Press, 1950.

Bridges, Amy. "Becoming American: The Working Classes in the United States before the Civil War." In *Working-Class Formation: Nineteenth-Century Patterns in Western Europe and the United States,* ed. Ira Katznelson and Aristide R. Zolberg. Princeton: Princeton University Press, 1986.

Brody, David. "The Old Labor History and the New: In Search of an American Working Class." *Labor History* 21 (1980): 485–512.

Brown, Thomas. "The Southern Whigs and Economic Development." *Southern Studies* 20 (1981): 20–38.

Brownell, Blaine A., and David R. Goldfield. *The City in Southern History: The Growth of Urban Civilization in the South.* Port Washington, N.Y.: Kennikat Press, 1976.

Bruchey, Stuart, comp. and ed. *Cotton and the Growth of the American Economy: 1790–1860.* New York: Harcourt, Brace and World, 1967.

———. *The Roots of American Economic Growth, 1607–1860: An Essay in Social Causation.* New York: Harper and Row, 1965.

Buck, Paul H. "The Poor Whites of the Ante-bellum South." *American Historical Review* 31 (1925): 41–54.

Burgess, Hugh Otis. "A Study of Prosperity in Georgia, 1840– 1850." Master's thesis, Emory University, 1926.

Burton, Orville Vernon. *In My Father's House Are Many Mansions: Family and Community in Edgefield, South Carolina.* Chapel Hill: University of North Carolina Press, 1985.

Burton, Orville Vernon, and Robert McMath, eds. *Class, Conflict and Consensus: Antebellum Southern Community Studies.* Westport, Conn.: Greenwood Press, 1982.

Byrne, William Andrew. "The Burden and Heat of the Day: Slavery and Servitude in Savannah, 1733–1865." Ph.D. diss., Florida State University, 1979.

Campbell, Randolph B. "Planters and Plain Folks: The Social Structure of the Antebellum South." In *Interpreting Southern History: Historiographical Essays in Honor of Sanford W. Higginbotham,* ed. John B. Boles and Evelyn Thomas Nolen. Baton Rouge: Louisiana State University Press, 1987.

Cash, W. J. *The Mind of the South.* New York: A. A. Knopf, 1941.

Cashin, Edward J. *Colonial Augusta: Key to the Indian Country.* Macon, Ga.: Mercer University Press, 1986.

———. *An Informal History of Augusta.* Augusta: Richmond Board of Education, n.d.

———. *The Story of Augusta.* Augusta: Richmond County Board of Education, 1980.

Castlen, Harriet Gift. *That Was a Time.* New York: E. P. Dutton, 1937.

Cawthon, William Lamar, Jr. "Clinton: County Seat on the Georgia Frontier, 1808–1821." Master's thesis, University of Georgia, 1984.

Cecil-Fronsman, Bill. "The Common Whites: Class and Culture in Antebellum North Carolina." Ph.D. diss., University of North Carolina, 1983.

Censer, Jane Turner. "Planters and the Southern Community: A Review Essay." *Virginia Magazine of History and Biography* 94 (1986): 387–400.

Channing, Steven A. *Crisis of Fear: Secession in South Carolina.* New York: Simon and Schuster, 1970.

Chaplin, Joyce E. *An Anxious Pursuit: Agricultural Innovation and Modernity in the Lower South, 1730–1815.* Chapel Hill: University of North Carolina Press, 1993.

Coleman, Kenneth, ed. *Confederate Athens.* Athens: University of Georgia Press, 1967.

———. *A History of Georgia.* Athens: University of Georgia Press, 1977.

Coleman, Kenneth, and Charles Stephen Gurr, eds. *Dictionary of Georgia Biography.* 2 vols. Athens: University of Georgia Press, 1983.

Commons, John R., Ulrich B. Phillips, Eugene A. Gilmore, Helen L. Sumner, and John B. Andrews, eds. *A Documentary History of American Industrial Society.* Vol. 2,

Plantation and Frontier, ed. Ulrich B. Phillips. 1910. Reprint, New York: Russell and Russell, 1958.

Cooper, William J., Jr. *Liberty and Slavery: Southern Politics to 1860.* New York: Knopf, 1983.

———. *The South and the Politics of Slavery, 1828–1856.* Baton Rouge: Louisiana State University Press, 1978.

Cordillot, Michel. "Les Origines du mouvement ouvrier dans le Sud des Etats-Unis." Thèse de Doctorat d'Etat, Université de Paris-VII, 1984.

Corley, Florence Fleming. *Confederate City: Augusta, Georgia, 1860–1865.* Columbia: University of South Carolina Press, 1960.

Cory, Earl Wallace. "Temperance and Prohibition in Antebellum Georgia." Master's thesis, University of Georgia, 1961.

Couch, Dale L. "John Riley Hopkins: A Nineteenth-Century Georgia Cabinetmaker." *Atlanta Historical Journal* 28 (1984–85): 43–55.

Coulter, E. Merton. *College Life in the Old South.* 2d ed. Reprint. Athens, University of Georgia Press, 1951.

Curry, Leonard P. *The Free Black in Urban America, 1800–1850.* Chicago: University of Chicago Press, 1981.

Cutten, George Barton. *The Silversmiths of Georgia, 1733–1850.* Atlanta: Pigeonhole Press, 1958.

Daniels, Christine, "'Wanted: A Blacksmith Who Understands Plantation Work': Artisans in Maryland, 1700–1800," *William and Mary Quarterly,* 3rd series, 50, no. 4 (Oct. 1993): 743–67.

Davis, Harold E. *The Fledgling Province: Social and Cultural Life in Colonial Georgia, 1773–1776.* Chapel Hill: University of North Carolina Press, 1976.

Davis, Robert Scott, Jr. "As Good as the French: The Georgia Buhr Stone Industry and Its French Competition." Unpublished paper in the possession of the author.

———. "Robert Findlay: Antebellum Iron Founder of Macon." *Journal of Southwestern Georgia History* 3 (1985): 17–43.

Dawley, Alan. *Class and Community: The Industrial Revolution in Lynn.* Cambridge: Harvard University Press, 1976.

Debats, Donald A. *Elites and Masses: Political Structure, Communication and Behavior in Ante-Bellum Georgia.* New York: Garland Publishing, 1990.

De Treville, John Richard. "The Little New South: Origins of Industry in Georgia's Fall-Line Cities, 1840–1865." Ph.D. diss., University of North Carolina, 1986.

Dew, Charles B. *Bond of Iron: Master and Slave at Buffalo Forge.* New York: Oxford University Press, 1994.

Dixon, Jefferson Max. "The Central Railroad of Georgia, 1832–1892." Ph.D. diss., Georgia Peabody College for Teachers, 1953.

Dodd, Donald B., and Wynelle S. Dodd. *Historical Statistics of the United States, 1790–1970.* Tuscaloosa: University of Alabama Press, 1973.

Doyle, Don Harrison. *The Social Order of a Frontier Community: Jacksonville, Illinois, 1825–1870.* Urbana: University of Illinois Press, 1978.

Dunlop, J. B. "A Scotsman Visits Georgia in 1811," ed. Raymond A. Mohl, *Georgia Historical Quarterly* 55 (1971): 259–65.

Dunn, Durwood. "Apprenticeship and Indentured Servitude in Tennessee before the Civil War." *West Tennessee Historical Society Papers* 36 (1982): 25–40.

Durey, Michael. "Thomas Paine's Apostles: Radical Emigres and the Triumph of Jeffersonian Republicanism." *William and Mary Quarterly*, 3rd series, 44 (1984): 666–88.

Earle, Carville V. "A Staple Importation of Slavery and Free Labor." *Geographic Review* 68 (1978): 51–65.

Earle, Carville V., and Ronald Hoffman. "The Foundation of the Modern Economy: Agriculture and the Costs of Labor in the U.S. and England, 1800–1860." *American Historical Review* 85 (1980): 1055–94.

————. "Staple Crops and Urban Development in the Eighteenth-Century South." *Perspectives in American History* 10 (1976): 7–78.

Easterlin, Richard A. "Regional Income Trends, 1840–1950." In *American Economic History,* ed. Seymour Harris. New York: McGraw-Hill, 1961.

Eaton, Clement. *The Growth of Southern Civilization, 1790–1860.* New York: Harper and Row Publishers, 1961.

————. "Mob Violence in the Old South." *Mississippi Valley Historical Review* 26 (1942): 351–70.

Egerton, Douglas R. "Gabriel's Conspiracy and the Election of 1800." *Journal of Southern History* 56 (1990): 191–214.

Ernst, Joseph A., and H. Roy Merrens. "Camden's turrets pierce the skies! The Urban Process in the Southern Colonies during the Eighteenth Century." *William and Mary Quarterly,* 3rd series, 30 (1973): 549–74.

Faircloth, Robert Watson. "The Impact of Andrew Jackson in Georgia Politics, 1828–1840." Ph.D. diss., University of Georgia, 1971.

Faler, Paul G. *Mechanics and Manufacturers in the Early Industrial Revolution: Lynn, Massachusetts, 1780–1860.* Albany: State University of New York Press, 1981.

Ferlager, Louis. "Capital Goods and Southern Economic Development." *Journal of Economic History* 45 (1985): 411–18.

Fields, Barbara Jeanne. *Slavery and Freedom on the Middle Ground: Maryland during the Nineteenth Century.* New Haven: Yale University Press, 1985.

Fishbein, Meyer H. *The Censuses of Manufactures, 1810–1890* Refer. Inform. Paper. No. 50. Washington, D.C.: National Archives and Records Service, 1973.

Flanders, Ralph B. "The Free Negro in Antebellum Georgia," *North Carolina Historical Review* 9 (1932): 250–72.

———. *Plantation Slavery in Georgia*. Chapel Hill: University of North Carolina Press, 1933.

Fogel, Robert William. *Without Consent or Contract: The Rise and Fall of American Slavery*. New York: W. W. Norton and Company, 1989.

Fogel, Robert William, and Stanley L. Engerman, *Time on the Cross: The Economics of American Negro Slavery*. Boston: Little, Brown, and Company, 1974.

Foner, Eric. *Free Soil, Free Labor, Free Men: The Ideology of the Republican Party before the Civil War*. New York: Oxford University Press, 1970.

———. *Tom Paine and Revolutionary America*. New York: Oxford University Press, 1976.

Foner, Philip S. *History of the Labor Movement in the United States from Colonial Times to the Founding of the American Federation of Labor*. New York: International Publishers, 1947.

Ford, Lacy K. *Origins of Southern Radicalism: The South Carolina Upcountry, 1800–1860*. New York: Oxford University Press, 1988.

Fox-Genovese, Elizabeth. *Within the Plantation Household: Black and White Women of the Old South*. Chapel Hill: University of North Carolina Press, 1988.

Fox-Genovese, Elizabeth, and Eugene D. Genovese. *Fruits of Merchant Capital: Slavery and Bourgeois Property in the Rise and Expansion of Capitalism*. New York: Oxford University Press, 1983.

Fredrickson, George. *The Black Image in the White Mind: The Debate on Afro-American Character and Destiny, 1817–1914*. New York: Harper and Row, 1971.

Freehling, Alison Goodyear. *Drift Toward Dissolution: The Virginia Slavery Debate of 1831–1832*. Baton Rouge: Louisiana State University Press, 1982.

Frey, Sylvia. *Water from the Rock: Black Resistance in a Revolutionary Age*. Princeton: Princeton University Press, 1991.

Frisch, Michael H., and Daniel J. Walkowitz, eds. *Working-Class America: Essays on Labor, Community, and American Society*. Urbana: University of Illinois Press, 1983.

Galenson, David W. "White Servitude and the Growth of Black Slavery in Colonial America." *Journal of Economic History* 41 (1981): 40–41.

Garrett, Franklin M. *Atlanta and Environs: A Chronicle of Its People and Events*. Vol. 1. New York: Lewis Historical Publishing Company, 1954.

Gates, Ben. "Mutual Aid or Monopoly: Artisanal Republicanism in Charleston, South Carolina, 1793–1822." Unpublished paper, University of Tennessee, 1990.

Genovese, Eugene D. *The Political Economy of Slavery: Studies in the Economy and Society of the Slave South*. New York: Vintage Books, 1967.

———. *Roll, Jordan, Roll: The World the Slaves Made.* New York: Pantheon, 1974.

Gifford, James M. "The African Colonization Movement in Georgia, 1817–1860." Ph.D. diss., University of Georgia, 1977.

Glickstein, Jonathan A. *Concepts of Free Labor in Antebellum America.* New Haven, Conn.: Yale University Press, 1991.

Goldfield, David R. "The Business of Health Planning in the Old South." *Journal of Southern History* 42 (1976): 557–70.

———. *Urban Growth in the Age of Sectionalism: Virginia, 1847–1861.* Baton Rouge: Louisiana State University Press, 1977.

Goldin, Claudia. *Urban Slavery in the American South, 1820–1860: A Quantitative Analysis.* Chicago: University of Chicago Press, 1976.

Govan, Thomas P. "Banking and the Credit System in Georgia, 1810–1860." *Journal of Southern History* 4 (1938): 164–84.

Gray, Lewis Cecil. *History of Agriculture in the Southern States to 1860.* 2 vols. Washington, D.C.: Carnegie Institute of Washington, 1933.

Green, Fletcher M. *Constitutional Development in the South Atlantic States, 1776–1860.* Chapel Hill: University of North Carolina, 1930.

Green, Henry D. *Furniture of the Piedmont Before 1830.* Atlanta: High Museum of Art, 1976.

Gregg, William. "Practical Results of Southern Manufactures." *De Bow's Review* 18 (1858): 777–91.

Griffin, Richard W. "The Augusta Manufacturing Company in Peace, War, and Reconstruction, 1847–1877." *Business History Review* 32 (1958): 23–31.

———. "The Origins of the Industrial Revolution in Georgia Cotton Textiles, 1810–1865." *Georgia Historical Quarterly* 42 (1958): 355–75.

Gutman, Herbert G. "The Reality of the Rags-to-Riches Myth: The Case of the Paterson, New Jersey, Locomotive, Iron, and Machinery Manufactures, 1830–1880." In *Nineteenth-Century Cities: Essays in the New Urban History,* ed. Stephen Thernstrom and Richard Sennett. New Haven: Yale University Press, 1969.

Hahn, Steven. *The Roots of Southern Populism: Yeoman Farmers and the Transformation of the Georgia Upcountry, 1850–1890.* New York: Oxford University Press, 1983.

Hansen, Marcus Lee. *The Atlantic Migration, 1607–1860.* Cambridge: Harvard University Press, 1940.

Harris, J. William. *Plain Folk and Gentry in a Slave Society: White Liberty and Black Slavery in Augusta's Hinterlands.* Middletown, Conn.: Wesleyan University Press, 1985.

Haskins, Charles H. "The Yazoo Land Commission." *Papers of the American Historical Association* 5 (1891): 61–103.

Haunton, Richard H. "Savannah in the 1850s." Ph.D. diss., Emory University, 1968.

Hawke, David Freeman. *Nuts and Bolts of the Past: A History of American Technology, 1776–1860.* New York: Harper and Row, 1988.

Heath, Milton Sydney. *Constructive Liberalism: The Role of the State in Economic Development in Georgia to 1860.* Cambridge: Harvard University Press, 1954.

Henderson, Archibald. *Washington's Southern Tour.* Boston: Houghton Mifflin, 1923.

Henson, Stephen Ray. "Industrial Workers in the Mid-Nineteenth-Century South: Atlanta Railwaymen, 1840–1870." Ph.D. diss., Emory University, 1982.

Higgs, Robert. *Competition and Coercion: Blacks in the American Economy, 1865–1914.* Cambridge: Cambridge University Press, 1977.

Hirsch, Susan E. *Roots of the American Working Class: The Industrialization of Crafts in Newark, 1800–1860.* Philadelphia: Temple University Press, 1978.

History of Newton County. Covington, Ga.: Newton County Historical Society, 1988.

Hoffman, Charles, and Tess Hoffman. "The Limits of Paternalism: Driver-Master Relations on a Bryan County Plantation," *Georgia Historical Quarterly* 57 (1973): 321–35.

Hoffman, Nelson, Jr. "Godfrey Barnsley, 1805–1873: British Cotton Factor in the South." Ph.D. diss., University of Kansas, 1964.

Hofstadter, Richard. *The Idea of a Party System: The Rise of Legitimate Opposition in the United States, 1780–1840.* Berkeley: University of California Press, 1970.

Holt, Michael F. *The Political Crisis of the 1850s.* New York: Wiley, 1978.

Huffman, Frank J., Jr. "Town and Country in the South, 1850–1880: A Comparison of Urban and Rural Social Structures." *South Atlantic Quarterly* 76 (1977): 365–81.

Hunt, Alfred N. *Haiti's Influence on Antebellum America: Slumbering Volcano in the Caribbean.* Baton Rouge: Louisiana State University Press, 1988.

Hynds, Ernest C. *Antebellum Athens and Clarke County, Georgia.* Athens: University of Georgia Press, 1974.

Jackson, Harvey H. "Consensus and Conflict: Factional Politics in Revolutionary Georgia, 1774–1777." *Georgia Historical Quarterly* 59 (1977): 388–401.

———. *Lachlan McIntosh and the Politics of Revolutionary Georgia.* Athens: University of Georgia Press, 1979.

Jackson, Harvey H., and Phinizy Spalding. *Forty Years of Diversity: Essays on Colonial Georgia.* Athens: University of Georgia Press, 1984.

Jernegan, Marcus Wilson. *Laboring and Dependent Classes in Colonial America, 1607–1783.* Chicago: University of Chicago Press, 1931.

Johnson, Michael P. *Toward a Patriarchal Republic: The Secession of Georgia.* Baton Rouge: Louisiana State University Press, 1977.

———. "Work, Culture, and the Slave Community: Slave Occupations in the Cotton Belt in 1860." *Labor History* 27 (1985–86): 325–55.

Johnson, Michael P., and James L. Roark. *Black Masters: A Free Family of Color in the Old South.* New York: W. W. Norton and Company, 1984.

————, eds. *No Chariot Let Down: Charleston's Free People of Color on the Eve of the Civil War.* Chapel Hill: University of North Carolina Press, 1984.

Johnson, Whittington B. *Black Savannah, 1788–1864.* Fayetteville: University of Arkansas Press, 1996.

————. "Free Blacks in Antebellum Augusta, Georgia: A Demographic and Economic Profile." *Richmond County History* 14 (1982): 10–21.

————. "Free Blacks in Antebellum Savannah: An Economic Profile." *GHQ* 64 (Winter 1980): 420–27.

Jones, Alice Henson. *Wealth of a Nation to Be: The American Colonies on the Eve of the Revolution.* New York: Columbia University Press, 1980.

Jones, Charles C., Jr. *Memorial History of Augusta, Georgia: From Its Settlement in 1735 to the Close of the Nineteenth Century.* Syracuse: D. Mason and Company, 1890.

Kelley, Ariadne Lea. "The Plantation Homes of John Wind." Master's thesis, University of Georgia, 1977.

Klein, Rachel N. "Frontier Planters and the American Revolution: The South Carolina Backcountry, 1775–1782." In *An Uncivil War: The Southern Backcountry During the American Revolution,* ed. Ronald Hoffman, Thad W. Tate, and Peter J. Albert, 37–69. Charlottesville: University Press of Virginia, 1985.

————. *Unification of a Slave State: The Rise of the Planter Class in the South Carolina Backcountry, 1760–1808.* Chapel Hill: University of North Carolina Press, 1990.

Koch, Mary Levin. "A History of the Arts in Augusta, Macon, and Columbus, Georgia, 1800–1860," Master's thesis, University of Georgia, 1983.

Kornblith, Gary J. "From Artisans to Businessmen: Master Mechanics in New England, 1789–1850." 2 vols. Ph.D. diss., Princeton University, 1983.

Kulikoff, Allan. *The Agrarian Origins of American Capitalism.* Charlottesville: University Press of Virginia, 1992.

————. "Growth and Welfare in Early America." *William and Mary Quarterly,* 3rd series, 39 (1982): 359–65.

————. *Tobacco and Slaves: The Development of Southern Cultures in the Chesapeake, 1680–1800.* Chapel Hill: University of North Carolina Press, 1986.

————. "The Transition to Capitalism in Rural America." *William and Mary Quarterly,* 3rd series, 46 (1989): 120–44.

————. "Uprooted Peoples: Black Migrants in the Age of American Revolution, 1790–1820." In *Slavery and Freedom in the Age of the American Revolution,* ed. Ira Berlin and Ronald Hoffman, 143–71. Charlottesville: University Press of Virginia, 1983.

Lamplugh, George R. *Politics on the Periphery: Factions and Parties in Georgia, 1783–1806.* Newark: University of Delaware Press, 1986.

Larson, Daniel. "A Historic Survey of Outstanding Examples of Federal and Greek Revival Architecture in Milledgeville, Georgia." Master's thesis, Auburn University, 1968.

Laurie, Bruce. *Artisans into Workers: Labor in Nineteenth-Century America*. New York: Hill and Wang, 1989.

———. *Working People of Philadelphia, 1800–1850*. Philadelphia: Temple University Press, 1980.

Lebsock, Suzanne. *The Free Women of Petersburg: Status and Culture in a Southern Town, 1784–1860*. New York: W. W. Norton and Company, 1984.

Leslie, Kent Anderson. *Woman of Color, Daughter of Privilege: Amanda America Dickson*. Athens: University of Georgia Press, 1995.

Lewis, Johanna Miller. *Artisans in the North Carolina Backcountry*. Lexington: University Press of Kentucky, 1995.

———. "Women Artisans in Backcountry North Carolina, 1753–1790." *North Carolina Historical Review* 68 (July 1991): 214–26.

Link, Eugene Perry. *Democratic Republican Societies*. New York: Octagon Books, 1965.

Magrath, C. Peter. *Yazoo: Law and Politics in the New Republic: The Case of Fletcher versus Pleck*. Providence: Brown University Press, 1966.

Margo, Robert A., and Georgia C. Villaflor. "The Growth of Wages in Antebellum America: New Evidence." *Journal of Economic History* 47 (1987): 873–95.

Marks, Bayley E. "Skilled Blacks in Antebellum St. Mary's County, Maryland." *Journal of Southern History* 53 (1987): 537–64.

Martin, Harold. *Atlanta and Environs: A Chronicle of Its People and Events*. Vol 3: *Years of Change and Challenge, 1940–1976*. Athens: University of Georgia Press, 1987.

Mason, Laura. "Ca Ira and the Birth of the Revolutionary Song." *History Workshop* 28 (1989): 22–38.

McComb, David G. *Houston: A History*. Austin: University of Texas Press, 1981.

McCurry, Stephanie, *Masters of Small Worlds: Yeoman Households, Gender Relations and the Political Culture of the Antebellum South Carolina Low Country*. New York: Oxford University Press, 1995.

———. "The Two Faces of Republicanism: Gender and Proslavery Politics in Antebellum South Carolina." *Journal of American History* 78 (1992): 1245–64.

McGuire, Peter S. "Athens and the Railroads." *Georgia Historical Quarterly* 18 (1934): 1–26, 118–44.

McKusker, John J., and Russell R. Menard. *The Economy of British America, 1607–1789*. Chapel Hill: University of North Carolina Press, 1985.

McPherson, James B. *Battle Cry of Freedom: The Civil War Era*. New York: Oxford University Press, 1988.

Merrill, Michael. "Cash Is Good to Eat: Self-Sufficiency and Exchange in the Rural Economy of the United States." *Radical History Review* 4 (1977): 42–71.

Miller, Randall M. "Daniel Pratt's Industrial Urbanism: The Cotton Mill Town in Antebellum Alabama." *Alabama Historical Quarterly* 34 (1972): 5–35.

―――. "The Enemy Within: Some Effects of Foreign Immigrants on Antebellum Southern Cities." *Southern Studies* 24 (1985): 30–53.

Miller, Roberta Balstad. *City and Hinterland: A Case Study of Urban Growth and Regional Development.* Westport, Conn.: Greenwood Press, 1979.

Mohr, Clarence L. *On the Threshold of Freedom: Masters and Slaves in Civil War Georgia.* Athens: University of Georgia Press, 1986.

Montgomery, David. "The Working Classes and the Pre-Industrial American City, 1780–1830." *Labor History* 9 (1968): 3–22.

Montgomery, Horace. *Cracker Parties.* Baton Rouge: Louisiana State University Press, 1950.

―――. "The Two Howell Cobbs: A Case of Mistaken Identity." *Journal of Southern History* 28 (1962): 348–355.

Morgan, Edmund S. *American Slavery, American Freedom: The Ordeal of Colonial Virginia.* New York: W. W. Norton, 1975.

Morgan, Philip D. "Black Society in the Lowcountry, 1760–1810." In *Slavery and Freedom in the Age of the American Revolution,* ed. Ira Berlin and Ronald Hoffman, 83–142. Charlottesville: University Press of Virginia, 1983.

Morris, Richard B. *Government and Labor in Early America.* New York: Alfred Knopf, 1946.

―――. "Labor Militancy in the Old South." *Labor and Nation* 4 (1947): 32–36.

Murray, Paul. "Party Organization in Georgia Politics, 1825–1853." *Georgia Historical Quarterly* 29 (1945): 195–210.

―――. *The Whig Party in Georgia, 1825–1853.* Chapel Hill: University of North Carolina Press, 1948.

Nash, Gary B. *The Urban Crucible: Social Change, Political Consciousness and the Origins of the American Revolution.* Cambridge: Harvard University Press, 1979.

North, Douglass C. *The Economic Growth of the United States, 1790–1860.* New York: W. W. Norton and Company, 1966.

Oakes, James. *The Ruling Race: A History of American Slaveholders.* New York: Knopf, 1982.

―――. *Slavery and Freedom: An Interpretation of the Old South.* New York: Knopf, 1990.

Olton, Charles. *Artisans for Independence: Philadelphia Mechanics and the American Revolution.* Syracuse: Syracuse University Press, 1975.

Owens, Leslie. *This Species of Property: Slave Life and Culture in the Old South.* New York: Oxford University Press, 1976.

Owsley, Frank L. *Plain Folk of the Old South.* Baton Rouge: Louisiana State University Press, 1949.

Phillips, Ulrich B. "The Economic Cost of Slaveholding in the Cotton Belt." *Political Science Quarterly* 20 (1905): 257–75.

————. *Georgia and State Rights: A Study of the Political History of Georgia from the Revolution to the Civil War, with Particular Regard to Federal Relations.* Washington, D.C.: Government Printing Office, 1902.

————. *A History of Transportation in the Eastern Cotton Belt to 1860.* New York: Columbia University Press, 1908.

Pocock, J. G. A. "The Classical Theory of Deference." *American Historical Review* 81 no. 3 (June 1976): 516–23.

————. *The Machiavellian Moment: Florentine Political Thought and the Atlantic Republican Tradition.* Princeton: Princeton University Press, 1975.

————. "Virtue and Commerce in the Eighteenth Century." *Journal of Interdisciplinary History* 3 (1972): 119–34.

Pred, Allan R. *Urban Growth and City-Systems in the United States, 1840–1860.* Cambridge: Harvard University Press, 1980.

————. *Urban Growth and the Circulation of Information: The United States System of Cities, 1790–1840.* Cambridge: Harvard University Press, 1973.

Price, Jacob M. "Economic Function and the Growth of American Port Towns in the Eighteenth Century." *Perspectives in American History* 8 (1974): 123–86.

Purdue, Robert E. *The Negro in Savannah, 1865–1900.* New York: Exposition Press, 1973.

Pyle, Barbara C. "The Free Negro in Bibb County, Georgia, 1850–1860." B.A. honors thesis, Emory University, 1974.

Rabinowitz, Howard N. *Race Relations in the Urban South, 1865–1900.* New York: Oxford University Books, 1978.

Range, Willard. *A Century of Georgia Agriculture, 1850–1950.* Athens: University of Georgia, 1954.

Reese, Trevor R., ed. *The Clamorous Malcontents: Criticisms and Defenses of the Colony of Georgia, 1741–1743.* Savannah: Beehive Press, 1973.

Reidy, Joseph Patrick. "Masters and Slaves, Planters and Freedmen: The Transition from Slavery to Freedom in Central Georgia, 1820–1880." Ph.D. diss., Northern Illinois University, 1982.

Reps, John William. *Tidewater Towns: City Planning in Colonial Virginia and Maryland.* Williamsburg: Williamsburg Foundation, 1972.

Roberts, Lucien E. "Sectional Factors in the Movements for Legislative Reapportionment and Reduction in Georgia, 1777–1860." In *Studies in Georgia History and Government,* ed. James C. Bonner and Lucien E. Roberts, 94–122. Athens: University of Georgia Press, 1940.

Rock, Howard B. *Artisans of the New Republic: The Tradesmen of New York City in the Age of Jefferson.* New York: New York University Press, 1979.

Roediger, David. *The Wages of Whiteness: Race and the Making of the American Working Class.* London: Verso Press, 1991.

Rogers, W. McDowell. "Free Negro Legislation in Georgia before 1865." *Georgia Historical Quarterly* 16 (1932): 27–37.

Rorabaugh, W. J. *The Craft Apprentice: From Franklin to the Machine Age in America.* New York: Oxford University Press, 1986.

Ross, Steven J. *Workers on the Edge: Work, Leisure and Politics in Industrializing Cincinnati, 1788–1890.* New York: New York University Press, 1985.

Russell, James Michael. *Atlanta, 1847–1890: City-Building in the Old South and the New.* Baton Rouge: Louisiana State University Press, 1988.

Russo, Jean B. *Free Workers in a Plantation Economy: Talbot County, Maryland, 1690–1759.* New York: Garland Press, 1989.

———. "Self-Sufficiency and Local Exchange: Free Craftsmen in the Rural Chesapeake Economy." In *Colonial Chesapeake Society,* ed. Lois Green Carr, Phillip D. Morgan, and Jean B. Russo. Chapel Hill: University of North Carolina Press, 1984.

Saunders, Robert. "Modernization and the Free Peoples of Richmond: The 1780s and the 1850s." *Southern Studies* 24 (1985): 237–72.

Saxton, Alexander. *The Rise and Fall of the White Republic: Class Politics and Mass Culture in Nineteenth-Century America.* London: Verso Press, 1990.

Saye, Albert B. *A Constitutional History of Georgia, 1732–1968.* Athens: University of Georgia Press, 1940 (rev. ed. 1970).

Schlereth, Thomas J. "Artisans and Craftsmen: A Historical Perspective." In *The Craftsman in Early America,* ed. Ian M. G. Quimby. New York: W. W. Norton, 1984.

Schultz, Ronald. *The Republic of Labor: Philadelphia Artisans and the Politics of Class, 1720–1830.* New York: Oxford University Press, 1993.

Sears, Joan Niles. *The First One Hundred Years of Town Planning in Georgia.* Atlanta: Cherokee Publishing Company, 1979.

Sellers, Charles Grier. *The Market Revolution: Jacksonian America, 1815–1846.* New York: Oxford University Press, 1991.

———. "Who Were the Southern Whigs?" *American Historical Review* 59 (1954): 335–46.

Sheller, Tina. "Artisans in Baltimore Politics." In *The American Artisan: Explorations in Social Identity,* ed. Gilje, Kaufman, and Rock. Baltimore: Johns Hopkins University Press, 1995.

Shirley, Michael. *From Congregation Town to Industrial City: Culture and Social Change in a Southern Community.* New York: New York University Press, 1994.

Shoemaker, Edward M. "Strangers and Citizens: The Irish Immigrant Community in Savannah, 1837–1861." Ph.D. diss., Emory University, 1990.

Shyrock, Richard Harrison. *Georgia and the Union in 1850.* Durham, N.C.: Duke University Press, 1926.

Siegel, Fred. "Artisans and Immigrants in the Politics of Late Antebellum Georgia." *Civil War History* 27 (1981): 221–30.

Simkins, Francis Butler, and Charles Pierce Roland. *A History of the South.* New York: Knopf, 1947.

Smith, Jane Webb. *Georgia's Legacy: History Charted Through the Arts.* Athens: University of Georgia Press, 1985.

Smith, Julia Floyd. *Slavery and Rice Culture in Low Country Georgia, 1750–1860.* Knoxville: University of Tennessee Press, 1985.

Soltow, Lee, and Aubrey C. Land. "Housing and Social Standing in Georgia, 1798." *Georgia Historical Quarterly* 64 (1980): 448–58.

Spalding, Phinizy. *Oglethorpe in America.* Athens: University of Georgia Press, 1977.

Starobin, Robert S. *Industrial Slavery in the Old South.* New York: Oxford University Press, 1970.

Statom, Thomas R., Jr. "Negro Slavery in Eighteenth-Century Georgia." Ph.D. diss., University of Alabama, 1982.

Steel, Edward M., Jr. "Flush Times in Brunswick, Georgia, in the 1830s." *Georgia Historical Quarterly* 39 (1955): 221–39.

Steffan, Charles. *The Mechanics of Baltimore: Workers and Politics in the Age of Revolution, 1763–1812.* Urbana: University of Illinois Press, 1984.

Still, Bayrd. *Urban America: A History with Documents.* Boston: Little, Brown, and Co., 1974.

Stone, James H. "Economic Conditions in Macon, Georgia in the 1830s." *Georgia Historical Quarterly* 52 (1968): 209–52.

Strong, Mrs. Paschal M., Jr. "Glimpses of Savannah, 1780–1825." *Georgia Historical Quarterly* 33 (1949) 26–35.

Sweat, Edward F. "The Free Negro in Ante-bellum Georgia." Ph.D. diss., Indiana University, 1957.

Sydnor, Charles S. *The Development of Southern Sectionalism, 1819–1848.* Baton Rouge: Louisiana State University Press, 1948.

Takaki, Ronald. *A Proslavery Crusade: The Agitation to Reopen the African Slave Trade.* New York: Free Press, 1971.

Temin, Peter. *The Jacksonian Economy.* New York: W. W. Norton and Company, 1969.

Terrill, Tom E. "Eager Hands: Labor for Southern Textiles, 1850–1860." *Journal of Economic History* 36 (1976): 84–99.

Theus, Will M. *Savannah Furniture, 1735–1825.* N.p., 1967.

Thornton, J. Mills, III. *Politics and Power in a Slave Society: Alabama, 1800–1860.* Baton Rouge: Louisiana State University Press, 1978.

Tryon, Rolla Milton. *Household Manufactures in the United States, 1640–1860*. Chicago: University of Chicago Press, 1917.

Van Doren, Mark, ed. *Travels of William Bartram*. New York: Dover, 1955.

Vipperman, Carl J. *William Lowndes and the Transition of Southern Politics, 1782–1822*. Chapel Hill: University of North Carolina Press, 1989.

Wade, John Donald. *Augustus Baldwin Longstreet: A Study of the Development of Culture in the South*. 1924. Reprint, Athens: University of Georgia Press, 1969.

Wade, Richard C. *Slavery in the Cities: The South, 1820–1860*. New York: Oxford University Press, 1964.

————. *The Urban Frontier: Pioneer Life in Early Pittsburgh, Cincinnati, Lexington, Louisville, and St. Louis*. 1959. Reprint, Chicago: University of Chicago Press, 1971.

Wallenstein, Peter. *From Slave South to New South: Public Policy in Nineteenth-Century Georgia*. Chapel Hill: University of North Carolina Press, 1987.

Walsh, Richard. *Charleston's Sons of Liberty: A Study of the Artisans, 1763–1789*. Columbia: University of South Carolina Press, 1959.

Watson, Harry L. *Jacksonian Politics and Community Conflict: The Emergence of the Second American Party System in Cumberland County, North Carolina*. Baton Rouge: Louisiana State University Press, 1981.

Wax, Donald. "New Negroes are Always in Demand: The Slave Trade in Eighteenth-Century Georgia." *Georgia Historical Quarterly* 68 (1984): 193–220.

Weaver, Herbert. "Foreigners in Ante-bellum Savannah." *Georgia Historical Quarterly* 37 (1953): 1–17.

Weiman, David F. "Farmers and the Market in Antebellum America: A View from the Georgia Upcountry." *Journal of Economic History* 47 (1987): 627–47.

————. "Petty Commodity Production in the Cotton South: Upcountry Farmers in the Georgia Cotton Economy, 1840 to 1880." Ph.D. diss., Stanford University, 1984.

————. "Urban Growth on the Periphery of the Antebellum Cotton Belt: Atlanta, 1847–1860." *Journal of Economic History* 48 (1988): 259–72.

Wesley, Charles. *Negro Labor in the United States, 1850–1925: A Study in American Economic History*. New York: Vanguard Press, 1927.

Wiebe, Robert H. *The Opening of American Society: From the Adoption of the Constitution to the Eve of Disunion*. New York: Knopf, 1984.

Wilentz, Sean. "Artisan Republican Festivals and the Rise of Class Conflict in New York City, 1788–1837." In *Working-Class America: Essays on Labor, Community, and American Society*, ed. Michael H. Frisch and Daniel J. Walkowitz, 37–77. Urbana: University of Illinois Press, 1983.

————. *Chants Democratic: New York City and the Rise of the American Working Class, 1788–1850*. New York: Oxford University Press, 1984.

Williford, William Bailey. *The Glory of Covington.* Atlanta: Cherokee Publishing Co., 1973.

Wood, Betty. *Slavery in Colonial Georgia, 1730–1775.* Athens: University of Georgia Press, 1984.

———. *Women's Work, Men's Work: The Informal Slave Economies of Lowcountry Georgia.* Athens: University of Georgia Press, 1995.

Wood, Kirk. "From Town to City: Augusta's First Mayoral Election." *Richmond County History* 15 (1983): 8–12.

Wood, Peter. *Negroes in Colonial South Carolina from 1670 through the Stono Rebellion.* New York: W. W. Norton and Company, 1974.

Wood, W. K. "The Georgia Railroad and Banking Company." *Georgia Historical Quarterly* 57 (1973): 544–61.

———. "A Note on Pro-Urbanism and Urbanization in the Antebellum South: Augusta, Georgia, 1820–1860." *Richmond County History* 6 (1974): 23–31.

Woodman, Harold. *King Cotton and His Retainers: Financing and Marketing the Cotton Crop of the South, 1800–1925.* Kentucky: University of Kentucky Press, 1968.

Wooster, Ralph A. *The People in Power: Courthouse and Statehouse in the Lower South, 1850–1860.* Knoxville: University of Tennessee Press, 1969.

Works Project Administration. *Georgia: A Guide to Its Towns and Countryside.* Athens: University of Georgia Press, 1940.

Wright, Gavin. *Old South, New South: Revolutions in the Southern Economy since the Civil War.* New York: Basic Books, 1986.

———. *The Political Economy of the Cotton South: Households, Markets, and Wealth in the Nineteenth Century.* New York: W. W. Norton, 1978.

Wyatt-Brown, Bertram. *Southern Honor: Elites and Behavior in the Old South.* New York: Oxford University Press, 1982.

Young, Alfred F. *The Democratic-Republicans of New York: The Origins, 1763–1797.* Chapel Hill: University of North Carolina, 1967.

———. "George Robert Twelves Hewes (1742–1840): A Boston Shoemaker and the Memory of the American Revolution." *William and Mary Quarterly*, 3rd series, 38 (1981): 561–623.

———. "The Mechanics and Jeffersonians: New York, 1789–1801." *Labor History* 5 (1964): 247–76.

Index

Naileries, 80
Native Americans, 3, 6, 13–14, 69–70
Needleworkers, 7; slave, 12. *See also*
  Milliners
Newton County, 118–20, 140
Newton County Mechanics' Society,
  140, 148–50, 152

Ocmulgee Iron Foundry, 90, 91. *See
  also* Iron foundries

Paine, Thomas, 45, 55
Painters, 7, 99, 100; slave, 169
Panic of 1837, 75, 90, 118–20
Panic of 1857, 91–92
Parsons, Ed, 106–7
Party politics, 135. *See also entries for
  specific political parties*
Pioneer Paper Manufacturing
  Company, 125
Political consciousness, among
  artisans. *See* Republicanism
Pool, Baxter, 47, 48, 59
Poor whites, 11–12, 166
Potters, 33, 34, 79
Pratt, Daniel, 109–10
Primrose, Edward, 59
Prince, Oliver Hillhouse, 105
Production. *See* Domestic production;
  Household production
Pulaski County, manufactures in,
  83–84

Railroads, 73–76, 86, 88, 100, 125,
  147, 157
Republicanism, 42, 104–5; Jeffersonian, 39, 149; artisanal, 36–39,
  45–47, 61–64, 104–5, 136; and
  prison labor, 153
R. G. Dun and Company, 91, 114
Rice mills, 164

Richmond Academy, 48
Richmond County, 81–82, 87–89, 144
Richmond Manufacturing Company,
  139
Royal, Elizabeth, 124, 126
Royal, John, 124, 126

Saddlers, 126; and harnessmakers, 26
Sanson, Thomas, 111–12
Savannah, 3, 7, 10–12, 36, 74;
  architecture of, 8; artisans in, 11,
  21–28, 169; competition in, 12, 60;
  demographics of, 21–22, 27, 77–78,
  157–58, 162; economy of, 9–13; fire
  in (1796), 53; immigrants in, 161,
  167–70; manufactures in, 84–87,
  89–90; mechanics in, 49–50; Nelson
  Incident in, 50–52; paper money act
  in, 48–49; skilled free blacks in, 26–
  28, 128–29; slave artisans in, 25–
  27, 128–29
Savannah House Carpenters'
  Association, 60–61
Savannah Mechanics' Association, 37,
  39–40, 50–52, 56–59, 60
Savannah River Anti-Traffick
  Association, 166–67
Saw mills, 58, 79, 92, 123, 165;
  protective legislation for employees
  of, 146
Sawyers, 9, 20, 25; slave, 25, 169
Services. *See* Crafts and services, of
  artisans
Shaffer, Balthasser, 52, 56
Shinglers, 99
Shipwrights, 9, 15. *See also*
  Boatbuilders, slave
Shoemaker, Josiah, 39–43, 47
Shoemakers, 1–2, 8–9, 21, 23, 29, 48,
  59, 106, 111, 113
Silversmiths, 7–8, 21, 25, 48, 59, 149